10 09 08 07 06   6 5 4 3 2 1

Distributed in Canada by Fraser Direct
100 Armstrong Avenue
Georgetown, ON, Canada L7G 5S4
Tel: (905) 877-4411

Distributed in the U.K. and Europe by David & Charles
Brunel House, Newton Abbot, Devon, TQ12 4PU, England
Tel: (+44) 1626 323200, Fax: (+44) 1626 323319
E-mail: mail@davidandcharles.co.uk

Distributed in Australia by Capricorn Link
P.O. Box 704, Windsor, NSW 2756 Australia
Tel: (02) 4577-3555

Library of Congress Cataloging-in-Publication Data

The portable MFA in creative writing : improve your craft with the core essentials taught to MFA students / by the New York Writers Workshop.
    p. cm.
  Includes index.
  ISBN-13: 978-1-58297-440-8 (hardcover : alk. paper)
  ISBN-10: 1-58297-440-3 (hardcover : alk. paper)
  ISBN-13: 978-1-58297-350-0 (pbk. : alk. paper)
  ISBN-10: 1-58297-350-4 (pbk. : alk. paper)
  1. English language--Rhetoric--Problems, exercises, etc. 2. Creative writing--Problems, exercises, etc. I. New York Writers Workshop.
  PE1408.P665 2006
  808'.042--dc22
                                                        2005033667
Permissions for works excerpted in the book are on file.

Editor: Michelle Ehrhard
Designer: Claudean Wheeler
Production Coordinator: Robin Richie

fw
F+W PUBLICATIONS, INC.

the portable

MFA in
creative writing

improve your craft

with the core essentials

taught to MFA students

THE NEW YORK
WRITERS WORKSHOP

WRITER'S DIGEST BOOKS

writersdigestbooks.com
Cincinnati, Ohio

THE NEW YORK
WRITERS WORKSHOP
MEMBERS

Marci Alboher	Coleman Hough
Beth Ann Bauman	Kaylie Jones
Maureen Brady	Jonathan Kravetz
Susan Brennan	Regina McBride
Peter Bricklebank	Hermine Meinhard
Nicole Burdette	J.B. Miller
Patty Dann	Carol Rial
Elaine Edelman	Charles Salzberg
Allison Estes	Charlie Schulman
Corie Feiner	Don Shea
Rita Gabis	Rachel Sherman
Juliann Garey	Alex Simmons
Doug Garr	Daniel Stern
Richard Goodman	Alix Strauss
Mary Stewart Hammond	Tim Tomlinson
Bronwen Hruska	Sarah Van Arsdale

Acknowledgments

PETER BRICKLEBANK thanks Sarah Van Arsdale for her editorial wisdom and for allowing him to clog her voice mail. He thanks Jessica Treat, Arlene Bensam, Deborah Ungar, JR Roessl, Lydie Raschka, Harriet R. Goren, Nicole Quinn, Darryl Graff, Kathleen Locke, Rosie Blitchington, and Barry Ramus, for their words and insights. And he thanks all his students, named or otherwise, who have worked, thought, and laughed right along with him.

RITA GABIS thanks her students and Donna Masini for her valuable input.

CHARLES SALZBERG thanks Helen Zelon, Nicole Tucker, Shannon Barr, Joslyn Matthews, and the rest of his students from whom he's learned so much. He also thanks Charles Leerhsen and John Lombardi for their skill as magazine writers and their generosity in allowing him to use their work. And he thanks Bill Glavin of the S.I. Newhouse School of Public Communications, for giving him the opportunity to teach in the "major leagues."

CHARLIE SCHULMAN thanks Ryan Dewit, Florence Prenga, and Laura Weiss, and especially thanks Juliet Bellow for her expertise and guidance.

For the opportunities they've given the New York Writers Workshop to conduct workshops abroad, **TIM TOMLINSON** would like to thank Vim Nadera, Director, Institute of Creative Writing, University of the Philippines, Diliman Campus, Quezon City, Philippines; Ed Lejano, Director, Film Institute, University of the Philippines, Diliman Campus, Quezon City, Philippines; Erich Sysak, Director, Professional Writing Program, Webster University, Cha'am, Thailand; Heng Li

Lang, Senior Assistant Director (Capability Development), Industry Development Division, the Media Development Authority of Singapore; Tan Lay Ping, Senior Management Executive (Capability Development), Industry Development Division, the Media Development Authority of Singapore; Tony Chow, President, Digital Media Academy, Singapore; Linda Mironti and Michael Mele, Founders, Il Chiostro, New York and Tuscany, Italy. And for the opportunity she's given him to live, love, and work at home, he would like to thank Lourdes Barrion Rodriguez.

THE NEW YORK WRITERS WORKSHOP thanks Rabbi Joy Levitt, Isaac Zablocki, Karen Sander, and the rest of the staff of the JCC-Manhattan; Adele Heyman at the Open Center; Denis Woychuk, owner of the KGB Bar; Michael Neff of the Algonkian Workshop; and Ducts.org.

And a special thanks to editor Michelle Ehrhard who put up with five writers, when even one is sometimes too much.

Contents

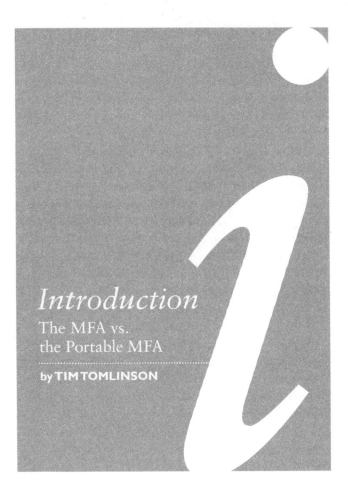

Introduction
The MFA vs.
the Portable MFA

by TIM TOMLINSON

Several years ago, I asked the then up-and-coming literary agent Noah Lukeman (he has now very much come up) to speak to my advanced group of students at the New York Writers Workshop. At that meeting, Noah was asked his opinion of the Master of Fine Arts degree in creative writing. He gave us, he said, the same answer he gives every one who asks that question: "Take the $35,000–$50,000 you're going to spend on the degree, buy yourself a good laptop and printer and a bundle of paper, and go off to a cabin and write. At the end of two years, the worst that can happen is you have nothing. Less than nothing is what you'll almost certainly have at the end of your MFA program, because, besides nothing, you'll also have a mountain of debt."

That may seem like a harsh assessment of the value of MFA programs; it is certainly not uncommon, especially among MFA graduates.

Interestingly, Noah was asked another FAQ at that meeting: What is the possibility of publishing a collection of short stories? To that, Noah gave the answer we've been hearing since the 1970s: slim to nonexistent. Unless, he said, your work meets with one of three exceptions: (1) you were already an established novelist, in which case a publishing house might begrudgingly run your collection; (2) your collection came packaged together with a novel, in which case the novel would be published first; or (3) one of your stories had appeared in one of the major story venues (*The New Yorker*, *The Atlantic*, *Harper's Magazine*, perhaps *The Paris Review* or *The Missouri Review*), and/ or you happened to have come out of one of the several high-profile MFA programs (at that time, Iowa, Columbia, Stanford, and a select few others). *Aha!* we all thought—there is some value to the MFA after all.

And there is. While much of what I have to say about the MFA is negative— perhaps even harsh—all of it is supported by experience and widespread testimony. It's also true, however, that there are quite a few legitimate and contradictory assessments, some of them in the pages of this book. Let me run through what was wrong with my program and so many other programs like it, and then I'll attempt to leaven my assessment with the possible benefits of the MFA.

THE FLAWS

I'll run through the flaws of the MFA one by one.

1. **The Pretense That MFA Candidates Are Already Full-Blown Artists.** MFA candidates are not full-blown artists in control of their craft. Many of them are unaware of their craft, on any level. Many of them are *merely* talented or have had the good or bad luck to write one piece interesting enough to impress a member of the admissions committee.

   Why is this pretense a flaw? Because it enables lazy teaching by promoting the idea that manuscripts submitted are fully considered representations of the best a particular writer has to offer, instead of what they most often are: desperate first drafts whipped off the night or morning before their workshop due date. Amazingly (and sadly), despite the fact that this is the nature of many workshop submissions, many participants still invest a lot of emotion in how well their stories are received by the workshop. And if the manuscripts are treated as

if they're anything more than exercises in the training process, the responses can be damaging.

MFA candidates need to learn craft, just as dancers and painters and musicians do. And their manuscripts should be assessed, at least in the first year, on the basis of how well they master a craft consideration (say, dialogue).

2. **Teachers Who Purport to Believe That Writing Can't Be Taught.** When you hear a teacher say that writing can't be taught, run to another workshop. Again, the craft of writing—just like the crafts of music, dance, painting, film, theater, etc.—can be taught. Have you ever heard someone say, "Why on earth are you taking piano instruction? Music can't be taught"? Of course not, but you hear this nonsense all the time about writing.

What is especially pernicious about this pervasive idiocy is that many of the teachers hired (often by the most high-profile institutions) purport to believe this. Why do I say *purport to believe*? Because the idea is something that only stupid people would actually believe, and none of these writers is stupid. But if you believe that writing can be taught, then you have to figure out a way to teach it, and that requires work—and a lot of it—even before the workshops begin. Teaching then requires a significant amount of work per manuscript. That means instructors would actually have to earn their salaries.

And why should they, if they don't have to? Often it appears that instructors have just barely read the students' manuscripts; sometimes it appears as if they put together their comments during the workshop session itself, first by listening to what others say, and then by throwing out a few of the usual generalities about writing what you know or cutting out adjectives. Many institutions have no fail-safe against this egregious lack of integrity—at least not in the middle of a workshop. And so the hapless MFA candidate can very easily pass through two years of workshops and never once have a discussion about scene construction or narrative payoff. Many people find it hard to believe that I passed through two years of an MFA program, four separate workshops, and received not so much as a comma written back on a manuscript. But it's true, and my case was not exceptional. I've received form rejection letters with more ink on them.

3. **Teachers With a Moses Complex.** Teachers with a Moses (he handed down the ultimate laws) complex are the other side of the coin. These teachers believe that writing *can* be taught—at least *their* ideas or laws of writing. Anything that doesn't fit into their narrow definition is treated as an abomination. Ask anyone who's ever studied with Gordon Lish. (Of course, after charging exorbitant fees for his workshops, Lish made his students sign statements of confidentiality that forbade them to whisper even a syllable's worth of what actually went on in his class. I've nurtured many damaged Lish refugees who had been taught to worship Lish and his writing, and who, after months with him, had no idea whatsoever about the mechanics of scene construction, dialogue, or story structure. When you consider the fragility of the writer's ego, especially at the developmental stage, and that part of the writer's "education" occurs in public, this type of teacher might be the very worst.

I have had students in beginning workshops that started out barely able to write a coherent paragraph, but wound up selling stories or novels (in progress) before the end of the ten-week session. There is a method to teaching, to cultivating talent, and that's the least that MFA candidates should get for the astronomical fees they lay out, and for the level of trust they necessarily bring to the workshops.

With this kind of brutalizing teacher, full of self-aggrandizing fire and brimstone, salvation must often be found far from the purview of the workshop or the campus. Think of the writer David Foster Wallace. He was told over and over by his workshop instructor that his work didn't make the grade. Wallace tried to please this Moses, but failed repeatedly until he gave up. Luckily for Wallace (and his many fans), David Lynch's *Blue Velvet* appeared near Wallace's campus, and after seeing that mind- and rule-bending film, Wallace felt vindicated. The rest is, well, an astonishingly successful career. Both Rick Moody (*The Ice Storm*) and Helen Schulman (*P.S.*) were told by their Moses that they weren't going to make it as writers, since they were failing to write like their Moses.

4. **Bias Toward the Pantheon and Prejudice Against the Marginal.** Because MFA programs are hosted by universities, the tendency to focus exclusively on a certain few "classic" writers is widespread. I think everyone should read Leo Tolstoy and Marcel Proust and Edith

Wharton and Herman Melville. But in a writing class, you want to read writers who stimulate your desire to write, not writers whose diction and content and worldview are so removed from your personal experience that they read like the literary equivalent of museum pieces. Instead of Samuel Johnson, how about Denis Johnson? Instead of Virginia Woolf, how about Tobias Wolff?

When MFA programs want to get contemporary, they often reach for the current critical/academic darlings, the Barthelme-Coover-Pynchon kinds of writers whose work is often antistory. Learning to write by studying these models would be like learning to make movies by studying the films of Stan Brakhage and Andy Warhol.

5. **An Elevation of the Lyrical Writer as Opposed to the Narrative.** A preference for lyrical writing might be a prejudice I share with MFA instructors. I gravitate more toward James Salter than Irwin Shaw, more toward Denis Johnson than John Irving. But again, we do a disservice to MFA candidates by advancing the scintillating sentence over the ambitious story. One shudders to think what this emphasis would have done to Tolstoy.

In the end, MFA programs that emphasize this type of lyrical writing produce stories recognizable for their shimmering surfaces, their elegant lines, and their completely unmemorable characters set in completely unconvincing narratives, since they are really only about shimmering surfaces and elegant lines, and not at all about anything that matters to people other than other students of shimmering surfaces and elegant lines. When the virtuoso voice or the quirky vision (both by definition rare) are elevated so above the well-told story, you wind up with perfectly made nothings.[1]

6. **A Focus on Immediate Product Rather Than Literary Process.** A workshop story is rarely (if ever) a finished product. It should be

---

[1] Even as I write this, I feel myself getting defensive about story, which is absurd. Let me provide a musical analogy. If John Lennon had studied only the work of electronic composer Karlheinz Stockhausen, no one would remember his name, no one would have listened to a measure of his music—if he'd been moved to compose any. Fortunately for him and for us, Lennon absorbed less lofty, less idiosyncratic artists such as Chuck Berry, Buddy Holly, and Hank Williams, and these helped him produce many of the songs we're still singing, such as "Norwegian Wood (This Bird Has Flown)," "Imagine," and "Revolution." As it is, Lennon did, for a short period, study the works of Stockhausen, and their influence led him to produce "Revolution 9," perhaps the most skipped track in the history of vinyl.

treated as a work in progress, and the workshop should assess its merits and flaws in relation to an already understood and shared set of aesthetic criteria. This type of approach removes the ego as much as possible from the process and minimizes the cruelty so often a part of workshop "critiques." Nearly every manuscript can be improved (some are so bad that nothing can salvage them except the wastebasket, and some—maybe one every ten years—are so good, so perfect in their own design, that nothing can or should be done to them except publication), and it's the instructor's job to identify how—not just for the benefit of the writer but for the entire group.

7. **A Failure to Establish Any Critical Vocabulary With Which to Assess Manuscripts.** If the instructor fails to provide guidelines for workshop critique, the critiques are almost guaranteed to be either dull or chaotic or both. It is easy to guide the discussion and to train writers to read as writers. If you can't get a sense from the program or the instructor of how manuscripts are going to be critiqued, then beware.

8. **A Highbrow Disdain for Anything Not in (or Deemed Destined for) the Canon.** This common attitude is the *This-is-not-[Tolstoy, Woolf, Borges, Gide, etc.];-therefore-it's-no-good* syndrome. This kind of approach eliminates discussion of all the writers whose work might clock in at A- or less, but who may inspire and teach—writers such as W. Somerset Maugham, Ellen Gilchrist, Raymond Chandler, Tom Perrotta, Richard Wright, and on and on. You can't hit a home run every time up, and it's important to recognize and appreciate the value and the validity of the single, the double, the base on balls.

9. **Writing by Committee or by Consensus.** Writing by committee is what happens when a group aesthetic forms and everyone attempts to meet it. Out the window go the authentic concerns and stylistic tendencies of the individuals, and instead you see the homogenous MFA story with whatever inflection it's taking at the moment. We've seen the riot-of-language Cormac McCarthy stories, the I'm-so-catatonic Ann Beattie stories, the I'm-so-stoned Denis Johnson *Jesus' Son* stories, the Dorothy Allison I've-been-molested stories, the

smart-alecky Lorrie Moore stories, the magical realism stories, the distilled-unto-meaninglessness Gordon Lish–derived stories. The committee of the workshop demands that a certain tone prevail, or the individual writer must wander off in isolation and loneliness (maybe not such a bad thing).

10. **The Damage to the Psyche Facilitated by All of the Above.** The point of all this dirt is that it's hard enough—and virtuous enough—to fail on your own dime; you don't need to pay $35,000–$50,000 for the privilege. Many talented aspiring writers are silenced in the MFA programs, and that's a rotten shame. Writing programs should nurture voice as well as sensitivity. They should demonstrate good habits, and they should address issues pertaining to a career in writing. But too many programs get away with doing few or none of those things. Why? Because they say that writing can't be taught, or because what goes into the making of a writer is so nebulous that there can't be a systemized, somewhat guaranteed approach.

THE PERKS

So, how about the positives of the MFA? These might include:

1. **Time.** This is the most important thing the MFA candidate is buying: the time to suspend all "real-life" concerns, and to write. Time is a luxury, and while the gradual passage of time, with its potential accrual of wisdom and craft, might be on the writer's side, the tick-tick-ticking away of the immediate present is definitely the writer's enemy. MFA programs offer you a lot of the immediate present, and that can prove to be invaluable.

2. **Community.** The MFA program is a place to cultivate a community of writers. Some of the people in my old program still look at my work, and I theirs, and it's helpful to know where someone's critique is coming from. It's also useful to know that others are sharing the same struggles. (This must be lacking in the low-residency programs, except when the participants convene, which is only once or twice a year.)

3. **Connections.** Getting something on an agent's or editor's desk is one of the hardest and most necessary skills to develop, and connections from an MFA program can facilitate that. If you're attending one of

the high-profile programs, useful connections will be either working there already (teaching, lecturing) or coming through as guest lecturers, panelists, readers, or instructors. No matter where your MFA program is, however, there is a way to capitalize on the connections offered by guest lecturers, panelists, readers, or instructors' guest speakers (no matter how jealously most guard them). Don't be afraid to hustle yourself—it's the only way. (In my program, one participant tried to give manuscripts to Jorge Luis Borges; of course, Borges read only Braille. That participant, while laughed at then, is now a highly successful novelist—and is getting the last laugh; her blind persistence, as it were, if not Mr. Borges, paid off.)

4. **The Degree Itself.** The MFA can open doors. It can get you jobs teaching. Two years in the woods cannot. Is that worth $35,000–$50,000? (Of course, these days, what is?)

5. **Progress.** Over time, many writing programs have developed strategies, programs, and courses designed to address many of the flaws discussed here. For example, many now require craft courses as part of the overall program.

If you must attend an MFA program, you should know beforehand who's teaching and how. What are the guarantees that some significant amount of time will be spent on craft? Again, to use music as an analogy: If you were studying music composition, you wouldn't want a program whose sole methodology was to put you in front of a piano keyboard and let you bang away. The same is true for writing. What are the exact craft concerns that will be addressed? How will they be addressed? In what depth?

A FINAL WORD ABOUT THE MFA EXPERIENCE

Finally, a word about the title: Why *The Portable MFA*?

We offer the book as a substitute for the MFA program. Instead of carrying debt, you can carry the book. If the book intrigues you, if its approach works, if you feel you want more, you can find us at www.newyorkwriter sworkshop.com.

The Portable MFA in Creative Writing can save aspiring writers about $55, 980. It may also save aspiring writers a lot of time and a lot of mistakes

by offering, in a clear, fun, results-oriented, craft-based manner, instruction on the craft of writing prose fiction, poetry, non-fiction, and drama.

First: What is the New York Writers Workshop? The New York Writers Workshop is a collective of working writers and teachers with a long list of publishing credits and long experience in teaching. Our workshops and consultations cover the gamut from writing for children to refining the villanelle, and we've taught from Spring Street in lower Manhattan to Singapore down by the equator. We're dedicated to the cultivation of good writing, and good writing practices, everywhere, and our principal medium, up until the release of the book you now hold in your hands, has been our workshops.

The Portable MFA in Creative Writing derives from the craft-based workshops we've been teaching for the past fifteen years, and from our experience writing in our own disciplines. It covers fundamentals and advanced techniques in fiction, non-fiction, poetry, and playwriting. The book proceeds from the premise that there is a craft in writing and that, like the craft in any art, can be taught. As is also the case in any art, after the craft is taught the artist is on his or her own. Talent, determination, endurance, and luck are outside the purview of this book, although many of the exercises are designed to cultivate talent, encourage determination, and train for endurance. As for luck, we offer the insight of golf champion Arnold Palmer, who said: "The more I practice the luckier I get."

The book is laid out in five sections: Fiction, Personal Essay and Memoir, Magazine Writing, Poetry, and Playwriting. The sections reflect the individuality of our instructors and the broad teaching philosophy of the New York Writers Workshop, which might be best summed up by a line from Tom Waits: "Any way's the only way." Each of us represented in this book approaches his or her class and topic differently, but all of us repeat the same basic truths: write, read, reflect, revise.

The individual chapters are lively, accessible, instructive, and user-friendly. Each chapter has taught me something, or reminded me of something that I once knew or thought I knew but had forgotten. Each chapter makes me want to stop reading and start writing. Each chapter makes me want to pursue its particular discipline.

And that might be the only problem with the book: You might not be able to decide what you want to write first, a poem, or a play, a profile or a prolegomenon. An obvious solution is to try them all, and with *The Portable MFA* you can. If you need to conduct an interview, we cover that. If you want to revise a novel, we cover that, too. (We could be weak on prolegomena.) The book facilitates experimentation, exploration, first attempts by new writers, and deep revision by more experienced writers. In short, the chapters provide the kind of workshop many of us wish we'd had and all of us now offer.

MFA programs are, *ahem*, curious things. They can work, and they should, but from the accounts we've gathered over the years, many don't. When I was in an MFA program—one of the most respected, highly touted, expensive, and therefore, one of the most flawed—structure was a dirty word and craft was something for carpenters, or the rubes upstairs in the film school. The education I received for over $30,000 can be condensed to eight easy-to-forget points, and I offer them all for the price of this book.

1. Write what you know; don't write what you don't know.
2. Flashy style or language without a story to tell is "all dressed up with nowhere to go."
3. Writing can't be taught.
4. Cut out adverbs.
5. Never use the word "always."
6. "You will never be fictionists."
7. Don't write screenplays; they will destroy your ability to write prose fiction.
8. There are kinds of stories.

Aside from the vapid number three and the asinine number six, none of these is wrong, but they're all useless. Your first exercise: Tear out the gray box, crumple it up, find a wastebasket, and practice your sky hook because with these eight MFA "rules" as your guidelines, you have a better chance making it in the NBA.

Good. Now we can get down to work.

Fiction

by TIM TOMLINSON

TIM TOMLINSON (MFA, Columbia University School of the Arts) is president and a founding member of the New York Writers Workshop. He has been teaching both fiction and screenplay workshops since 1991 at such institutions as the New York Writers Workshop, the Writer's Voice, the University of the Philippines, Webster University in Cha'am, Thailand, and the Media Development Authority in Singapore. At New York University's General Studies Program, he is master teacher of writing and contemporary culture. His short stories, film reviews, articles, and haiku have been published in numerous venues, including *The New York Times*, *North American Review*, *The Missouri Review*, *Downtown Express*, and *Time Haiku*.

Foreword

The best books and stories can change our lives. I have my list of life-changers,[1] and I'm sure you have yours. If it's true, as Saul Bellow said, that writers are readers moved to emulation, then it might also be true that we write fiction we hope will change our lives or the lives of others. That's a noble and lofty ambition.

It's probably a good idea to try to write the life-changers every time out. I mean, otherwise, why bother? But it's important to recognize and accept that each effort cannot be a life-changer, for you or the reader.[2] Each piece should have its own integrity. A good short story is better than a bad novel. A good short story will make the reader crave more short stories, more fiction, whereas a bad novel will make the reader reach, once again, for the TV remote.

As Thom Jones (*Cold Snap*, *The Pugilist at Rest*) has indicated, you can't write *Sgt. Pepper* every time out. Occasionally, you even write one for Ringo. Graham Greene, an excellent and professional liar, said that he alternated between serious novels (*The Heart of the Matter*, say) and "entertainments" such as *Our Man in Havana*. Beethoven wrote Symphony No. 9 in D minor. He also wrote bagatelles—short, light musical pieces. He didn't feel bad about the bagatelles. He understood an important truth: that a bagatelle can be a good bagatelle, but it can't be any kind of symphony except failed.

What follows is a discussion of the craft of prose fiction, regardless of category (mystery, romance, literary, chick lit, etc.). Whatever your ambition or project, the elements of craft as presented here can help tighten your prose, increase your character depth, invigorate your scenes, and accelerate your story velocity. Hopefully this instruction will also enable you to recognize what kinds of projects are bagatelles, and what kinds might be symphonies; it offers insights into the craft of fiction in order to ensure that your bagatelles are good bagatelles, your symphonies good symphonies.

[1] For the record, they are: *On the Road*, Jack Kerouac; *Tropic of Cancer*, Henry Miller; *A Fan's Notes*, Frederick Exley; *Bad Behavior*, Mary Gaitskill; *Fear and Loathing in Las Vegas*, Hunter S. Thompson; *Remembrance of Things Past* (later accurately translated as *In Search of Lost Time*), Marcel Proust; *The Flowers of Evil* (poems), Charles Baudelaire; *Light Years*, James Salter; *Dog Soldiers*, Robert Stone; *The Beautiful Room Is Empty*, Edmund White; *Liars in Love*, Richard Yates; and many of the short stories of John Cheever and Raymond Carver.

[2] For example, look at my list of life changers. I mention *On the Road*, but not any of the many, shall I say, weaker books of Kerouac. I mention *Tropic of Cancer*, not *Plexus*. I mention *Liars in Love*, but not *Cold Spring Harbor*. And in reference to stories, I say *many* of the stories of Cheever and Carver, not *all*.

Getting Started

WRITING FROM LIFE

A good place to begin your fiction is out of your own experience. This is not to say you should write autobiography. Instead, look at your own life and to try to make sense of certain moments—perhaps small moments that represent some larger truth.

Regarding the autobiographical impulse in fiction, one of the questions I hear most often in workshops is a variation of this: At which point might I enter the morass of my life and write a story? A handy answer to anyone who asks that question: At a point when something significant changed. A graduation. A marriage. A death. First love. First sex. First heartbreak. Another answer: At a moment that has universal or widespread resonance. Christmas. A birthday. The fourth of July. The festival of Diwali. Tet.

Make a list of five turning points in your own life and note the years in which those turning points occurred. Now make a list of historical connections to those years. What happened in the news, in sports, in politics, in entertainment? Think about how (if at all) your life was influenced or impacted by those apparently surface events. You may discover that moments in your life that felt divorced from the march of history were actually quite connected with the larger picture on some level.

When I recall 1970, for instance, I see myself as a confused and vaguely sad adolescent; in the pictures I form in my memory from that time, I see a certain listlessness and passivity. I'm sure all the marijuana didn't help, but I also recall that that was the year the Beatles broke up. In 1964, when I was eight years old, the Beatles entered my life and the lives of others as a powerful, positive, joyful, rebellious influence. Over the next six years, their music and their lives affected many people on a deeply personal level, often on a daily basis. What did it mean to me then, in 1970, that they had disintegrated in acrimony? With what awareness did my stoned, fourteen-year-old consciousness confront this fact? And what did it mean to others, since I was by no means the only one affected? Autobiography and its connection to history can lead to resonant fiction.

Many stories are built upon life turning points. Tim O'Brien's "On the Rainy River" concerns a character's receipt of his draft notice. Mary Gaitskill's

"Secretary" focuses on a first job. Beth Nugent's "Locusts" involves the first time its protagonist is molested by a relative.

Many stories are built around historical connections. Marly Swick's "The Summer Before the Summer of Love" takes place in Ohio in 1966, when the Beatles are making their final concert tour. Gary Krist's "Giant Step" uses the first moon landing. An early Philip Gourevitch story, "Desiree in Escrow," conflates a child's loss of his mother with television images of the first Gulf War.

I once had a student who said that, to him, writing from personal experience was an indication of a broken imagination. For him, and to others with similar delusions, I offer the following significantly abbreviated list of fiction writers whose work places them in the front ranks of the Broken Imagination Club: Dorothy Allison, Melissa Bank, Toni Cade Bambara, Thomas Beller, Saul Bellow, William S. Burroughs, Raymond Carver, Sandra Cisneros, Michael Cunningham, Edwidge Danticat, Frederick Exley, Jonathan Franzen, Mary Gaitskill, Isabel Huggan, Gayl Jones, James Jones, Kaylie Jones, Thom Jones, James Joyce, Jack Kerouac, Henry Miller, Susan Minot, Rick Moody, Walter Mosley, Marcel Proust, Philip Roth, James Salter, Mona Simpson, Amanda Stern, Robert Stone, Edith Wharton, Tobias Wolff, Richard Wright, Richard Yates.

RETELLING STORIES

Another place to start is with a story you were told by someone else. How would you represent that story if you had to write it? Where would the emphasis be? How would you render the setting? How would you capture the voices of the participants?

The first story I ever wrote was really a transcription of a story that had been told to me by my brother about something that had happened to him, not me. He had recently graduated boot camp at the U.S. Marine Corps' Parris Island training grounds. While there, the worst trouble he'd gotten into occurred when the drill instructor discovered that my brother had left his footlocker unlocked. In a rage, the DI overturned the footlocker and spilled its contents onto the floor, where he found, rolling about in the mess, several plums my brother had taken from the mess hall. If failing to lock a footlocker is a misdemeanor, taking food from the mess hall is a high crime. If you know anything about the Marine Corps, boot camp, or drill instructors, you can imagine the paroxysms of outrage the DI went into over the issue of the unauthorized plums.

I knew something about all three—the Marines, boot camp, and DIs. My father was a Marine and served for six years. He went through Parris Island's boot camp not once, but twice (the Corps nullified his first graduation when they discovered that he'd enlisted under an alias while underage), and he returned to Parris Island as a DI several years after his second graduation. I wrote a story of sorts (a bagatelle?) called "The Poor Boot's Fruit," in which I imagined my father as the DI (of course) and myself (mixed with my brother) as the poor boot.

I attempted to write the story from the third-person omniscient point of view. The only rules I knew about writing were rules I'd gleaned from my reading, and since my reading consisted largely of books that had been published in the 1960s and early 1970s (Richard Brautigan's *Trout Fishing in America*, Tom Wolfe's *The Electric Kool-Aid Acid Test*, and everything by Kurt Vonnegut up to *Breakfast of Champions*, I didn't know much about rules. That helped me. I later learned that my story had violated some rules (I was working with a selective omniscience, which is generally reserved for one point of view, but I used several points of view at will and at random), and I then understood why the story didn't fully work—why the story wasn't really a story, but an anecdote, a vignette, a bagatelle. However, I had managed to come up with a piece that did a little of what my brother's story did for me: It made me laugh. And I recognized in it certain character types: a decent enough guy who violates a small, seemingly senseless rule, and a maniacal tyrant who goes ballistic at the slightest infraction. And I recognized certain themes inherent in what had captured my imagination: brutal, perhaps arbitrary authority; rebellion; father-son conflict (later, I would call it Oedipal drama); the world of men, order, regimentation, and physicality; and that world's impositions on the imagination and pleasure.

You can't make discoveries about character types, humor, personal themes, the nature of your imagination, and a whole lot of other things critical to the development of a writer if you don't get the material on the page. And you can't get the material on the page if you're hung up about rules.

I think that starting with a story that makes you laugh is a good idea. Starting with your parents is even better.

Showing Others Your Work

Be careful about showing your work. When I was a student, one of my fellow students asked a teacher what the writer should do if a story might hurt the writer's parents. The teacher said, "Every word I write is an attempt to hurt my parents." Some of us might want to tread more easily on those who raised us, for better or worse. At the least, protect parents and siblings and friends and spouses and partners from early drafts. Don't show them a story until it's finished—hopefully published. Then it has a life of its own, and because it is an already existing something or other, it's harder for those near to you to see themselves in it.

Another good reason not to show your work to people you know is to protect the most important person in the process: yourself. Any negative criticism can hurt, but it's especially important to avoid negative criticism from those who know how to hurt you, or from those who might be most prone to hurt feelings themselves.

If you are uneasy about including someone you know (or aspects of someone you know) in your work, keep in mind Tom Wolfe's assertion: The only way to hurt someone you know is to leave him out of your book.

POEM, DREAM, CONFLICT

The purpose of this exercise is to get started writing by using personal experience, personal habit, and that rich reservoir of material, the dream life. This exercise also encourages you to hustle through moments; you don't have to expect the individual moment to "solve" the story or to point the direction your writing should take. Instead, move on and wait for connections to materialize, if they ever do, and don't worry if they don't. In fact, *not* knowing how things fit together is a very good place to be. It allows you to play around, and this kind of play has a way of skipping past inner censors and critics and allowing the work to flow out of the unconscious. You don't need to see the full painting from the first brushstroke.

An absence of connections in your manuscript can raise questions in the mind of the reader, thereby engaging him. The earlier that questions are raised, the sooner you'll have a reader turning pages. This exercise will help you create material that raises questions.

Select a line from a poem that resonates with you. You can substitute a line from anything: a biography, a scientific treatise, a speech. Next, consider a recent (perhaps troubling) dream. Then, recall a problem you're having with another person.

Once you have each of these items firmly in mind, begin a fictional account that weaves these three apparently disparate strands together, following the steps below.

1. Poem. Write one or two paragraphs based on the resonant line of poetry (or prose) you chose. Then skip a line.

2. Dream. Write one or two paragraphs using fragments or themes from your dream. (It's unnecessary to make any explicit reference to the text you used for step one.) Again, skip a line.

3. Conflict. Write one or two paragraphs concerning the conflict you thought of. (Again, it's unnecessary to make any explicit reference to steps one or two.) Skip a line.

4. Putting it all together. Begin weaving together elements from steps one through three. Follow your impulses. Something is probably already occurring to you.

As an example, I have provided my own attempt at this exercise.

1. *Poem*

   From a shelf labeled "Staff Picks," she blindly removed a narrow volume of Stephen Dunn's poems which fell open to: "It was the hour of simply nothing, / not a single desire in my western heart…" Further down the page: "There was even an absence of despair." She rolled her eyes; even in random books selected by nearly illiterate clerks, she was finding her experience rendered. So much for uniqueness.

   She piled her arms with magazines and took a seat on the staircase leading to texts on science.

2. *Dream*

   Her just-before-waking dream had involved horses, horses with their heads over a fence. She had extended her fist, and a yearling's thick white teeth had scraped skin from her knuckles. At first she'd recoiled, but then she offered the knuckles again. *What in God's name could that mean?* she wondered.

She looked at her hand now, half expecting to find scabs.

3. *Conflict*

The night her brother called, she found her attention wandering. She held the receiver in one hand, the TV remote in the other, and she surfed through the channels, half-listening to his litany of investment successes.

"I bought at lunchtime," he told her, "called in a put by afternoon, sold in the morning."

This appeared to have some meaning for her brother.

"That's good," she told him. "Very good."

She stopped at *Lou Dobbs' Moneyline*, then *Jeopardy*.

4. *Putting It All Together*

At the checkout counter, she was almost surprised to find the slim volume of poems among her purchases.

"Great collection," the salesman said.

The salesman had a horsey face. Reflexively, she covered her knuckles.

"Do you know anything about investing?" she asked him.

He frowned. "Would I be working the register at a bookstore," he said, "if I knew anything about investing?"

They agreed to meet for coffee the next afternoon.

Story Structure and Plot

A discussion of the basics of story structure must begin with plot. Why? Because effective fiction raises a question in the mind of the reader. The reader turns the pages, and continues to turn the pages, in the interest of answering the question. How early the fiction (story or novel) raises that question, how dramatic that question is, how desperate the reader is to know the answer to that question, how long the writer can delay answering that question—all of these are functions of plot.

This is not to say that fiction can't succeed (with certain readers) if it lacks a plot, or that stories must be structured a certain way. But by focusing first on story structure, you stress perhaps the most critical story function—one that appears in the vast majority of stories, from the best-sellers to small-press esoterica. (Because it appears far less frequently, and because its choices seem to be deliberately in opposition to the rigors of plot, the plotless story can be discussed in relation to its more abundant cousin.[3])

One hears all sorts of definitions of plot and its distinction from story. Story, according to E.M. Forster, is "The king died, and then the queen died." Plot is "The king died, and then the queen died of grief." Plot, to Forster, is motivation.

Story, according to David Mamet, is "the essential progression of incidents that occur to the hero in pursuit of his one goal." In other words, story is the protagonist making choices, taking actions.

So plot involves (1) motivation, (2) choices, and (3) change. The engine of these plot elements is conflict. If you find those qualities in your manuscript, you will be on your way to drafting a well-told story, one that readers will want to finish.

CLASSICAL STORY STRUCTURE

In classically constructed fiction (short story or novel), the opening section (passage, chapter, act) introduces character and setting (the exposition), the conflict, and it provides the event that sets the story moving forward in present action. The longer second act will rise and fall, often twice, in an event-crisis-climax pattern. The third act, usually the shortest, might provide a resolution of sorts, and will certainly answer the Major Dramatic Question. So, in the big picture, you have (1) set-up, (2) increasing complications, (3) climax and reversal, and (4) resolution.

Classical structure provides the writer with a checklist, and the checklist provides a fail-safe. Questions you can put into your story's structure are:

1. **Has your opening section provided** *the set-up?* That is, has it introduced principal characters and setting. Has the conflict been introduced? Does the inciting incident, the event that kicks the story into present

---

[3] *Plotless* is not a pejorative, it's a choice. Good examples of plotless stories can be found in the collections of Lydia Davis.

action, appear? Does that incident raise the Major Dramatic Question, the question that the reader needs to see answered?

2. **Do the *complications* of the set-up increase in urgency?** Does the protagonist's struggle increase? Are the obstacles in the protagonist's way more and more difficult to hurdle?

3. **Does the struggle build to a *climax*?** Does the climax involve the protagonist taking an action that is dramatized on the page? Does the outcome of that action address the Major Dramatic Question? **Does the outcome involve a *reversal*?**

4. **Does the conclusion *resolve* the story's tensions?** Has the Major Dramatic Question been answered?

When is it advantageous to plot classically? Probably always. It's a bit like asking when it is advantageous to make the wheel round. Round wheels roll; plotted fiction compels.

But, are some wheels rounder than others? In fiction, yes. In the so-called *minimalist* fiction of the late 1970s through the 1980s, set-ups and resolutions were often effectively abbreviated. Raymond Carver's "Neighbors" sets up in two paragraphs:

> Bill and Arlene Miller were a happy couple. But now and then they felt alone among their circle had been passed by somehow. ... They talked about it sometimes, mostly in comparison with the lives of their neighbors, Harriet and Jim Stone. It seemed ... that the Stones lived a fuller and brighter life.
>
> The Stones lived across the hall from the Millers. ... on this occasion the Stones would be away for ten days. In their absence, the Millers would look after the Stones' apartment, feed Kitty and water plants.

In this set up, Carver introduces principal characters (Bill and Arlene), the setting (an apartment building, Anywhere, USA), the conflict (Bill and Arlene envy their neighbors, the Stones), and the inciting incident (Bill and Arlene will be looking after the Stones' apartment). By the third paragraph, "Neighbors" is into its complications. It concludes at the climax; its resolution is implied. But even with the abbreviated set-up and the lopped off resolution, "Neighbors" still rolls. Why? Because the elements of the checklist are there. (For further discussion, see the sidebar, "A Plot Troubleshooting Device" on page 28.)

STORY-OPENING STRATEGIES

Stories are usually built around a three-part structure: acts one, two, and three or the beginning, middle, and end. Each part of the structure has its own purpose.

The purpose of the beginning of a story is to introduce character and conflict. Another purpose is to catch and hold the reader's interest. One way to do so is to raise a question in the mind of the reader. Another way is to quickly immerse the reader in the action of the story, to eliminate boring exposition. Frank O'Connor said that "short stories begin where everything but the action has already taken place. Only the action remains." This is a useful tip to remember. Exposition is implicit in action; action is exposition. The old *show, don't tell* rule, in other words. By telling—that is, by providing a résumé or a psychological profile for your character—you are providing information in a form that glides past the reader like a software terms-of-use agreement. By showing—that is, by allowing the reader to observe your character in action—you are dramatizing information, and information provided through action stays with the reader. Compare the following approaches to the same story opening.

> In college, Janice studied to become a pharmacist. After school she acquired her license and began work in a small town drugstore (she hated that term) in New Hampshire. At twenty-six, she married Neil Pilbow, a commercial pilot eleven years her senior. A lot of people thought she'd be unhappy to turn thirty, but Janice was A-okay with that milestone. In fact, she felt at the prime of her life.

> Janice Pilbow slid her lab coat over her head, hung it on a dressing room hook, and studied herself in the mirror. In her yoga outfit, a body-length leotard that she wore underneath her lab coat, she looked the same at thirty as she'd looked at nineteen. "One day," her husband Neil had told her that morning, fixing his pilot's cap on his head, "I'm going to open the cockpit door, and you'll be standing there in that outfit, and oh boy, those passengers better have their seat belts buckled."

Conflict, when effectively dramatized, also catches the attention of the reader. The following commonly used story-opening strategies (SOS) capture the reader's interest by presenting immediate conflict. For each premise type,

I have created my own brief story-openings. The openings amount to the first few strokes of paint on the canvas—a strategic stroke designed to get the picture painted convincingly and efficiently.

ROUTINE-DISRUPTION

How do you get plot into a story? It's as easy as creating a routine, then disrupting it. Routine-disruption creates plot. It makes the protagonist struggle to restore the order that's been disrupted, or it makes the protagonist accept that the order can never be restored. It causes the protagonist to make choices and take actions, and the actions characters take are what define them. Most of the other story structures discussed here are variations of the routine-disruption premise.

1. Every morning for ten years, Jim Dorsey ran through his well-manicured suburban neighborhood for exactly six miles. One morning, closing in on mile five, something in the area of his ankle snapped. ...

2. Betty Indick never saw her mother in midtown, until one afternoon, on her lunch break, there her mother was, looking in the windows of boutiques.

3. Joan Comfort hadn't had a drink in five years. Then, one night, she met an intriguing man with a tempting bottle of ...

(Example one is the premise of John Cheever's "O Youth and Beauty." Example two is the premise of Edwidge Danticat's "New York Day Women." Example three is the premise of Kate Braverman's "Tall Tales From the Mekong Delta.")

THE CHANCE ENCOUNTER

The chance encounter is a variation of routine-disruption. The routine is that the protagonist never sees someone anymore. The disruption is when that someone appears. The chance encounter premise provides something of setting (where does the encounter take place?) and something of the exposition (what is the protagonist doing at the time?), and into that setting it slams a character out of the past. That character will introduce necessary backstory and an old issue in the protagonist's psychological development that's been left unresolved. It injects a past problem into a present situation. (And that is the working method of many a Raymond Carver story. Carver, who divided his life into "Good Raymond" and "Bad Raymond" periods, often jammed Bad Raymond experiences into Good Raymond settings. The story "Cathedral" is a classic example.)

1. He was about to take his dinner on the verandah overlooking the sea when he saw a familiar figure emerge from the shallows, stop ankle deep, and throw back her long, unmistakable hair.
   "Scotch," he said to the waiter. "Double."

2. She was preparing to go home for the evening when a knock came at her office door. Without waiting for a response, the knocker entered. Ken, whom she hadn't seen in eleven years, whom she'd believed was dead, stood big as life in front of her desk. He did not appear to recognize her.

3. One day, while returning from the gym, Bobby heard his name shouted several times before he stopped. From across the avenue trotted Zee, an old college roommate who'd mastered a dozen old ways and invented several new ways to cheat on exams, all while his girlfriend was cheating on him ... with Bobby.

(Example one is the premise of Jennifer Egan's "Why China?" Example two is the premise of Helen Schulman's *P.S.* Example three is a variation of a premise that launches several stories by Mary Gaitskill including the aptly named "Chance Encounter"; it also happened to me.)

ENTER: MYSTERIOUS STRANGER

Enter: mysterious stranger is the name Robert Penn Warren gave to his story strategy for "Blackberry Winter." The early drafts of "Blackberry Winter" contained lyrical passages and moving descriptions, but nothing was happening to advance the story. So, into those lyrical passages and moving descriptions, Warren introduced a mysterious stranger, a guy who walks up the path toward the house, carrying a switchblade.

Enter: mysterious stranger is a close relative of the chance encounter and routine-disruption. It involves the introduction of a new element into the story's world—an element dynamic enough to cause a significant disruption.

1. That summer, the office workload increased almost daily. By mid-July, the manager hired a new secretary, but once hired, that secretary refused to work.

2. Janet didn't like handicapped people—or cripples, as she insisted on calling them. She didn't like the way they bungled about, banging into things or slowing down the progress of the bus. She didn't like the way they just assumed they had to be deferred to. One evening, her husband came home from work with his handicapped friend, a woman in a wheelchair, whose feet had to be braced not to curl inward.

(Example one is the premise of Herman Melville's "Bartleby, the Scrivener." Example two is the premise of Raymond Carver's "Cathedral.")

THE SHATTERING STATEMENT

Routine: The protagonist has never heard a particular point of view, a particular "truth" before. Disruption: Now he hears it. The shattering statement creates plot by forcing the characters to address a truth that is now out on the table.

1. On their tenth anniversary, Colin Hough's wife, Deb, informed him, without rancor, without accusation, that she had never had an orgasm with him, and that she didn't believe she ever would.

2. On a family drive into Brooklyn for a Thanksgiving visit, Tommy leaned into the front seat and said, "I hate Grandma."

   His mother and father exchanged looks.

   "You don't hate Grandma," his mother told him.

   "I do, too," Tommy insisted. "I hate her guts."

   "Hey," his father told him, "that's enough."

(Example one is the premise of Richard Yates's "A Natural Girl." Example two is something that could have happened, and maybe should have, on one of the dreaded visits my family made to visit with my father's mother.)

A first cousin to the shattering statement is the shattering discovery.

The day after her father's funeral, Karen gathered the belongings in his apartment. In a photograph album buried below balls of socks, she discovered pictures of her father naked, in the company of men. In some of the pictures, naked men were doing things to other naked men. Some of the naked men were boys.

EXPECTATION VS. ACTUALITY

This setup establishes what a character thinks a new situation will entail and how that expectation collides with reality. Sometimes the routine is explicitly stated, explicitly delineated, elaborately established. Sometimes the routine is implicit in the portrayal of the disruption. In Raymond Carver's "Neighbors," a couple has always been curious about the lives of their more successful, high-living neighbors. That's the routine. The routine is implicit in the zeal the couple brings to the opportunity to apartment-sit for the neighbors; it is never explicitly stated.

1. On moving to New York, Jim expected to land a soap in one week, a Broadway show in two, and a first-class ticket to LAX in three. But by his fourth week, without an agent, without an audition, without even a cattle call, he took a job with a furniture-moving company where all the furniture movers were like him—actors—only older.

2. Billie had always dreamed of the day when she could cross the boulevard and hang around the parking lot of the diner, where the boys all leaned against the hoods of their cars and smoked cigarettes and cracked jokes about the girls who passed dangerously and deliberately close by. She dreamed how one of those boys would study her, would follow her with his eyes, shyly smile, and one day break away from his friends to ask her, awkwardly, if he might buy her a soda.

   She hadn't dreamed that one day, while her parents were gone and she was all alone, that boy would show up at the house with one of his friends.

(Example one is the premise of Jennifer Egan's "Emerald City." Example two is the premise of what might be the most widely anthologized story in English, Joyce Carol Oates's "Where Are You Going, Where Have You Been?")

THE ROAD STORY

This is an old and crowded field—think Homer's *The Odyssey*, Hermann Hesse's *The Journey to the East*, Jack Kerouac's *On the Road*, Richard Ford's "Rock Springs," Tobias Wolff's "Desert Breakdown, 1968," and pretty much any other story or novel in which the characters start in one place and head for another. That's basically the setup: Your characters are in location A, they set out for location B, and things happen between departure and arrival. Once they arrive, the story is over, and that's one reason why it's such an easy and appealing setup. (Of course, they don't have to arrive.)

In this premise, the trip is the disruption of routine. Of course, a routine might be established on the trip, and then that routine might be disrupted. For instance, a couple on their way out of New York to New Orleans might argue all the way from New Jersey through Virginia, but then stop arguing once they approach the border of Tennessee.

A common flaw in the road story is inherent in its nature: Road stories in which the protagonist visits several destinations tend to be episodic. Places (and the characters connected to them) drop out of the narrative once the protagonist gets back in the saddle. The concern then becomes to build resonance through association or contrast. Once you've shown aspects of your character through his interaction with the saloon-keeper in location B, how will you show your character's development through his encounter with the saloon-keeper in location G? If a dog chases the runner at location A, how do you use the dog that appears at location C?

THE PLOTLESS STORY

A good question to ask yourself is *How soon does my manuscript raise a question in the mind of the reader?* If it doesn't raise a question, the reader won't urgently need to know the answer. Why should the reader continue to turn pages?

W.B. Yeats said that the further music strays from the dance, and poetry from the song, the deeper those forms are in trouble. Story and plot are the simplest components of prose fiction, and the further you stray from them, the more difficult it will be for you to sustain the interest of readers.

That said, there are other elements of fiction that can sustain readers: tone, language, idea, atmosphere, and character. If the tone of a story matches the reader's inner voice, the reader might stick around till "About the Author." For instance, if a story or novel seems ironically hip, it might appeal to readers who share that sensibility.

Florid or virtuoso language, too, can keep a reader involved. However, a common workshop pitfall is the writer with language but no story. Robert Stone said that fiction requires both elevated (convincing, literary, musical) language and gripping story. One without the other diminishes the fiction. In relation to the Coen brothers filmmaking team, the critic Stanley Kauffmann wrote that they appeared to have become articulate before they became mature. That is the case, I'm afraid, with a lot of voice-driven, *Look, Ma, I'm writing* diction-fiction that crowds the pages of the small presses and that is championed inside many MFA workshops.

Keeping the reader engaged with an idea is tricky. Most ideas are better expressed in forms like the essay, the tract, and the monograph. However, Milan Kundera's hugely successful novels are idea laden, perhaps even idea driven. He is less interested in characters working out their struggles than he is in characters illustrating his ideas.

Atmosphere can mean either exterior or interior setting. The exterior setting of Ernest Hemingway's "The Big Two-Hearted River, Part One" pulls you in and keeps you because of its lyric specificity, its distillation in prose of the natural world. Many Lydia Davis stories pull you in with interior setting—the intellection of a wounded heroine, a jilted lover, a waiting spouse. What Davis follows, then, is not a character in action who makes revealing choices, but the ripples of thought and emotion in a character pinned, for one reason or another, in stasis.

Many a book introduces a wonderful character, but little drama or action. Depending on the nature of the character, a reader will toss the book or turn the pages. Frederick Exley's *A Fan's Notes* might be driven more by character than by plot.[4] Henry Miller's *Tropic of Cancer* is a book that seems to provide everything but plot: voice, tone, character, language, setting, idea, rant, erudition, spleen, bile, and humor. It is, at best, intermittently plotted. I have read it through to the end at least a dozen times.

[4] In "The Art of Fiction," Henry James says, "What is character but the determination of incident? What is incident but the illustration of character?" And David Mamet says that to discuss plot-driven as opposed to character-driven stories is nonsense. Perhaps in the greatest books and stories there is a perfect marriage of character and action, and I agree that that's a marriage worth proposing and, as long as possible, remaining faithful to. But I don't think it's controversial to suggest that in some stories we're more hooked by character than action, or vice versa. Andre Dubus's "A Father's Story" might be an example of a character-driven story; it's because we care about the protagonist that we wait around so long for the action. The little twists and jolts in the action of a Somerset Maugham story are often more interesting than the often one-dimensional characters. The argument really boils down to semantics because in the end, all story elements are inextricably linked. Yet I daresay that *Finnegans Wake* is more voice than plot driven, the comments of James and Mamet notwithstanding.

As Flannery O'Connor stated about fiction, you can do whatever you can get away with, but you'll probably find you can't get away with very much.

A Plot Troubleshooting Device

Every writer should plug the following troubleshooting device—from Frank O'Connor's book on writing, *The Lonely Voice*—into his every manuscript. In his book (transcriptions, actually, of lectures) O'Connor says that there are three things a story requires: exposition, development, and drama. You know that the plot portion of the beginning of your story is strong if you can summarize your story in three lines, with each line relating to one of these elements. This device can help you determine if you've established a routine, created a compelling disruption, and given your protagonist something to struggle for. O'Connor's example appears below.

> *Exposition:* John Fortescue was a solicitor in the little town of X.
>
> *Development:* One day, Mrs. Fortescue told him she was leaving him for another man.
>
> *Drama:* "You'll do nothing of the kind," he said.

In line one, the exposition, you learn who the story is about: John Fortescue. You learn what John Fortescue does for a living: He's a solicitor (lawyer). From that piece of information, you can form reasonably accurate impressions of the Fortescues' relative income and social milieu. And you know where the Fortescues live: in the little town of X (not the big town of London). From all this information—quite a lot for one line—you can intuit a routine: the married life of a small-town attorney.

In line two, development, you see the inciting incident of the story—the disruption of the routine. You now know what's at stake in the story: a marriage, and everything connected with the marriage—the routine, the reputation, the self-esteem, perhaps the career.

In line three, drama, you learn what the protagonist will struggle for: the marriage. John Fortescue wants to restore the order—the routine—that's been disrupted.

One of the most important questions you can put to your character is *What does my character want?* This question should be followed by *What's in the way of my character getting it?* You can already answer those questions about the Fortescues: John Fortescue wants to save his marriage and the routine that it represents. What's in the way of him getting that? Mrs. Fortescue.

If you try to create an exposition line for your manuscript (X is an X in X), and you can't come up with all the information needed to fill in the blanks, then your story has a problem with exposition. The reader needs to know something about the characters and the world of the story in order to appreciate fully the struggle the characters are about to undergo.

If, when assessing development, you cannot find the one day or the one time that something happened to disrupt a routine, you might have a problem with plotting. Instead of a piece that moves dramatically, a piece in which a character struggles for something, you might have a series of routines without drama.

If you come up blank for drama (or if the drama seems vague), then your story has a problem with conflict and motivation.

If your story withstands the exposition-development-drama test, then you're probably well on the way to telling a solid story.

MOVING FORWARD TO THE SECOND ACT

Probably the most challenging part of writing a solid story will be making the middle, the second act, as vital and focused as the opening. In discussing plot, John Barth borrows language from physics and calls this middle section the section of increased perturbations. In other words, what was problematic in the opening of the story grows more so in the middle until, finally, the problems become so urgent that a climax is forced through choices the character makes and actions she takes. This is the section where a lot of stories—and even more novels—go awry. It's the section where the writer would do well to recall the David Mamet definition that "story is the essential progression of incidents that occur to the hero in pursuit of his one goal." If it's not essential, dump it. If there is more than one goal, cut it or them. If the work in question is a novel with subplots decide if the subplot's protagonist has more than one goal; if so, cut it or them.

Easier said than done, but then nothing about writing is easy. There are, however, a few tricks you can try, and a few wrenches you can twist, to help figure out that perilous middle. One trick is to skip it—skip the middle entirely. As Flannery O'Connor put it, stories do have beginnings, middles, and ends, but not necessarily in that order. If that's the case, they don't have to be written in that order, either. If you're stuck, jump forward: *How does your story end?* Other questions toward the same solution: *What's the best possible ending for my character? What's the worst? What's the craziest?* Have fun, write to these questions, and then ask: *What events are required to get my character from here (the end of the beginning) to there (the beginning of the end)?*[5]

Those are useful terms to remember: *the end of the beginning* and *the beginning of the end.* Your beginning ends because something has happened—an event, a revelation, a shift in awareness—and now your middle caroms off that event. And your ending begins where the middle ends, and your middle ends because something happened. What? Where? Who was there? What time was it? How did it smell? How did your character feel when it happened? What will she do now that it has?

The beginning is the setup, the place where the principal characters are introduced, the setting is established, and the conflict is triggered. In Pam Houston's "Selway," the principal characters decide to set out on a rafting journey against the warnings of park rangers. The middle is their journey, during which events occur that force choices that reveal character and lead to a climax. In Mary Gaitskill's "Tiny, Smiling Daddy," Stew learns over the phone that his daughter Kitty has come out as a lesbian in a national magazine. The middle is Stew's journey into town to get that magazine and to learn what his daughter has said about herself and her family. In these examples, the beginning has established a decision or a course, and the middles follow through quite naturally.

Follow-through is an important idea. Decisions and events cause the next decisions and actions. In the middle, don't forget what came before. If a dog

---

[5] The problem with writing is writing. The discoveries in writing will be made in writing. The solutions to story problems—structural, motivational, existential—will be found in writing. If the pages of the story are a locus of anxiety, get out of them—do an exercise for which there is no right or wrong. Just get writing. Your middle will not arrive through thinking, and while it may arrive in dreaming, dreaming is more likely to produce results if you fall asleep while writing.

bites the protagonist in act one, and act two is set in a high-stakes poker marathon, the middle would do well to address how that dog bite affects the protagonist's game. The middle is where you follow through on the beginning's complications, and where you set up the ending (which follows through on the middle).

If you're working on a long short story (say, twenty-five or more manuscript pages) or anything longer, remember that middles have their own beginnings, middles, and endings. That is, an event sets the action in motion, the action leads to some kind of crisis, and the crisis leads to a climax. In "Selway," when the stakes have risen with the water, the crisis involves the last chance to abandon the journey, and the climax depicts the results of the choice the characters make. In "Tiny, Smiling Daddy," Stew's private anguish is exposed more and more as he ventures into town to buy the magazine, and once he's made the purchase, his private understanding of the nature of his relationship with his daughter is threatened more and more as he reads. Incremental perturbations, turns of the screw, complications—these are the characteristics of your story's middle.

Reversal

Sometimes the writer gets stuck in a manuscript, wondering where to turn. A good exercise is to turn around, hang a U-ey, reverse direction. Ask: What did my protagonist believe in the story's opening? How can I make that exactly the opposite by the end? What did my protagonist value? How can I have her destroy that thing? What are the circumstances of my protagonist? How can I make those exactly the opposite?

Reversal is a plot element that goes all the way back to the beginning. Remember Oedipus searching for the person responsible for the plague and then discovering that it's himself? In contemporary stories, you'll find reversals in abundance. At the beginning of Tim O'Brien's "The Things They Carried," Lieutenant Jimmy Cross values nothing so much as the letters he's received from a girl back home; by the end, he burns those letters. In the beginning of Tom Perrotta's "You Start to Live," Buddy sits in the back, Laura Daly drives; by the end, their positions have reversed. In Angela Patrino "Sculpture I," a young woman

> with a negative self-image moves to a country where she's compared favorably to Julia Roberts.
>
> If your story is stuck somewhere in the middle, try reversal, and go the other way. The trick, finally, is to make the reversal less a mechanical thing and more an organic outgrowth of the story, of why the story is being told. But forcing reversals on stalled stories is good practice for when the real thing comes along.

STORY ENDINGS

The short story is, to use writer David Lodge's term, end-oriented, meaning that one picks up a short story with the expectation of soon reaching its conclusion (whereas, with a novel, the ending is some distance away). The impact of a short story is significantly affected by its ending, a novel's perhaps less so. There are many good (and some great) novels with weak or bad endings: Leo Tolstoy's *War and Peace*, which moves out of fiction and becomes a history lesson; Graham Greene's *The End of the Affair*, which limps with weak motivation to the finish line from the pivot at the act-two story turning point; Alberto Moravia's *Contempt*, which solves a crucial story problem with a deus ex machina (as does the volume of Marcel Proust called *The Fugitive*). Still, these are books worth reading. (For balance, a few novels with great endings: Edith Wharton's *The Age of Innocence*, James Welch's *The Death of Jim Loney*, Scott Spencer's *Endless Love*.)

Whether you're working on a novel or a short story, ask yourself some of the following questions about your ending:

1. What is the last action that the reader sees? How can this final action encapsulate, reinforce, and underscore the story's themes?

2. What is the final language of the story? The last sentence? The concluding phrase? How do these resonate? How do they evoke the story's theme?

3. In dialogue, does a character express his destiny?

4. Does the image or action or language work on more than one level (is it both literal and symbolic)?

Basic Manuscript Evaluation

In workshop, the following questions can help troubleshoot the manuscript under discussion and help the writer of the piece (and all the other writers) return to work with a sense of how to approach revision.

1. What is the world of the story and how convincingly are its details rendered?

   The **world** of the story is its setting in time and place. How well is the story's place established? Are the descriptive details adequate to paint a mental picture? Are there too many details—do you get lost in them? How well do the details participate in telling the story? How convincing is the story's setting in time? *Convincing* is related to *accurate*, but not wholly: You wouldn't expect a story set in eighteenth-century New England to include discussion of the Oedipus complex, but you might allow for loose play with facts and history if the license taken creates a more convincing story.

2. Who is the story about and (a) are we convinced by them, and/or (b) do we care about them?

   For **characters**, dimensionality is the main concern. Do they feel fully formed, complex, fully human? Are they capable of surprising you? Do they convince you (in their speech, habits, costume, thoughts, desires)? Or are they one-dimensional? Are they caricatures? Stereotypes?

3. Do the events of the story challenge the characters? Ultimately, are the characters' true natures revealed as a result of the story events?

   What kinds of **events** does the story throw at the characters? Do those events sufficiently challenge the characters and thereby reveal their truest nature? Or do the events feel random, ornamental, nonessential? Further, how well are events dramatized? Do they convince? Do they raise questions? Are they representative of more than just the literal action?

4. How well does the language of the story communicate the story's theme? Is the tone appropriate for the content? Is the writer glib (a common approach in workshops) when he needs to be neutral?

   Language is to a story what paint is to a canvas—it's the medium through which the message is communicated. Does the story's language communicate the story convincingly? Are there glitches in the language? If there are unintended grammatical errors, the story will probably suffer. But more important in this category is the syntax—the tone, the voice, the efficiency of the sentences, the music of the prose. The sensitive reader needs the prose and the dialogue to sound exactly right.

5. What are the stakes of the story? Does the protagonist stand to gain or lose something by story's end? How clear are the stakes?

   A critical concern for a story is what's at **stake** for the characters. The higher the stakes, the more intense the drama. In Pam Houston's "Selway," Tim O'Brien's "The Things They Carried," and Edmund White's "Running on Empty," the stakes are life-or-death. Those kinds of stakes rivet a reader. Of course, most literary fiction does not concern life-or-death stakes; literary fiction more frequently deals with less urgent issues. The stakes still need to be clear, and felt. What does the principal character stand to gain or lose by the end of the story?

And one final important question to ask: Does the story raise a question in the mind of the reader? How early?

An Example: Pam Houston's "Selway"

In "Selway," a single woman goes on a whitewater rafting trip with her boyfriend, a man who seeks greater and greater danger in his rafting, and who refuses to commit to his girlfriend.

The world of the story is the river, the raft, and the riverbanks. These are all persuasively rendered. You feel the cold of the water, its violence; you feel the vulnerability of the raft as well as its graceful glide over the less turbulent patches of river. You are provided with details of the camp settings, the particulars of riverbanks. The setting in time is the early to mid-1990s, and the story is true to that time.

The characters are fully dimensional. The boyfriend is something of an outdoor macho man. He is a recognizable type in his relation to danger—he seeks it, he attempts to master it. And he is a recognizable type in relation to women—he wants one in his life, but he refuses to make a place for her. He's complex (or complicated) because he embodies a paradox. So does the girl—the narrator. She wants a man to make a place for her in his life, but she is only attracted to men who won't. These characteristics are, of course, related to the stakes of the story.

The events of "Selway" are relatively straightforward: Against the advice of river guide officials, a couple sets out on a raft journey on a dangerously turbulent river. The things that happen to the characters are the things that happen on rafting trips: variations of calm and turbulence, rolling and camping, talking, observing. The story events build to a convincing climax as the raft approaches the most dangerous of all the whitewater patches. The answer to the question of whether the events challenge the characters sufficiently enough to reveal who they really are is a resounding yes.

The language of the story convincingly represents the consciousness of the girlfriend. The prose renders that consciousness with authority, insight, and eloquence. It also handles the particulars of the descriptive details with authority.

Stakes are clear right from paragraph one: If the characters go out on a raft in this river, their lives will be imperiled. The magnitude of the stakes is convincingly reinforced as the couple proceeds downriver and the water becomes more and more turbulent and casualties of that turbulence are encountered or observed.

These five broad categories—world, characters, events, language, stakes—apply, more or less, to the critique of every piece of fiction. One or two may be more important than others in a given story. (Nuanced characters might not be terribly important in action stories, which tend to be event driven. Nuanced characters are critical, however, in most literary fiction.) Evaluate these categories in your own manuscripts and see how your work fares.

Jumping the Time Frame

FLASH FORWARD

Flashing forward—that is, jumping the time frame of the story—can work a number of wonderful effects on a manuscript. One, it can take the writer out of the anxiety of figuring out what comes next in the course of events. Instead, the question becomes *What is the later effect of the events that have already transpired?* Two, even if the answer to that question does nothing for the story, it can lead the writer right back into the story by somehow revealing what comes next in the story's time frame. Three, it delays gratification—it suspends. By answering the question of what happens in the future, the writer delays answering the question of what happens now at the moment of the story climax. What happens now is what the reader wants to know, and the flash forward can effectively delay that gratification and thereby increase its impact.

For example, in Junot Diaz's "The Sun, the Moon, and the Stars," Yunior (the narrator) is on vacation with his Cuban girlfriend in the Dominican Republic, Yunior's birthplace. The trip is Yunior's attempt to patch up a relationship that his earlier infidelity had sent heading toward the rocks. On the trip, it appears as if the girlfriend is plotting some nasty payback. Right at the moment when the tension between the narrator and his girlfriend becomes unbearable—right at the act-two climax, when we'll learn what the girlfriend is going to do, the action that will answer the Major Dramatic Question (MDQ)—Diaz flashes forward to the next period in the protagonist's life. It's about six months in the future, and things have changed. We're dying to know how, and why. Diaz doesn't let us down, he just makes us wait a little longer before the story returns to answer the Major Dramatic Question. This choice created another wonderful effect; while the reader savors the new moment (for its language, for its feeling and tone, for its information about character), the reader is also impatient for the answer to the MDQ. The Major Dramatic Question is the question that drives the story, that turns the pages, that the reader needs to have answered. In "Selway," will the couple survive? In "The Sun, the Moon, and the Stars," will Yunior lose his girlfriend? The reader is like a dog in front of two bowls, and a kind of anxious dizziness is induced by the richness of choice.

Give it a try in your story. Jump forward ten days, ten weeks, ten months, ten years. What has happened because of what had happened? How does that new situation inform the past? Is there a way to go back into the story—the past you've jumped from—and address its hanging issues?

THE FLASHBACK

A flashback is an event that happened in the past and is presented as a scene, that is, in real time with all the devices real-time scenes might deploy, including dialogue. Flashback is an overused device with many potential pitfalls. If flashback appears early in the story, there is probably a problem with the story entry point; maybe the story needs to begin earlier. If you recall the Frank O'Connor idea that the short story begins where everything but the action has already taken place, you know that the action itself—what you see the protagonist do in the present time—should be sufficient to reveal the inexorable nature of the character and the essential theme of the story.

If a flashback appears later in the story, it may have the effect of reducing present action conflict to a 2 + 2 = 4 arithmetic: The character is behaving like *this* in the present because *that* happened to her in the past. *Because* equals explanation, and explanation is to be avoided. It's antithetical to fiction.

Those caveats aside, flashback can be used effectively. Midway through *The Death of Jim Loney*, a backstory event concerning Jim Loney's girlfriend, Rhea, is presented in a flashback; this flashback adds to your understanding of Rhea and your sense of foreboding for Jim as the novel moves toward its climax.

Flashback is not the same as backstory. Backstory is information in the story's or character's past, and it can be parceled out effectively in the narration as the story progresses. See, for instance, John Cheever's "The Swimmer," a story in which the protagonist, Neddy Merrill, decides to swim home, using the pools of his county as a kind of continuous stream. At each pool, through his actions and through his interaction with others, we learn a little bit more of Neddy's past, and that new information helps us better understand Neddy's present. Cheever parcels out that information little by little as the story progresses; not once does he use flashback.

Character

CHARACTERIZATION THROUGH ACTION AND DETAIL

Stories are about events that happen to people. If we like the people, if we identify with the people, if we recognize the people, we are likely going to be compelled to read about those events. The question is, how do we create characters readers will be interested in? How do we avoid clichés, stereotypes, or one-dimensional caricatures?

First, try to provide information about the characters without appearing as if you're providing information. In other words, it's not just the information, it's the way you present the information. You don't want to provide a formal résumé or a psychological profile of a character. Instead, you want to show the character in action; from that action, the reader will determine the traits and qualities of the character.

For instance, compare these two sentences about the same character.

> Bernstein cared a lot about his golf game.

> Bernstein slammed his Ben Hogans into the trunk of his Toyota.

In the first example, we have information, plainly stated. What we don't have is effective characterization, which is achieved through action and detail. Example two provides those. Action is exposition: Bernstein is slamming golf clubs into the trunk of a car. This action provides information without explicitly stating the information (as in the first example). That action conjures several possible suggestions about Bernstein: (1) He's careless; (2) he's angry about his game (he lost, he played poorly); or (3) he's angry about something else, and a round of golf has not soothed him.

Details also characterize. Ben Hogans are a type of golf club; they say something about the type of golfer (they are linked to the point of view of the golfer and suggest the amount of investment the golfer has in the game). A Toyota is a type of car, and again, that type suggests something about the owner. Balzac said, "Show me what a man owns, and I'll show you what he believes." Details work on more than one level. The details are the literal circumstances of the moment, but they also point to deeper truths about the character.

The first example above tells us one piece of information about Bernstein, but the second example actually characterizes him by *showing* us many pieces of information.

Forget the Rules

Perhaps the most important rule of all writing: Forget about all the rules. A friend of mine who's an avid (and very good) tennis player wanted to take his game to the next level. He hired a coach and began working with the coach twice a week. The coach ran him ragged on the court and constantly made micro-corrections to his form. In less than a month, my friend found his game falling apart, and after two months he complained to his coach. "I get out on the court, I try to remember everything you've taught me, and I can't return a ball over the net." The coach said, "When we practice, practice as hard as you can. Do every drill, integrate every correction. Then, when you play, forget you ever had a coach, forget every drill, every instruction. Just play your game. The drills and the instructions will filter into your game if you just forget about them and play." My friend followed the coach's advice, and soon he was at the top of his club, looking for more advanced players to challenge from other clubs.

The same principle applies to writing. Practice hard and often, attempt to do the exercises and the drills while you're practicing. Then, forget everything you've learned and write straight out of the fever (or the grind) of writing. Once you've got a stack of pages, read them, see how they're going, *then* think about the "rules."

AVOIDING CLICHÉS, STEREOTYPES, AND ONE-DIMENSIONAL CHARACTERS

Characterization through action and detail is one way to avoid creating flat characters. Here are a few additional tips (not rules) to help you avoid clichés, stereotypes, and one-dimensional characters:

I. **RESEARCH CHARACTERS THE WAY ACTORS DO.** I don't mean read an entry in Wikipedia (although you can), and I don't mean pile up a stack of books in the library (although you can). Get out among the type of character you're writing. For instance, if you're writing about truck drivers, get in a truck with one. Take a ride, or several. What's in the cabin? What's on the radio? The CB (if they even still have those things)? What does the trucker wear? How does he sound? What kinds of jargon does the trucker use? What's in his glove compartment?

What's in his cooler? Does he lie in his logbook? (If he doesn't, he's not a trucker.) Drop in to a truck stop. Listen. Observe. Don't rely on reading a couple of chapters of John Steinbeck's *The Grapes of Wrath*. Get out there with the real people and study them.

A good case in point: Compare the renderings of prostitutes in Mary Gaitskill's "Trying to Be" with those in Lorrie Moore's "Vissi d'Arte." One rendering is complex, dimensional, convincing; the other is false, hackneyed, invented.

Lorrie Moore, "Vissi D'Arte"

... Deli was hovering in his doorway. "Mornin', Harry," said Deli.

"Isn't it afternoon?" asked Harry.

"Whatever," said Deli. "You know Harry, I been thinking. What you need is to spend a little money on a girl who can treat you right." She inched seductively toward him, took his arm with one hand and with the other began rubbing his buttocks through his jeans.

Harry shook her off. "Deli, don't pull this shit on me! ... Don't start your hooker shit with me now."

"Fuck you," said Deli. And she walked away, in a sinuous hobble, up to the corner to stand.

Mary Gaitskill, "Trying to Be"

Stephanie wasn't a "professional lady" exactly; tricking was just something she slipped into, once a year or so, when she was feeling particularly revolted by clerical work, or when she couldn't pay her bills. She even liked a few of her customers, but she had never considered dating one; she kept her secret forays into prostitution neatly boxed and stored away from her real life. She was thus a little dismayed to find herself standing in front of the smeared mirror in the "Shadow Room," handing her phone number to Bernard the lawyer.

In the Moore story, the prostitute is a flat secondary character with no inner life. So far, okay. Flat secondaries are useful. But this one's straight out of an old Shirley MacLaine movie. You can almost hear the gum cracking and the phony nasal Bronx accent. Her name, "Deli," makes her a joke—someone the reader can laugh at from a considerable height. Her "sinuous hobble" at the passage's conclusion is an attempt to make the fake character appear real.

In the Gaitskill piece, the prostitute is the protagonist, and by clause two, line one, she's already a complicated figure. She is at odds with the work and with the setting. She has a dual life, a split consciousness. By the conclusion of the passage, the duality of her life is challenged.

2. **PLAY AROUND WITH YOUR ORIGINAL CONCEPTIONS.** I remember some good advice I received in grad school from an actress I'll call C.C. I had shown her a few screenplays, and she said that they were really male-oriented. She asked if I wrote any stories about women. I told her I had a hard time writing women—I didn't know them—and C.C. frowned as though she'd just heard something idiotic. She said, "Write a character named Dick. When you finish, change the name to Wilma and adjust all the pronouns."

   I can't say that that helped me know women any better, but it sure helped me write them. Basically, she was saying that women aren't any less complex and dimensional than men.

3. **WRITE SYMPATHETICALLY ABOUT ALL CHARACTERS.** If you have a villain, make sure the villain has some positive quality. Anton Chekhov called the scene revealing the good in the villain the petting-the-dog moment. You've seen this principle at work in James Bond movies, in which the villain often has a sympathetic bond with an animal.

4. **GIVE HEROES OR HEROINES A FLAW.** Tobias Wolff pointed out the mileage to be gained by creating a narrator or protagonist who has done something wrong. So, just as you give the villain positive attributes, make sure you reveal flaws (or a flaw) in the protagonist.

5. **AVOID SENTIMENTALITY.** J.D. Salinger said that a writer is being sentimental toward characters when he loves them more than God loves them. To invoke Chekhov again, maintain absolute neutrality. Don't lead the reader to like or dislike a character. Instead, just show the character in action and the reader will make his own determination.

WRITING CHARACTER FLAWS

Virginia Woolf said that a writer can't write about the flaws of others until she is ready to acknowledge the worst things about herself. That is, of course, a difficult task. On one level or another, you will be implicated in your work, or you will be seen to be avoiding something, leaving something out. To write from the deepest, most vulnerable part of the self is a struggle that most of us try to avoid—by sharpening pencils, checking the mail, answering the phone, going to the gym; or, in the writing, going for the easy laugh, stopping at the second or third level of self-awareness, and not really digging in to what Robert Olen Butler calls the white hot center of the unconscious. Part of this avoidance has to do with its potential discomfort, part with what might be revealed (to others and ourselves), and part with the intrusions of everyday life and our obligations to them. Eventually the writer has to confront hard truths. The success of your writing will depend significantly on how skillfully, how readily you are able to access those deepest, most vulnerable parts.

THE INTERVIEW

This exercise is designed to enable you to skip past the inner censor and access the depths of your characters—their truest nature, truest voice, deepest fears, and most guarded secrets. In so doing, you will probably engage some of your own personal demons.

Imagine you are an interviewer on assignment. Your point-of-view character (or a secondary character) is your subject. Before beginning the interview proper, provide some backstory for the character. Write one paragraph of setting (Where does the interview take place? I recommend setting it where your character lives, "now" or at the time of the story), one paragraph concerning conditions (What day is it? What is the the weather like during the interview? What is around: pets, liquor bottles, etc? What is the subject wearing?), and one brief paragraph highlighting significant events or accomplishments in the character's life. Keep each paragraph short (five lines maximum). Then begin the interview with a series of questions designed to help your character relax, to trust you. *Where do you live? Work? Where do you see yourself in five years?* You ask the questions, the character answers. And in the answers, you'll hear your character speak.

As the interview proceeds, make the questions increasingly tough: *For you, what defines love? Is there anything your creator doesn't know about you? Is there a secret you're keeping from him? Is he preventing you from revealing that*

*secret in the story? Is he being fair to you? If you could tell the story, what would
be different?*

Take a look at the small-press publication *The Paris Review*. Find the "Craft
of Fiction"/"Writers at Work" interview and study the format. Then use
that format for the interview you conduct with your character.

Besides helping you get to know your character better, to learn his secrets and his fears (and to confront, perhaps, some of your own), the interview exercise also enables you to step out of the anxiety of the perfect
scene, the perfect sentence, and to allow your character to speak in his
own voice—and for you to hear it. Students often tell me that this exercise
unlocked the story for them. Give it at least thirty minutes, although you'll
probably find that thirty minutes is nowhere near enough.

The writer of *Oldest Living Confederate Widow Tells All*, Allan Gurganus,
was troubled by a tic of speech the novel's narrator had, but he continued writing until he had about two hundred pages. The narrator is a
privileged woman from the antebellum South who, in the writing, uses
the grammatically incorrect word *ain't*. Gurganus thought that it was odd
for a woman of her position, and from that time, to use the word *ain't*,
and when the habit bothered him enough, he stopped writing the book,
took out a legal pad, and across the top page wrote the heading *Why I Say
Ain't*. His answer—actually, *her* answer—became the 120-page section of
the novel called "Why I Say Ain't." Your interview is similar in intent to
Gurganus's exercise. (This is not to say you'll wind up with 120 pages of
useful fiction, but you might.)

MAKING YOUR CHARACTERS BELIEVABLE

Your goal in characterization is not only to create a multidimensional character,
but a believable one. How? The answer, once again, is Flannery O'Connor's
assertion that you can do whatever you can get away with, but that you'll
probably find you can't get away with very much. On the other hand, you
might be surprised at what you *can* get away with. For instance, you might
not think you could get away with a small-time boxing coach who reads
Nietzsche, but with some readers, Thom Jones did (see *The Pugilist at Rest*).
You might not think you could get away with an unbathed, rum-sodden
alcoholic having a wild carnal affair with a vivacious young career woman,
but with some readers, Frederick Exley did (see *A Fan's Notes*).

Getting away with it means the reader stays with the story or the book without tossing it across the room or using to it to level the kitchen table. It means that the character you've drawn is convincing enough for the reader to accept the character's actions as convincing, even inevitable, at the same time that they're surprising.

There are a few things to avoid when creating a believable character:

1. Don't overdetermine your character by providing too much information. In other words, provide neither a résumé nor a psychological profile (or provide as little of each as necessary); let the actions the character takes demonstrate who the character is.

2. Watch out for stereotypes. If everything you know about prostitutes came from Shirley MacLaine movies, don't write prostitutes.

3. Don't tell everything about your character. Keep a secret that only you know, and imagine another secret that the character is keeping from you.

Beginning writers often think that characters are what the narrator tells us about them. That's a mistake. What narrators tell us about characters is merely information: *Dr. Sibelius loved the symphonies of Brahms.*

Beginning writers often think that characters are what they say about themselves. This is also a mistake. What characters say about themselves is their way—one of their ways—of getting what they want: *"I am a sober and trustworthy man," the young drunk said at the job interview.*

Characters are the choices they make, and the actions they take: *When the homeless man entered the subway car, Dr. Sibelius buried his head behind the score of Brahms's Symphony No. 3 in F major.*

Dialogue

Agent Noah Lukeman says that when he's still not certain whether he'll represent a manuscript, he flips forward to a passage of dialogue. If the writer can handle dialogue, Noah will read another five or so pages before making a decision. But if the dialogue sounds artificial, inert, or dead, the manuscript gets tossed into the rejections heap. So, for one of the hottest agents on the scene today, a lot rides on the element of dialogue.

Over the years, the fear of dialogue has been my students' biggest fear. They know they have to use it—it makes scenes—but they think that when they write it, it sounds artificial or dead. And they're right. (Dialogue is dead in dozens of "literary" books on the shelves right now, and in a few moments I'll show you why.) Their inability to write dialogue baffles them because they speak and hear dialogue themselves every day, all day, even in their dreams. And they recognize it when they see it on the page, and when it's working it looks so easy, looks … just like talking.

TYPES OF DIALOGUE

There are several types of dialogue: direct dialogue (also called dramatic or real-time dialogue), indirect (or reported) dialogue, stylized dialogue, and asynchronous dialogue. The writer needs to deploy each, to varying degrees, throughout a novel. In my opinion, the most critical form of dialogue to master is direct dialogue. Mastery of direct dialogue requires an ear for all sorts of speech (pick up any Robert Stone novel and you'll see what I mean), from staccato street jive to the dry sherry tones of Oxford. Without excellent direct dialogue, an entire book will feel less authentic—when the characters speak, they will sound as if they're speaking lines, not participating in dramatic scenes.

DIRECT (DRAMATIC/REAL-TIME) DIALOGUE

Direct dialogue happens in a scene, in the present action, in something like real time. To write effective direct dialogue, it's important to remember that on the page, the flow of natural speech can be interrupted with exposition, description, and characterization, all without compromising the immediacy of the moment. Interruptions work like beats in a measure of music. Often, the asides, descriptions, behavioral tags, attributions, and observations provide the beat and anchor the reader. Without them, the piece would look like a play script and feel like a play without actors or direction.

In the passage from Robert Stone's "Helping," below, a recovering alcoholic enters a bar he hasn't visited in eighteen months.

> Jackie G. greeted him as if he had been in the previous evening. "Say, babe?"
>
> "How do," Elliot said.

A couple of men at the bar eyed his shirt and tie. Confronted with the bartender, he felt impelled to explain his presence. "Just thought I'd stop by," he told Jackie G. "Just thought I'd have one. Saw the light. The snow ..." He chuckled expansively.

"Good move," the bartender said. "Scotch?"

"Double," Elliot said.

When he shoved two dollars forward along the bar, Jackie G. pushed one of the bills back to him. "Happy hour, babe."

"Ah," Elliot said. He watched Jackie G. pour the double. "Not a moment too soon."

INDIRECT DIALOGUE

In indirect dialogue, the narrator reports that dialogue has been spoken. Altering the presentation of the dialogue is a way to take control of a scene with runaway direct dialogue. It's also a way to accelerate through moments of dialogue that are largely inconsequential. Take a look at this example from Anton Chekhov's "The Lady With the Pet Dog." A womanizer named Gurov is walking and chatting with a young woman on vacation.

> They walked and talked about the strange light of the sea, the soft warm lilac color of the water, and the golden pathway made by the moonlight. They talked of how sultry it was after a hot day. Gurov told her he came from Moscow, that he had been trained as a philologist, though he now worked in a bank. ... From her he learned that she had grown up in St. Petersburg and had been married in the town of S—, where she had been living for the past two years, that she would stay another month in Yalta. ...

STYLIZED DIALOGUE

Of course, all dialogue is stylized—it's an illusion. But some dialogue creates a sense of real time passing, while stylized dialogue flows through time without attempting a cinematic full picture. In Kate Braverman's "Tall Tales From the Mekong Delta," a drug dealer takes a woman struggling with sobriety to a house with a pool and asks her to dive in. (And it's not his pool.) How much time does it take to read the passage? How much story time elapses? And why might the writer give the speaker, Lenny, this kind of steam-roller dialogue (which is really a monologue)?

"Don't tell nobody, okay?" Lenny was pulling his shirt over his head. He stared at her, a cigarette in his mouth. "It's private. It's walled. Just a cliff out here. ... Come on. Take off your clothes. What are you? Scared? You're like a child. Come here. I'll help you. ... Here. See? Over your head. Over baby's head. Did that hurt? What's that? One of those goddamn French jobs with the hooks in front? You do it. What are you looking at? I put on a few pounds. Okay? I'm a little out of shape. I need some weights. I got to buy some weights. What are you? Skinny? You're so skinny. You one of those vomiters?"

ASYNCHRONOUS DIALOGUE

Tension and drama in dialogue increase when characters disagree with each other and when they respond in an unscripted way—when they throw the other speaker(s) a conversational curve ball. In the following scene from Joan Didion's novel *Play It as It Lays*, Carter confronts his unhappy wife, who has run away from him. He speaks first. His question is apples; her answer, oranges. When characters respond directly all the time, the dialogue can appear scripted. Discordant dialogue captures the sense of real speech while performing a narrative function.

"What do you weigh now? About eighty-two?"

Maria opened her eyes. The voice was Carter's but for an instant in the bright afternoon light on the sun deck she could not make out his features.

"I didn't know you'd be here today," she said finally.

"Helene told me you were coming out."

"Helene is a veritable Celebrity Register."

"Just calm down. I want to talk about something." He looked back toward the house. BZ was on the telephone in the living room. "Let's walk down to the beach."

"We can talk here."

"Have it your way, we can talk here." He kicked aside her sandals and sat down.

Due 8/17/16

PRACTICING DIALOGUE

In this exercise, write dialogue between two characters in a disagreement. For example, in a sketch from *Monty Python's Flying Circus*, a man pays one pound for a five-minute argument. He enters an office and tells the man behind the desk that he came in for an argument. "No, you didn't," the man behind the desk tells him, and they're off. "Yes I did." "You most certainly did not." And so on. The sketch goes on, hilariously, for another five minutes.

All you need to do in order to get some charged, dramatic dialogue flowing on the page is to bring two characters together and have them disagree.

    "Nice weather we're having."
    "This?"
    "What's wrong with it?"
    "What's right with it?"
    "Well, it's not Florida, true, but—"
    "What in the hell do you know about Florida?"

Keep writing for ten minutes without stopping, and remember the primary condition: The characters must always disagree.

You know from experience that when you present an argument to someone and that person says, "You're right, I agree," the conflict is over. You can call out for pizza and reach for the remote because there's nothing further to discuss. Your characters must disagree.

As long as characters are in disagreement, you have conflict, and if you have conflict you have a scene, since the dramatic tension will be created by the questions in the readers mind: How will the conflict resolve? How will character A attempt to impose her will on character B?

Once you've written for at least ten minutes (since characters, like people, have a lot to argue about, ten minutes may not be nearly enough), go back through the scene and consider your usage of interruptions, attributions, asynchrony, and stylization. Dialogue should be fun, snappy, crisp, and it should reveal something about the people speaking it. The second your characters are in accord, your dialogue is in trouble.

Things That Kill Dialogue

1. When characters say to each other what they already know: "Hello, I'm your brother, who graduated top of his class at Yale."

2. When characters respond as if they expected to hear what the other said.

"Is there anything to eat here?"
"How about some eggs?"
"Yes, thank you. You know how I love eggs."
"I love them too."
"We have quite a lot in common."
"We share a love of eggs."
"I couldn't agree more."

3. When characters state the issues of the scene explicitly. Don't write:

"I'm angry at you for withholding emotionally."

This reads like the script for a Lifetime movie.

Instead, write:

"Would you pass the salt?"
"Get it yourself," he said, not looking up from the television.
She reached for the salt, and threw it through the TV screen.

"Now," she said, "would you pass the pepper?"

DIALOGUE TAGS (ATTRIBUTIONS)

Dialogue tags are part of the writer's arsenal. Their first function is to keep the reader aware of who's speaking and when, all without getting in the way. In most cases, the reader should and will experience dialogue tags like punctuation—as utterly unobtrusive—if they're used sparingly and if they keep clear who's speaking.

The second function of dialogue tags is to affect meaning. *"What are you doing?" she said*, feels different from *"What," she said, "are you doing?"* Use the tags to create the desired effect, to communicate the reality of the moment. The tags will still be unobtrusive, but the reader will register and interpret them.

Raymond Carver used dialogue tags to create both emotional and musical effects. By frequently repeating them (using *he said* for every line of dialogue), Carver created a sense of monotony and a kind of drunken emphasis. By moving them around (leading a sentence with *she said*, then following with *said he*, then dropping the tag, then placing it in the middle, etc.), he demonstrated how words on the page are like colors on the canvas: They're experienced by the reader and they can be deployed to certain effect. They are not solely to remind the reader of who's stating the line.

Summary and Scene

SUMMARY

A summary is narration that reports on the passage of time or the circumstances particular to a place.

> Early that summer, the heat became unbearable. By July 4, the lawns started to brown, and in August the front yards in the neighborhood resembled sandboxes.

In the above summary narration, a summer passes in one sentence. Summary can collapse time and accelerate narrative.

> In Helena's absence, Maris applied himself to the guitar. His fingertips went from sore and tender to callused and impervious by the time she returned.

Summary can eliminate the steps of an action or behavior and present the reader only with what is necessary. It's an efficient way to skip past, as Elmore Leonard puts it, the parts that the reader skips anyway.

Summary can also prepare a reader to enter a new space by providing some sense of what one might typically find there.

> The Lucky Strike featured a pool table with felt that looked as if it had been chain-sawed and a jukebox that stopped at 1959. On Thursday nights, "Ladies Night," women drank half-price. Of the dozen or so

regulars who weren't hookers, at least four would have black eyes. After Happy Hour, at least six. The men didn't fight the men until after ten.

SCENE

A scene is a dramatic unit that begins at one fixed point in time and ends at another. It depicts action, and that action can and often does include dialogue, although it doesn't have to. (For instance, in Ernest Hemingway's "The Big Two-Hearted River, Part One," the scenes of Nick Adams making camp and fishing are scenes without dialogue.) Scenes, in contrast to summaries, show us an action or sequence of actions in something that usually approximates real time—that is, they move forward the way we feel time moving forward. (Of course, that sense is an illusion created by effective prose rendering of actions.) Scenes are often constructed around a character or characters struggling for something—some objective. In order to achieve their objectives, characters use a variety of means, usually starting with the least expenditure of energy and building as required, in an individual scene or across several scenes, until the objective is either gained or lost, or until the outcome is put on hold by the author to create suspense.

A scene might cover five minutes of real time in about eight pages (as in Robert Stone's "Helping"), or it might cover three hours of real time in two hundred pages (as in Marcel Proust's *The Guermantes Way*).

SCENE RULES OF THUMB

There is no rule on how long a scene must be, but there are some general rules of thumb for composing effective scenes.

One rule of thumb is to get in late and leave early. That is, join a scene that's already in progress. If the scene involves a couple having an argument (as many great scenes do, including Raymond Carver's "Will You Please Be Quiet, Please," Ernest Hemingway's "Hills Like White Elephants," and Mary Gaitskill's "Stuff"), you don't need to show the husband pulling into the driveway, putting the car in the garage, then ignoring his kids on the front lawn as he makes his way up the path to the front door. Instead, you can begin the argument at the point when the husband pours his second scotch, or third. Join the scene in progress, and leave it early. And you don't have to wait until the argument is over to end the scene. Maybe the wife says something that encapsulates the whole meaning of the argument, of the scene, of the marriage. You might want to get out there, not at the point where the husband walks out of the room and picks up the TV remote.

Another rule of thumb is to intersperse narration in dialogue. Scenes, as I discussed in the dialogue section, can benefit from narration in their midst. In other words, don't rely solely on dialogue to drive your scenes. When you find your characters are talking too much (or more than you want them to), when you find that what they're saying is running away with the scene, take the control back from them. Report what one or the other says; don't use direct dialogue. For example, notice the difference in these two scenes:

> Daphne and Martin met for a dinner date at a quiet restaurant in the neighborhood. Their waitress had just placed their main courses.
>
> "I like potatoes," she said.
>
> "Marvelous," he told her.
>
> "I like carrots, too."
>
> "Imagine that," he said.
>
> "And celery. Asparagus. I can't say much for yams, but I do enjoy a beet now and then. A red beet. Turnips, too. Yes, asparagus, beets, turnips, too. Did you know that the turnip was a staple of Iroquois cuisine? Or was it Mohican? Or am I confusing the turnip with maize, which is really just another name for corn after all, isn't it? What's the difference between corn and Indian corn? Do you know, I mean botanistically speaking? I know it's different in color, but is it a different animal altogether? *Cornus Indianus* or something? But corn—I'm talking about regular corn now, not Indian—corn I'm rather fond of. Not creamed corn. Corn on the cob, fresh corn. You wrap it in tin foil and put it on the grill, or you boil it, then you drown it in butter. I love it when it's drowned in butter. You can ladle melted butter over the boiled ear, or you can twirl the ear along the top of the butter stick. Which method do you prefer? God—I just remembered candy corn!"

This scene would benefit if the author took back a little control.

> Daphne and Martin met for a dinner date at a quiet restaurant in the neighborhood. Their waitress had just placed their main courses.
>
> "I like potatoes," she said.
>
> "Marvelous," he told her.
>
> "I like carrots, too."
>
> "Imagine that," he said.

"And celery. Asparagus. I can't say much for yams, but I do enjoy a beet now and then. A red beet. Turnips, too."

Daphne continued to identify her vegetable preferences. Martin consumed the contents of his plate, nodding occasionally. He never cared much for vegetables, or at least the discussion of them. He thought they represented themselves rather well without the interference of language. His eye followed their waitress. What did she think about carrots, he wondered.

"But corn—I'm talking about regular corn now, not Indian—corn I'm rather fond of. Not creamed corn. Corn on the cob, fresh corn."

Martin stuck his fork into Daphne's pork chop and removed it to his own plate.

"I love it when it's drowned in butter."

"You don't say," he said, chewing.

HALF-SCENE AND SCENE SNIPPETS

Although it is often effective to insert a little summary into a scene, you can also do the exact opposite—inject scene-like devices in the midst of summary. Why? Because narrative summary veers dangerously close to the informational. Like boiled chicken, it requires a little spice. Not the red hot chili peppers of a Thai soup, but maybe just a few shakes of the salt and pepper.

Italo Calvino pointed out that in fiction, time doesn't take a lot of time. If a character walks across a room and looks out a window, we don't need a fastidious description of how she put her left foot in front of her right, then her right in front of her left, etc.: *The shouting startled Sally at her desk. From the window, she could make out forms at the edge of the yard. ...*

If a relationship of several years goes sour, it isn't necessary to detail each plodding step of growing dissatisfaction in order for the reader to grasp that the thrill is gone. Instead, the writer can cheat a little—by which I mean that the writer can tell, in narration, of the relationship's deterioration over time. But in order to get away with the narration, it is useful to sprinkle it with the salt and pepper of a half-scene or scene-snippets.

Half-scene refers to the use of scenic devices and present-action moments in the midst of summary or narration. Half-scenes and snippets make the summary more alive, less static or informational, and more dramatic; they can be used to characterize (a snippet may contain a behavioral tag that can be exploited); they can accelerate or facilitate movement through time. Snippets provide the scenic detail that makes a narrational moment more vivid. Compare the snippetless, *Their day passed in boredom and lassitude*, with, *Their days passed in boredom and lassitude, their half-drunk glasses of iced tea crowded the kitchen table*.

Consider the following consecutive passages of Melissa Bank's long short story "My Old Man." In the first passage, which addresses the routine of working at home, Bank uses no present action—that is, no *scene*—whatsoever. Instead, she tells us how things ordinarily were with this couple, and she makes that telling feel more immediate, more alive, by including what might ordinarily be said, or what might ordinarily be carried (the iced tea); in other words, she includes scene snippets, which create the sense of half-scene.

The second passage addresses the routine of lovemaking (or, perhaps more accurately, lovemaking and its discontents). Again, Bank works not with present time, but with *unparticularized* time. She's working in the conditional: This is what *would* happen, this is what *might* be said. This passage concludes with the only present action in the two passages.

> In the evenings, he'd work upstairs in his study, and I'd edit manuscripts at the big mahogany table, where I could worry a sentence for an hour.
>
> He'd come down to refill his iced tea and look in on me. "What is it?" he'd ask.
>
> Standing behind me, he'd read. He'd take the pencil out of my hand and cross out a word or a sentence or the whole page. "There," he'd say. It took about thirty seconds, and he was always right.

> Each time, Archie was mystified. Each time, he told me it had only happened to him once, years ago, when he was blind drunk. He'd light our cigarettes and lie there, staring straight ahead.
>
> "It's not you, babe," he said one night.
>
> I nodded, as though consoled. The thought had never occurred to me.

ROUTINE ACTION

The passages above depict routine action, action that takes place routinely, several or many times. Routine action is not the same as present action, which is the kind of action you see in a scene—an action taking place at one particular time. Routine action is the action of summary: *Every Saturday she would go to the bookstore*. Present action is the action of the particular time:

In the reference section of the bookstore, she perused Rocket Science for Dummies *and thought,* Of course, I can do that.

For this exercise, follow the model the Bank passages provide. Think of two routines that might define two characters—a couple. Bank's routines are working at home and lovemaking (and its discontents). What two routines might represent the reality, over time, of your couple? Using conditional constructions (*he would, she would*) or language that represents routine time as opposed to particularized time (*each time, every time*), create two consecutive half-scenes that open with routine action.

Describe the conditions of the routine: *Each time, she would be smoking. Each time, he'd be choking.* Include description of details typically there in the action (an ash tray, a magazine), and statements of what might typically be said: *"Each time,"* she'd say, *"I hate the way you choke when I'm smoking."* Braid the dialogue into the moment, then cut back to routine action.

Subtext

Larry Brown's story "Facing the Music" begins:

> I cut my eyes sideways because I know what's coming. "You want the light off, honey?" she says. Very quietly.

We don't know why the narrator cuts his eyes sideways—we don't know why he can't look the woman (his wife?) in the eye. And we don't know why she offers to turn out the light. So the story opens with two questions, and those questions remain unanswered all the way until the story's end. On the journey between question and answer, we learn enough about the characters to sympathize with them, despite their flaws (which are also delineated in the story).

With two unanswered questions operating just under the surface of the story's action, Brown generates effective subtext. We know the characters are doing what they're doing for a reason, but we don't know what the reason is.

You can create the same kind of effect in your fiction. Try following Brown's example. Begin a story with an action that suggests some kind of motivation, but don't disclose what that motivation is. As you work through your story, perhaps you'll discover why the character does what she does at the opening. When you make a discovery in fiction, you have a living piece.

CREATING TENSION WITH OFF-SCREEN EVENTS

In order for scenes to really play in fiction, they require a certain tension. One way to create tension in present-action scenes—in moments that occur, so to speak, on-screen—is to have some ongoing off-screen event affect the behavior of the character we're watching. The behavior we see occurs in the way it occurs *because* of the off-screen event(s). This device drives much of Leo Bloom's behavior in James Joyce's *Ulysses*, it drives much of Rabbit Angstrom's behavior in John Updike's *Rabbit Redux*. And it drives one of Raymond Carver's masterpieces, "Are These Actual Miles," in which a man waits at home drinking and contemplating his failure while his wife is out trying to sell a car—for cash, by any means necessary—to a slimy salesman.

As an exercise in creating this kind of tension, write a passage that follows the actions of character A while character B (someone she loves) is off doing something that might profoundly humiliate A. How is character A's behavior affected by something that's occurring many miles away?

Description

SETTING

In my teaching over the years, the biggest, most persistent problems I've seen concern the element of description. Description is often either ignored or botched. In order to create the fictional dream, the writer needs to render place effectively enough for it to convince the reader. A good way to practice descriptive writing is to look at examples of effective description and follow them. I often tell my students to take the focus off the character—off what the character does, says, thinks—and instead write at least three descriptive sentences about setting before the character is even referred to, then several more sentences of setting description (preferably elaborations of earlier description) without the character, then go back to the character again. This way you have the character entering a place that already exists in the reader's mind.

Another benefit of approaching a moment from this vantage point is that you can include metaphor or symbolism in your details. Further, you can present the details in a way that reveals point of view; that is, you can use the details to reflect how the character sees them, sees the world. So, finally, you don't have simply description, which runs the risk of sounding like a travel brochure. Instead you have description and characterization and metaphor.

Good examples of leading with description can be found in Ernest Hemingway's stories "The Big Two-Hearted River, Part One" and "Hills Like White Elephants," which opens like this:

> The hills across the valley of the Ebrol were long and white. On this side there was no shade and no trees and the station was between two lines of rails in the sun. Close against the side of the station there was the warm shadow of the building and a curtain, made of strings of bamboo beads, hung across the open door into the bar, to keep out flies. The American and the girl with him sat at a table in the shade. It was very hot and the express from Barcelona would come in forty minutes. It stopped at this junction for two minutes and went on to Madrid.

Notice how Hemingway starts out wide—that is, his focus in line one is some distance from the characters. In line two, he's closer, in line three, closer still. It's not until line four, after three full lines of setting, that the characters are introduced. Their introduction is linked to setting.

ZOOM IN

Your exercise: Select something you've written that begins with character and rewrite it, this time leading with three full lines of description before introducing characters. Start out wide, as Hemingway does, and line by line, bring your focus closer in toward the characters.

What will this do for your fiction? Well, in the immediate example, it will place your characters in an already clearly existing space. The fact that the place precedes the characters could say something about the characters' relationship to that space, as it does in the Hemingway story (they will be gone, and the place will still be there as it was before their brief interlude at the station).

PRIMARY AND SECONDARY INFORMATION

The poet, essayist, and novelist Steven Dobyns uses the terms *primary information* and *secondary information* to discuss movement through a piece of fiction. Primary information, he says, is *Bob shot Alice.* Secondary information is *It was the third week of a hot July and all the lawns had turned brown. Cars baked in the driveways and kids leapt into the weak pulse of sprinklers.*

Primary information advances the narrative. The reader wants to know primary information: why Bob shot Alice, how badly she's hurt, whether he'll be arrested. Secondary information provides context, metaphor, idea, etc. Although the reader is impatient to know the primary, without secondary, you have a flat, one-dimensional story in the spirit of, say, James Bond. Too much secondary, and you wind up boring the reader.

So much of the writer's job involves getting out of the head—getting out of thoughts, words, abstractions, figured-out solutions—and going into the senses. A good practice in your early revisions is to ask of each paragraph: *What am I giving the reader to see, feel, smell, hear, taste?* If you can't find details that appeal to the senses, add them.

Gustav Flaubert said that in order for an image to work it needs to appeal to three senses. To which I respond yes—but keep in mind that Flaubert lived with his mother. He had the time to conjure three appeals per sentence, and we in this terribly busy twenty-first century might not. For your prose fiction, try to include at least one sense per paragraph. And don't rely on sight always or primarily.

Some readers are interested solely in primary information (the James Bond novels sold very well). Some will tolerate massive amounts of secondary information (Marilynne Robinson's *Housekeeping* begins with about sixty-five pages of it). Most of us fall somewhere in between, with the more literary leaning toward the latter in varying degrees.

The point to remember is that description reinforces the fictional dream. If the fiction strays from the real world too far or for too long—that is, if the writer is stuck on providing information or explaining an idea or running a riff with language—the reader's immersion in the dream is imperiled. Even on page 299 of a 300-page novel, the writer is providing descriptive details (*proofs*, John Gardner calls them) that paint the picture and reinforce the reality of the story.

What is the right amount of description? How many details are enough? That answer changes for every story. In the twelve- or thirteen-page Raymond Carver story "What We Talk About When We Talk About Love," perhaps four or five details are provided to flesh out the setting. In Tim O'Brien's "The Things They Carried," there are often four or five details per sentence. Each story is brilliant, each is completely realized. In your own work, the idea is to determine what's needed and then to provide no less, and no more.

Remember the old Hemingway dictum: You can leave out what you know; you can't leave out what you don't know. Put in as much detail as you can imagine or remember and then take away as much as you can. In my own writing about scuba diving at coral reefs, I used to cram in every single marine biology detail I know, and I know a lot. Then I realized that I was just killing the story with stuff I loved (*the lower spines on the pectoral fins of roughspine sculpins extend well beyond the fin membrane*) but that had no real weight in the story. Little by little, I started trimming until I arrived at the requisite number of details to communicate the reality of a coral reef and of the worldview of the character diving at that reef.

Again, there are notable and abundant exceptions. I often say, *On every page of your story, your character is somewhere. Where? And how are the details of that place participating in telling the story?* But my admonitions to include these types of details aside, many stories successfully omit them. Denis Johnson's story "Dirty Wedding" ends with three description-free pages. Many Lydia Davis stories are tortured cerebrations without place or detail. Long passages in Alberto Moravia's works involve interior processes, not the things of the world.

I tell my students in session one that in session two I'll contradict some if not all of what I said in the first session. That's the nature of writing. While there are general guidelines for writing fiction, there are no hard and fast rules other than to make the reader want to turn pages. But beginning writers do themselves a disservice by worrying about readers turning pages. Beginning writers need to keep their focus on writing pages, and worrying about anything that sounds like a rule is self-defeating.

Sometimes I suggest a student try something a little different, and I hear, *But that's not my style.* And I have to say, respectfully, that at this point in your development, you don't have a style. Your style will emerge through practice. Your practice will reveal to you your eye for detail (just as it will reveal your ear for dialogue, your instinct for pacing, etc.). Some of what you discover from your practice will please you and some will not; your practice will also reveal weaknesses. That's what practice is for.

Think about the element of description, and how much attention it requires, once you have a stack of pages. Then think about the needs of your readers.

Point of View

Point of view (POV) refers to the perspective from which a story is told or narrated. The three broad categories of POV narrator are first-person, second-person, and third-person.

A first-person narrator tells the story from his point of view: *I was eleven years old when these events occurred.*

A third-person narrator tells the story from the perspective of another: *He was eleven years old when these events occurred.*

A second-person narrator, the least common, creates a curious effect by telling the story from the perspective of the person she's addressing, using the second person pronoun: *You were eleven years old when these events occurred.* The second-person narrator creates the sense that you are in the story. Second-person narration can also give the feel of a first-person narrator telling her story from the distance of a second-person narrator.

FIRST-PERSON NARRATOR

Although there is still much fiction told from the first-person POV, you often hear editors and agents say that they're not interested in first-person narrator fiction. To their trained and weary eyes, a first-person narrator reads like first fiction, like workshop stuff, like autobiography. Nonetheless, first-person narrator fiction still appears in great abundance and with great frequency. I wouldn't take too seriously the sweeping generalizations of editors and agents; they certainly don't.

The perspective of the first-person narrator is obviously limited. Since *I* is telling the story, the only consciousness *I* is privy to is her own. *I* cannot tell us the thoughts of others, but instead must rely solely on observation and speculation (observation is better, since clearly rendered behavior will communicate to the reader what the characters might be thinking about). First-person narrator work can seem young and coming-of-age autobiographical if it fails to fully address the larger world outside the head and behavior of the first-person narrator.

One of the great advantages of the first-person narrator is the intimacy it creates: Readers can form a deep bond with someone who is spilling her guts with apparent honesty, someone who might otherwise be repellant to readers. Two recent examples: Chappy from A.M. Homes's *The End of Alice*; Precious from Sapphire's *Push*.

THIRD-PERSON NARRATOR

There are at least as many liberties as there are restrictions attached to the third-person narrator. First, the liberties: The third-person narrator is not bound to one consciousness. It can know—and, in some cases, it can present—the thoughts of several, even many characters. The ability to relate the inner thoughts of other characters is called omniscience. Total omniscience is exemplified in Leo Tolstoy's *War and Peace*, a novel in which even the thoughts of Napoleon are available to the reader.

Tolstoyan omniscience is not very common today for a number of reasons. One reason is that we've developed the sense that all points of view are subjective, so it's inherently false to employ a narrator who purports to know everything. It's presumptuous. At best, the narrator knows his own world, and only from a perspective necessarily shaped, if not limited, by socioeconomic conditions—class, race, religion. A narrator's subjectivity often reflects the writer's subjectivity. A writer whose subjectivity remains unexamined may create narrators who share his limitations.

Great talent and great vision may, to some extent, transcend those conditions, but even great talent and vision are constructed in a particular context, a context whose "truths" may differ from the "truths" of another context. So a writer's stance toward her material is also, consciously or not, an ontological stance. Some writers, recognizing this, have their narrators communicate the sense that it's impossible to know anything with certainty, even one's own self. Other writers give the third-person narrator a limited (selective) omniscience, in which the narrator remains close to the consciousness of one character.

This brings up an especially critical element with the third-person narrator: modulation of distance. A third-person narrator closely linked to the consciousness of the protagonist is still distinct from the protagonist and therefore can know more than the protagonist. The third-person narrator knows the outcome of the story, while the protagonist does not. The third-person narrator might know the meaning of the story even if the protagonist doesn't. In order to communicate the distinction between narrator and protagonist, the narrator modulates the distance between herself and the protagonist. That is, the narrator steps back from, or out from proximity with the protagonist's consciousness and offers an insight, a speculation, a piece of information, or a perspective unavailable to the protagonist. Once that is accomplished, the proximity with the protagonist is reestablished.

Limited omniscience with effective modulation is demonstrated masterfully in John Cheever's "The Swimmer." In this story, protagonist Neddy Merrill's life is already in ruins, but Neddy is unaware of that fact. The third-person narrator knows, but although closely linked to Neddy's consciousness, it never lets on. Instead, the narrator follows Neddy through his swim across the county and presents all events through the filter of Neddy's awareness.

> Was his memory failing or had he so disciplined it in the repression of
> unpleasant facts that he had damaged his sense of the truth? Then in
> the distance he heard the sound of a tennis game. This cheered him,
> cleared away all his apprehensions and let him regard the overcast
> sky and the cold air with indifference.

Here the third-person narrator is very closely linked to Neddy's consciousness; the narrator is privy to all of Neddy's questioning, remembering (or lack of it), hearing, and regarding. When, however, Cheever needs to pull back and to comment on the nature of Neddy's journey, he does so in language that reinforces the fact that the third-person narrator is distinct from the consciousness with which it is so often closely linked.

> Had you gone for a Sunday afternoon ride that day you might have
> seen him, standing on the shoulders of Route 424, waiting for a
> chance to cross. You might have wondered if he was the victim of
> foul play, had his car broken down, or was he merely a fool.

Use of the third-person narrator creates a kind of contract with the reader. Once a point-of-view character has been established (that is, once it is clear to which consciousness the narrator is most closely linked), that character's POV will be the only POV, and to introduce another POV violates that contract (that rule). In a novel with multiple POVs, this "rule" might apply to a section. For instance, in Robert Stone's *Dog Soldiers*, three main characters have their own sections. When Hicks is the protagonist of the section, Stone gives us Hicks's POV, etc. In James Welch's *The Death of Jim Loney*, in which many POVs are deployed, the "rule" remains the same; each section has its own POV character. For instance, consider this story opening:

> Jimmy thought of himself as generally a decent guy, but today, for some reason, he felt the urge to get indecent.

The reader of this story will automatically assume that the point of view for the rest of the story will be Jimmy's. If on page eleven the point of view of Jane appears, the reader will experience a bump (to use John Gardner's term); the contract will have been breached. So a rule of thumb is, once you introduce a POV character, that character's POV can be the only POV.

How strict is that rule? Not very strict. Remember Flannery O'Connor's assertion that you can do whatever you can get away with, but that you'll probably find out you can't get away with very much.

One way to get away with dual or multiple POVs in a short story is to introduce the other POV(s) early so that the reader makes accommodations for the device right away. Another is to provide clearly marked, roughly equal sections for each POV. In "A Romantic Weekend," Mary Gaitskill shows the POVs of two young people about to engage in some sexual experimentation; Amy Bloom's "Faultlines" is an eleven-page story with four POVs.

The thing to remember is that any choice you make in a piece of fiction will have consequences. If it is your intention to enfold the reader as much as possible in the world of the story (and that is the prevailing intention in fiction), then you'll want to adhere to the conventions as much as possible. Any device that appears at all unconventional tends to knock the reader out of the story world, and switching POV is one such device. The negative effect is even greater if the switch in POV is mishandled.

SECOND-PERSON NARRATOR

The second-person POV is the least common, the most unorthodox, the most risky, and sometimes the most fun. Perhaps the most famous example of second person is Jay McInerny's delightful debut novel, *Bright Lights, Big City*, with its damaged second-person narrator marching though a coke-addled New York City in the mid-1980s. The second-person narrator is often used in "how-to" stories, that mini subgenre that every writer should give a try. Examples include Lorrie Moore's "How to Become a Writer," Pam Houston's "How to Talk to a Hunter," and Junot Diaz's "How to Date a Brown Girl."[6]

The risk of second-person narrator is its unorthodoxy—it's a gimmick, and some readers can never make the adjustment: *What does she mean "you"? Me? Her? The character?*

The unorthodoxy of the second-person narrator is also its pleasure. The gimmick becomes something of a high-wire act, and the reader is aware of both the tightrope walk and the story. That's why it's most often used for short stories; it's hard to sustain a gimmick for an entire novel. Readers don't have that kind of patience.

CHOOSING POINT OF VIEW

The choice of POV has to do with what works best for the material. Richard Ford once yanked a novel that was already in galleys and took a full year to rewrite it from another POV. Scott Spencer nearly went mad with *Endless Love*, trying several different POVs over the course of years, rewriting the book in its entirety several times before arriving at the voice that now tells the novel (first-person narrator). Sometimes the choice of POV has to do with a writer's predilections and/or strengths. Robert Stone rarely uses the first-person narrator, and never in novels. Mary Gaitskill, too, favors the third-person narrator. Junot Diaz, on the other hand, often writes in first person. These choices appear to be the writers' strengths; on the other hand, the choices serve the material well, and that's the biggest consideration.

I recommend playing with POV. If you've written mostly first-person narrators, try a second-person narrator, and so on. The rule of thumb used to be that the aspiring author had to write a million words before arriving at her authentic voice. You can do a lot of experimentation with a million words, and the practice of writing virtually demands it. Experiment on, and bring your monsters and angels to life.

[6] My own contribution to the genre is "How to Tell If Your Boyfriend Is Crazy," published in *Hampton Shorts*, Summer 1999.

Revision

With apologies to Jack Kerouac (a man and spirit I adore), good writing involves hard revision. That doesn't mean that the first draft (or second, fifth, tenth) got it wrong, it means that each draft is a step toward the finished product (as much as a piece of fiction *can* be finished), much like the rehearsals of a play. The audience sees the apparently effortless unfolding of a riveting drama. What they don't see is all the rehearsal, all the revision that went into making the production appear effortless. Revision resisters (and I think we all fall into that category at least at one point or another) think they stumble upon ammunition when they read the seemingly artless stories of Raymond Carver, or the drugged out wigginess of Denis Johnson's *Jesus' Son*. To borrow an expression from another wigged-out druggie, Dennis Hopper's photojournalist in *Apocalypse Now*, wrong! Raymond Carver's revisions were legendary: First, because they were manifold; second, because they never stopped; and third, because he published alternate versions of quite a few of his stories. And Denis Johnson's magnificent collection of stories began as poems, years before the publication of story one; he kept on revising the poems, trying to make them work, until finally, at the point of abandoning the material, he used the beginning of one poem as the opening of the piece of fiction that became "Car Crash While Hitchhiking." The rest spilled forth.

I've already discussed the advantages of experimentation, of mucking about in the fictional tool kit and changing around initial impulses—making a first-person narrator a third-person narrator, lopping off a story's beginning, changing character gender, that kind of thing. All of these suggestions are suggestions in revision, and they are all big, tectonic plate-shifting types of revisions, revisions that restructure the entire piece and create a brand new topography, not to mention a brand new (hopefully less volcanic) middle earth.

But smaller revisions are also essential, so I offer here a couple of suggestions for simple mechanical revisions to help you tweak what you have on the page, torque it up. These types of revisions can (and often do) open up elements in the psychology of the story of which you were hitherto unaware.

REVISION IN FOUR PARTS

1. *Motivation.* At every moment, every character in your story wants something. What? Go back through each one of your scenes and ask yourself: *What exactly is it that Q or X wants here? Is it clear that he wants it? What's in the way of his getting it?* Write the answers to those questions. If you can't answer them clearly, your scene might have a problem. Add at least one sentence per scene that somehow (subtly, explicitly) addresses the desire or issue most urgent in the scene.

   I was worried that she had told him about us, about me and her.

   —ROBERT BOSWELL, "GLISSANDO"

   I didn't want to be left alone with the blind man.

   —RAYMOND CARVER, "CATHEDRAL"

   She was thinking that he must be drawn to her vast emptiness, could he sense that she was aching and hot and always listening?

   —KATE BRAVERMAN, "TALL TALES FROM THE MEKONG DELTA"

2. *Significant details.* Look for your details (an ash tray, a fork, a drug, the name of a street). Choose at least one per scene and write one more piece of description that elaborates on that initial detail. Each time you do this, you'll be adding a full sentence between detail and whatever follows. The purpose of this exercise is to go deeper. Find something else to say about the detail that makes it earn its place. Is there something about it that your character might consider, might dwell on? Is there something about it that suggests themes of the story? Work it. But don't make it decorous. Think vertical, not horizontal: Go deeper.

   The paint had flaked off in spots, and a gray like bad skies shone beneath it.

   —ROBERT BOSWELL, "GLISSANDO"

   He imagined bare feet. Martha was a poet, with the poet's sensibilities, and her feet would be brown and bare, the toenails unpainted,

... and though it was painful, he wondered who had been with her
that afternoon.

—Tim O'Brien, "The Things They Carried"

3. *Repetition of detail.* Find a detail you mention on page one of your
   draft. Repeat it on page five and page ten, putting some new spin on
   it with each new appearance.

It was a boy with shaggy black hair. ...

... he had shaggy, shabby black hair that looked crazy as a wig. ...

He placed his sunglasses on top of his head, carefully, as if he were
indeed wearing a wig. ...

—Joyce Carol Oates, "Where Are You
Going, Where Have You Been?"

4. *Recounting of story events.* Somewhere in the middle of your story,
   in the territory of act two, have your POV character recount or ru-
   minate on the major story events up to that point. This can keep you
   well-anchored in the drafting, and the reader well-anchored in the
   reading.

I wondered why I had told Frederick that I thought he was nice. Probably for the same reason I had sweet dreams about a petty sadist. I
tried to think of my dead sex partner, but my memories of him were
truncated, and gray with elapsed time.

—Mary Gaitskill, "Turgor"

The Novel

Since the predominant mode of instruction in MFA programs is the short
story, why even bother discussing the novel? I'll attempt to answer that in a
moment. First, an explanation for the widespread focus on the short story:
It's shorter, and the majority of its concerns are the concerns of the novel as
well. Participants can get through a short story in a sitting (Alice Munro and
Harold Brodkey short stories perhaps excepted). They can learn structure,
scene, summary, voice, dialogue, setting, and any other issue of craft from

the short story. And they can try their hand at the short story (maybe several) in a single semester. The novel doesn't lend itself to such utility.

However, it is not uncommon to find MFA workshops devoted to the novel. Many MFA candidates submit novels (as did I[7]) for their thesis. And the novel is the form that, eventually, any career-minded writer will have to undertake, for better or worse. It's the nature of the business. I might add that the New York Writers Workshop has been conducting courses in the novel right from its inception, my own course being Fiction in General, the Novel in Particular. Other courses in the novel are taught by Maureen Brady, Sarah Van Arsdale, Sheila Kohler, and Kaylie Jones.

Those exceptions aside, the MFA focus on the short story can lead to problems in writing the novel. Several years ago, the novelist and short story writer Chitra Banerjee Divakaruni was asked to read the novels nominated for the National Book Award. It was a daunting task—if I remember correctly, she had some sixty novels to read in six months. What made it more daunting was a pattern Divakaruni discerned about one third of the way into her task, a pattern that sustained itself throughout the entire reading period. In the article she wrote describing her discovery, Divakaruni said that all the novels started out brilliantly. Their language was exquisite, their characters compelling, and their initial mechanics dynamic. Then, after somewhere between thirty and fifty pages, they all fell apart. Divakaruni was describing the effect of MFA programs on writing: their stress on the perfect surface and their tendency to homogenize prose. She was also noting one of the major differences between the short story and the novel, which might be called (to return to Flannery O'Connor) what you can get away with.

You can get away with a lot in short stories. From the reader's perspective, they're a minor investment, a short time. The flaws in a writer's vision, the limitations of a writer's skills, might not be so readily apparent in a short story. The novel, however, will turn the klieg lights onto flaws and limitations. Think of the pleasures of the poems and short stories of Charles Bukowski; now think of the puerile and static nature of his novels. A writer with razzle-dazzle language, a writer with a couple of interesting experiences and the acquaintance of one or two interesting characters, the writer with a quirky way of thinking, of living, might be able to get those strengths onto the page

---

[7] I use the term *novel* in the broadest sense, and only because that's what I called it then. I think of it now as a detestable impertinence.

and hold the reader's attention for the length of a short story. A short story (even an Alice Munro short story) is short, compared to a novel; it represents a small investment on the part of the reader, so its flaws won't be as crippling, its disappointments as profound.

One somewhat common circumvention of the novel's dangers is the so-called novel-in-stories, a collection of short stories, often told by the same narrator or POV character, that focuses on the same character or characters and builds, somewhat novelistically, over a period of time (say, childhood). Such is Isabel Huggan's *The Elizabeth Stories*, Susan Minot's *Monkeys*, Tom Perrotta's *Bad Haircut*, and so many others.[8] These are excellent books all, by excellent writers. And they're smart substitutes for the long haul of the novel. But their satisfactions are less than novelistic.

In general, the novel is less forgiving of flaws; it is more revealing of limitations. But the novel is more forgiving of certain specific tendencies than is the short story. If a reader has invested one or two hundred pages in a four-hundred-page book, he's not going to throw it aside just because the narrator takes a detour into the mythology of the whale, say, or into the socioeconomic history of Route 66 or into the rhapsodies of Mozart's Clarinet Quintet K.581. What a novelist knows, what he's studied, what he's passionate about, might find its way into a novel without killing the novel's ultimate impact. So the novelist can get away with a little instruction, a little rumination, a little denunciation, and the overall story might not suffer too terribly, if at all. Think of Russell Banks's wonderful novel *Continental Drift*, which thrives on the instruction it provides as its two separate stories draw nearer and nearer to intersection. But material like that would be terribly out of place in the taut and unforgiving form of the short story.

There is another difference that deserves our attention, and that is the difference between what the forms take out of you as a writer and as a person.

---

[8] The writers Gary Krist and Amy Bloom each began something along these lines, and it's interesting to see how far the strategy took them. In his collection *Bone by Bone*, Gary Krist has three interlinked stories called "The Ericcson Stories." These were initially intended to be part of a novel. In Amy Bloom's *Come to Me*, the two stories under "Henry and Marie" were intended to be part of a novel. It is always useful to look at writers at work, especially when we can see the thinking and the sweat and tears behind their decisions. Junot Diaz's work—his collection of stories called *Drown*, and the stories that appear periodically in *The New Yorker*—are at once excellent stories and illuminating examples of Diaz's struggle with the novel form.

The demands of the short story, cruel and debilitating as they are, are not on the same level as those of the novel. A good short story—its initial draft and even some revision—can be done in a sitting, a week, a month; the really tough ones may require longer. A novel, however—even a short one, even a bad one—takes a long time: assuming the best-case scenario and the shortest of novels, six months. More likely a year, and a year is short. Then there's the day-to-day struggle with the material. In a way, it's the difference between raising a family with a spouse and moving from lover to lover; the one is a long struggle with gratifications suspended and sacrifices common, the other a series of fun but perhaps repetitious and less productive challenges. Short stories might not challenge the writer on levels as deep as the novel does.

The novel is the oracular form, it's the opera as opposed to the parlor song, it's the place to declaim and decry and emote from the diaphragm up to the eyeballs. It's the place to present many sides and to wrestle with massive contradictions and to reconstruct ups and downs. It's the place to show the reader what you've got: What do you know? What have you done? What have you learned? How does this piece of the puzzle fit with that piece? What does that mean? These are not the demands of the majority of short stories. A failed short story is a few weeks of fruitless work; a failed novel is a dead child.

The short story is end oriented: If the ending's no good, the story suffers considerably, even fails. The novel is less dependent on the perfect ending. Consider Leo Tolstoy's *War and Peace*, for instance. Its ending fails for more than one hundred pages, but the novel is still considered classic. That's because the seven hundred or so pages that precede the failed ending are marvelous. The same is true of Marcel Proust's multivolume novel; the final two volumes are considerably less effective than the earlier four or five masterpieces, but that doesn't compromise the excellence of the earlier volumes. Nor does the failure of Lawrence Durrell's *Mountolive* and *Clea* undermine the excellence of *Justine* and *Balthazar*, volumes three and four and one and two (respectively) of his uneven Alexandria Quartet. In regard to more contemporary work, the disastrous end-strategy of Susanna Moore's *In the Cut* doesn't cancel out the finely observed and dynamically paced first 150 pages.[9]

---

[9] This novel might be a special case, since it aspires somewhat to genre fiction—it is an urban sex/crime mystery. Its ending, therefore—a literary gimmick that a good teacher would have saved her from, and a good editor should have—feels as if it landed from another planet: Planet MFA. The same type of MFA eureka-spasm occurs at the conclusion of a Dani Shapiro's *Picturing the Wreck*; did they have the same editor, one wonders?

Although novels and short stories differ in all these important aspects, they are similar in just about every other way. Concerns about language, about dialogue, about description are all identical. The novel as an art form accommodates as many experiments and permutations as the short story. The novel can deploy multiple points of view. The same story can be told four or five different ways by four or five different characters. It can be told in letters, in diary entries, in laundry lists. It can include newspaper clippings, existing poems, invented poems, movie reviews.

The novel as commercial art form resembles the conventional short story in that it tells a coherent story which can be charted like the structure of a film: in three acts, with tension-and-release devices sustaining interest over the long haul.

A well-paced novel is constructed on chapters that each raise a question, just like a short story, and then delay answering that question for as long as possible. But each chapter's answer hooks into the next chapter instead of ending the story. So, in novels, answers create questions—those questions are the inner dynamic of the novel, and they suspend the answer to the Major Dramatic Question, which was presented in the novel's opening.

THE LOOSELY PLOTTED VS. THE TIGHTLY PLOTTED NOVEL

For the most part, I have been discussing classically constructed fiction—stories and novels whose structures resemble the three-act structure of drama and film. In the classically constructed piece of fiction, the opening act introduces character, setting, and conflict, and it provides the event that sets the story moving forward in present action. The longer second act will rise and fall, often twice, in an event-crisis-climax pattern. The third act (usually the shortest) might provide a resolution of sorts, and will certainly answer the Major Dramatic Question. In the big picture, the novel contains (1) setup, (2) increasing complications, (3) climax, and (4) resolution.

How do you plot classically? That answer's easy as well: Create an order, or routine, then disrupt it. Some argue that there is really only one plot: to restore the order that's been disrupted. (This echoes Freud's notion of the pleasure principle's mandate to gratify appetite, eliminate tension, and to arrive at stimulus zero.) And again, it's useful to remember all the tips provided in the earlier sections:

1. Begin your story close to the point of its climax.
2. Begin your story where everything but the action has already taken place.
3. Give your protagonist one goal to pursue, and provide only the essential incidents of that pursuit.
4. Follow through on events—remember event C causes event D, etc.
5. Complete a process of change.

Not all stories and novels do those things, and not all stories and novels are classically constructed. Do they have to be? Absolutely not. Think of the symphony, which is in sonata form. Which musical forms do not adhere to the sonata? The impromptu, the nocturne, the bagatelle, the polonaise, the prelude, the fugue, the lyric, the ecossaise, the gnossienne, the pavane. You can make up your own forms. And you probably should. In the end, you'll probably find yourself working close to classical structure anyway (again, the round wheel rolls).

But when might you disregard classically plotted fiction? The best advice I have to offer here is: once you've written the draft. Consider Tim O'Brien's story collection, *The Things They Carried*, which is a sort of novel-in-stories. Here is a book that contains several classically plotted stories (the title story and a few others), and a whole bunch of impromptus, nocturnes, preludes, bagatelles, and maybe a fugue or two. There are journal entries, letters, lists. There is meta-fiction. O'Brien appears as a character in some; in others, the narrators are never identified. My guess is that this collection cohered when someone—and that someone might be Tim O'Brien—said, *Oh no, all the rules are broken here, but so what? It's still a beautiful read and a powerful experience.*

Some pieces of fiction satisfy their own internal orders. Chekhov and Hemingway, two "classical" writers who established the norms of the contemporary short story, gave themselves the liberty to do anything. While many of their stories are classically constructed ("The Lady With the Pet Dog," "The Short Happy Life of Francis Macomber"), many are not. Browse a collection and see what these two giants allowed themselves; you are allowed the same range.

Henry Miller's *Tropic of Cancer* is loose, so loose it threatens to fall apart in many places. The organization, such as it is, is thematic and associative rather than narrative. The novel's loosely constructed four sections are crammed (unequally) with rant, vision, and narrative. Its first section is the least narrative. Here, crablike, the Miller narrator scuttles back and forth across Paris, time, and characters. Still, an act one of sorts is achieved, since this opening section (some sixty or so pages) introduces all the major characters, themes, and conflicts. The opening rants create the liberty for Miller, later on, to interrupt the pacing of narrative moments for long speculations of a philosophical sort. The ideas are as important to Miller as the stories within the larger narrative.

Compare Miller's novel to James Welch's *The Death of Jim Loney*, a masterpiece of compact, three-act-structure storytelling. It comprises many short chapters with alternating points of view (all in third-person), each chapter advancing an inevitable story outcome that might be the example par excellence of the transcendent ending. Each voice and each section works close to character and event, and any commentary on action, setting, history, or context derives from a particular point of view.

Sandra Cisneros's *The House on Mango Street* uses a similar approach—the short-chapter mosaic—with a somewhat different intent. Welch's novel, a tragedy, joins the narrative in the same way taut short stories do: as close as possible to the point of climax. Cisneros's fragmented novel builds like pieces of a puzzle to form an impression of a family epic through the coming-of-age of a principal character. Its time frame is wider, more comprehensive. You might say that her trajectory is horizontal—across time and events—whereas Welch's is vertical—going deeply into fewer events. Of course, Cisneros goes vertical in each of the short sections, mining each for whatever ore is in them.

AFTERWORD

The question *What is the novel?* may have seen best answered by novelist Don DeLillo, who said, "The novel is whatever novelists are doing at a given time." That is, each novelist invents the form every time out, and every invention is legitimate. His message: Don't worry about what anyone says the form is, just write. You can do whatever you can get away with, and worrying about conforming to established conventions is tail-chasing.

The amateur's crisis of confidence as she begins her first short story is the writer's crisis of confidence at the outset of every new project. This is unique to writing. Once an architect knows how to design buildings, she designs buildings. On her next assignment, she doesn't wonder, *How do I design buildings? Maybe I'm not really an architect.* ... Once an orchestra conductor knows how to conduct orchestras, she conducts. Faced with a new score, she doesn't think, *Oh my god, how do I conduct symphonies? Maybe I'm not really a conductor.* But the writer faces that first vast empty page (or screen) of the new project and thinks, *I wonder if the mail's in. Jeesh, my pants are tight—should I go the gym? Who's on Oprah? I can do some sit-ups and watch* Oprah. *Maybe it's Maya Angelou. Or maybe there's something inspirational at the cineplex. And how the hell do I write this damn thing anyway? Who cares what I write? Why should they? Maybe I'm not really a novelist. Maybe I'm not really a writer. (Maybe I should have tried something easier, like designing buildings, or conducting symphonies.)*

That's the good news and the bad news. The bad news, because it means that confronting terror and humiliation is part of the job description. Good news, because it happens to everybody, it comes with the turf, and each time out will be like the first time. First love only happens once, but first-fiction terror and euphoria can happen again and again.

So haul out your Moleskine or boot up the iBook, and go scare the hell out of yourself. Then fall in love. Repeat when necessary.

RECOMMENDED READING

NOVELS

Coetzee, J.M. *Disgrace.*
Exley, Frederick. *A Fan's Notes.*
Kohler, Sheila. *One Girl.*
Miller, Henry. *Tropic of Cancer.*
Salter, James. *Light Years, A Sport and a Pastime.*
Stone, Robert. *Dog Soldiers.*
Welch, James. *The Death of Jim Loney.*
Wharton, Edith. *The Age of Innocence.*
White, Edmund. *The Beautiful Room Is Empty.*

SHORT STORY COLLECTIONS

Bloom, Amy. *Come to Me.*
Cameron, Peter. *The Half You Don't Know.*

Carver, Raymond. *Where I'm Calling From.*

Cheever, John. *The Stories of John Cheever.*

Gaitskill, Mary. *Bad Behavior, Because They Wanted To.*

Houston, Pam. *Cowboys Are My Weakness.*

Johnson, Denis. *Jesus' Son.*

Nugent, Beth. *City of Boys.*

O'Brien, Tim. *The Things They Carried.*

O'Connor, Flannery. *The Complete Stories.*

Paley, Grace. *Enormous Changes at the Last Minute.*

Perrotta, Tom. *Bad Haircut.*

White, Edmund. *Skinned Alive.*

Yates, Richard. *Liars in Love.*

USEFUL GUIDES TO WRITING

Burroway, Janet. *Writing Fiction: A Guide to Narrative Craft.* 5th ed. New York: Longman, 2000.

Checkoway, Julie, ed. *Creating Fiction: Instructions and Insights From Teachers of Associated Writing Programs.* Cincinnati, Ohio: Story Press Books, 1999.

Gardner, John. *The Art of Fiction: Notes on Craft for Young Writers.* New York: Vintage Books, 1985.

Hills, Rust. *Writing in General and the Short Story in Particular: An Informal Textbook.* Rev. ed. Boston: Houghton Mifflin, 1987.

Madden, David. *Revising Fiction: A Handbook for Writers.* New York: New American Library, 1988.

O'Connor, Flannery. *Mystery and Manners: Occasional Prose.* Sel. and ed. by Sally and Robert Fitzgerald. London: Faber and Faber Ltd., 1972.

Personal Essay & Memoir

by PETER BRICKLEBANK

PETER BRICKLEBANK has been published in *The American Voice*, *The Carolina Quarterly*, *Mid-American Review*, *Kansas Quarterly*, *Confrontation*, *Fiction*, *Global City Review*, and elsewhere. His work has been anthologized in *The Breast* and *Short Story Criticism*, and has appeared in *The New York Times Book Review*, the *American Book Review*, *The Chicago Tribune*, *The Minnesota Review*, *ACM* (*Another Chicago Magazine*), and others. He has been nominated for a Pushcart Prize, received a New York Foundation for the Arts fellowship in fiction, and held residencies at the Fundación Valparaiso (Spain) and the MacDowell Colony. He teaches at the New York Writers Workshop, New York University, Hunter College, and privately in Manhattan. He co-teaches a winter fiction and memoir workshop in Oaxaca, Mexico.

Introduction: Looking Forward to the MFA

MFA programs bring many benefits to aspiring authors. They buy them time to actually work, to attempt to be that elusive and impecunious thing, a writer. This is no small matter if that individual comes, as many of us do, from a background that encourages nothing unless it is pragmatic in the career department. Grad school also brings proximity to writers. One of the first wordsmiths I ever saw in the pallid flesh was at a science fiction convention. Gimlet-eyed, he returned my gawking as if he'd just stepped, blinking with jetlag, from his flying saucer, and I was the disappointing life form he'd stumbled upon. He was a creature from another universe—a literary one—and I had no earthly words by which to make my own needy embarrassment and awe intelligible. In grad school, you meet writers on a level less awesomely paralyzing—you try on the skin of being a writer—and that's certainly to the good.

You also find yourself among a few fellow students who also suffer from burgeoning bibliolatry and graphomania, and this is a wonder when you come from a cultural backwater where you find yourself addicted to words but unable to talk to anyone about them. Where I came from, girls preferred garage mechanics with their own cars rather than pedestrian wannabe scribblers; in grad school, there are book lovers to talk to about writing's miseries and marvels. All these are good aspects of any workshop.

And MFA programs also give out money and, along with it, the confidence, nay the fillip to ego that is a fellowship or an award won. These are all useful, as is the literary magazine you might get to work on. Doing so is a beneficially chastening experience and teaches tough truths that you don't learn hunkered in your own garret. So, yes: peers, established authors, experience in the literary world, awards, and the chance to come out as a writer. MFAs have merit, and a place.

But you don't have to have that award.

And those peers fade fast.

There are better ways to get a date (yes, fixing her car can't hurt).

Literary magazines—some great ones—exist outside the ivyed walls.

And when you get out of the program, you're either going to dry up and die off as do most (at least in my years), or you're going to have to find ways to buy time and earn your fix of that nasty writing obsession.

And probably most of the authors you first admired never went to MFA programs, but learned their craft and the business of being a writer outside of the academic sphere. An MFA is first and foremost a program in an educational institution, and, as such, it is *academic*. What you'll read is good, is great, is useful. But it also comes with an academic slant. That can mean an overemphasis on a restrictive literary canon at the expense of those small, quiet gems that didn't make it to apotheosis. Nothing wrong with the greats, and you should read plenty of them, but I don't measure myself as a failure because I'm not a "great" writer.

One of the things I learned early on—outside academia—was that there were unsung, underappreciated writers, writers who might never get in *The New Yorker* or publish regularly or at all with the big commercial presses, but who were wonderful and set a standard that I'd be happy to attain. These were writers who survived by publishing in obscure, weird, irregularly appearing mushrooms of publications called literary magazines, writers who might get taken up in venerable but penniless literary presses, springing up with next to nothing but their zest. Writers who might not ever publish a book at all. Yet they were still working. They lived in the obscure banality of the artist. They wrote and they said their thing, and no one called them promising or gave them awards, but they could knock out the pages, and they did. And they could move me, and they could be learned from. My education as a writer began when I took a leap of faith and committed myself simply to reading and writing as much and as well as I could. It had nothing to do with graduate school.

Along with the academic side of an MFA program comes an overreliance on theory. Schools of criticism or writing theory are fine, but when you're trying to develop craft, or deal with the fifty-ninth rejection of your story (I placed it on the sixtieth attempt), or cobble together ways to survive in the world and still write, or find the psychological strength to go on at all, theory is bad practice.

And there's also the intensified competition of grad school. I remember attending the first class of a very famous writer, held at his home. The room was packed. Two people read pieces aloud, and we were asked to comment. I couldn't critique without a manuscript in front of me, which did not endear me to the famous author's pedagogic ways (though he was obviously intellectually far beyond our keening yearning vapidity). And I recoiled from the deadly competitive spirit in that gathering, the intense mass delusion that if he liked your work he might pass it to his editor at the national magazine. It was simply too much. I sensed I couldn't get the mentoring or feedback I'd need there, and realizing that sitting at the feet (almost literally) of the great wasn't necessarily going to translate into insight, I dropped the class.

It's not just me. There are people in the top writing programs in the country miserable with the competition and the unfairness of it all. (It helps to be young and pretty, or so I hear.)

The money you spend on grad school—on credits and grades and the prestige of it all—can also buy a lot of time to bend seriously to your own work. It can buy classes unencumbered by academic mind-set, a lot more of them. There's always a price to be paid for being a writer, and there's a price to grad school beyond the mega-dollars for all their fine benefits.

But MFA or otherwise, what's most important is fostering a love of language and the lifelong process of learning to write insightfully and well. In this nonfiction chapter, you'll look at the essay and the personal narrative or memoir with that in mind. The essay as a vehicle for expressing the often suppressed individual voice and the memoir as a testament to the lessons of a life are what make nonfiction the vibrant and oh-so-relevant genre it is today.

The Personal Essay

WHAT ISN'T A PERSONAL ESSAY?

The common wisdom is that the essay is protean, a shape-shifter, that it has myriad forms and applications—the article, the op-ed piece, the book review, the complaint to the principal, the statement to the court, the declaration to the loved one, the philosophical musing, etc.—and that any attempt to rigidly define it is misplaced. Corral it in neat parameters and the spirited horse is no longer wild and free. But I'm sure all of us have come to the essay through this spirit of overdefinition and prescription: Didn't we all learn the joys of the five-paragraph essay in college or high school? You remember the formula: There's an introduction, which houses the thesis (the main idea) and sets out three points to be covered; and then there are (preferably) three paragraphs, each explicating one aspect of that original idea; and then there's a conclusion. In effect, you tell your readers what you're going to say, then you say it (with examples explicitly labeled as examples in case the reader isn't following the already well-worn path), and then you tell them what you've already told them (you know how that begins: *In conclusion*), and the reader glazes over at the regurgitated ideas and falls back asleep.

This method of writing doesn't work because it begins with the end, rather than the beginning. The writer is starting with his conclusion and simply attaching facts and anecdotes as exemplification. But if the writer is not discovering anything, how can he maintain interest? If everything is a foregone conclusion, aren't things going to drag along? Yes, you do have to have a sense of where you're going—even a good sense of what it might be that you're saying—but exactly what gets said depends on the process, on *how* it gets said, on the ideas that come along as you write. As with the feature article, you certainly want a sense of direction and purpose before you start, but you don't want to constrain the idea so much that it can't breathe. That's where so many college essays die—Decomposition 101 might be a better label for Composition 101—and it's why so many people end up hating writing. It's boring. There's nothing in it for the writers to discover about the world or themselves. And, of course, they think they have no ideas to voice anyway.

This is why we need to consider what elements form the elusive personal essay.

ESSENTIAL ELEMENTS OF THE ESSAY

In some sense, the personal essay attempts to give the reader the impression that the writer is on a voyage of discovery. The word *essayer* comes from the French, meaning "to attempt, to try." Notice that the word doesn't prescribe arriving at conclusions, solving weighty issues, or any mention of docking on Mt. Olympus in the section marked *Muses & Artists Only*. What that definition in fact suggests is engaging in the writing process, being willing to wrestle the inchoate ideas in your head into specific language and insight on the page.

But if we've only got a rough idea about where we're going—a general theme if not an articulable thesis—then maybe our journey is a mystery tour. Which also implies that the literary essay—as opposed to a journalistic article—can wander. But then what stops it from wandering all over the place? And what is actually filling the pages? This brings us to what characterizes the personal essay (and with acknowledgement to Phillip Lopate on many of these ideas).

- the personal presence of the author
- an engagement between self and the world
- the author's self-exploration/self-discovery
- the need to both show and tell

- veracity/authenticity
- the mutability of form
- a sense of intellectual plot, quest, engagement, or payoff

THE PERSONAL PRESENCE OF THE AUTHOR

A characteristic of the personal essay is a voice that seems to speak directly to the reader. It is an easy voice, a spoken voice, an intimate voice, that of a confidant. It is the voice of the writer. An essay gives the impression of a tête-à-tête between author and reader, the intimacy of the friendly, receptive ear cupped at the articulate mouth of an observant mind. A writer's experiences in life, filtered through the limitations and strengths of his character, articulated in his own words in his own singular way create a distinct vision of our shared existence as sentient beings. *Your* personal essay provides a window on the world, on *our* shared human experience.

In the sixteenth century, Michel de Montaigne, the patriarch of the essay, said, "It is myself I portray." He was not suggesting that the essay was a nesting box for narcissists. In an essay, you often deal with conflicts within yourself or with aspects of life as they come at you from without. In so doing, you reveal yourself, certainly, but the primary interest of the reader is not the self-exposure, not the confessional nature of such personal writing, but rather the way that life presses on everyone. When you, as a writer, express things that readers recognize as somewhat akin to their own experience, you confirm their humanity; where you differ from others, your individuality and the individuality of those reading you are enhanced by being acknowledged, voiced, described, made plain in the light of day. The essay, then, provides an inner dialogue in an outfacing form. In seeking to make discoveries about your own life in an essay, you find patterns, meanings, and understanding that extend beyond you.

> **TIP:** You don't have to look for your voice; it's already within you. And if you're writing with conviction and passion, the more you write, the more defined and deep that *you* becomes.

> **MANTRA:** "The essay is a haven for the private, idiosyncratic voice in an era of anonymous babble." —Scott Russell Sanders

AN ENGAGEMENT BETWEEN THE SELF AND THE WORLD

Surely, one of the reasons we read is to find universals, to reestablish that we're just loveably quirky rather than weirdos escaped from *Where the Wild Things Are*, and that our experiences fall into the terribly broad category of being more-or-less human. But character is formed in action (or in inaction). So we are what we do in certain situations, we are what we think or don't think about the smorgasbord of possibilities offered to us on cocktail sticks at the tedious dinner party of life. We're social creatures. If art provides a personal and social forum for issues of experience, then the essay is an incalculably valuable social form that requires and encourages intelligent expression in search of a greater understanding of what it is to be alive.

The writer isn't alone in the world. And wider issues have particular effects on individuals. The essay combines the isolated individual with the amorphous abstraction of society. And it is that interaction that provides spark, zest, flux, and the *frisson* that makes reading more than mere entertainment to kill time between reality shows but an enhancement of reality itself, our reality.

Phillip Lopate, in his essay "Confessions of a Shusher," engages an aspect of himself that he seems half-pleased and a quarter chagrined by: He is, he grinningly announces, one of those people who takes umbrage with inane unceasing nattering and rustled candy wrappers once the film begins. The implication is, of course, that many of us are similarly irritated in such situations; some would like to say something but decide not to, while others do say something, incurring the wrathful disdain of those upbraided (after all, can you shush someone in a nonthreatening, nonjudgmental way?). Lopate's essay is simply a meditation on attitudes toward the shusher, a creature we love or hate, depending on whether we're irritated or being irritating at the time. It provides no deep insight, but the mild enjoyment of experience recognized and explored.

By contrast, George Orwell's essay "A Hanging" describes the execution he had to take part in as a colonial military policeman. Between what Orwell observes in his immediate world (the barefooted condemned man steps around a puddle on the way to the gallows, a chilling reminder of his shared humanity with everyone there) and what he observes within his own thoughts (that in the moment the trapdoor opens, the man's body will be doing what all bodies do, the hair and nails growing, the body following its so-human imperatives, utterly oblivious to the arbitrary justice about to transform it simply because the man was a political opponent), the essay ultimately provides an argument against capital punishment, without ever using the phrase.

One essay with grinchy-grumpiness, one with gravitas—both created from the interaction of a mind that retains its sovereignty and alertness with a world that sleepwalks through the horrors of its own insensitivity.

> **TIP:** You can be sensitive, rational, and reasonable in an essay. But you don't have to be. In fact, just like in the real world, it often helps if you aren't. Aside from the times when you affect a particular disposition to attain a goal, don't feel obliged to be nice and well-behaved in an essay. No one's going to tell your mother.

> **MANTRA:** "For me, the drama of the essay is the way the public life intersects with my personal and private life. It's in that intersection that I find the energy of the essay." —Richard Rodriguez

THE AUTHOR'S SELF-EXPLORATION AND SELF-DISCOVERY

We live in the calloused, dented, impacted shells of ourselves, hating all manner of our parts while on some level overly smug with the clever little devils we think we are. Given the resilience of ego, that essayists manage any degree of honest self-exploration is wondrous (chalk another point up for the book-lined life). But if your writing is to surprise your readers, then you must surprise yourself, and that's achieved by unearthing just who it is you really are. And whenever there's excavation going on, people will watch, fascinated.

Part of the strength and appeal of the essay comes from the intimacy with the writer, the quirky, personal, conversational voice and the candor of that writer. When the author allows the reader to look deeply and with feeling into himself as he acknowledges the inadequacy and ignorance we all will find in ourselves if we care to honestly look, that openness and vulnerability is apt to convince the reader of the essential decency of the author. We discover who we are in the smithy of worldly experience, by what we do or don't, by what we think or refuse to countenance. The essay is a tool to explore that: who we were, who we are, who we are (or are in danger of) becoming.

Phillip Lopate, in his essay "The Moody Traveler," describes with a true curmudgeon's delight the distastefulness of traveling and being expected to enjoy oneself. Nothing much happens in the essay; while taking part in (and commenting on) the usual shuffling to scenic overlooks and the snapping of memories each as vapid as the next, the author attempts to avoid interactions with those who see nothing but a delight in such foot-dragging, brain-numbing tyranny. But the reader is there not for the travelogue, but for the pleasure of acquaintance with the amusing and ever-so-humanly dyspeptic writer. The joy is in the *schadenfreude*. The scenic view is into the self.

There's no cheaper, and richer, way of traveling. The essay is the passport.

> **TIP:** As essayist, you must be your own inquisitor, testing what in you is wise or foolish; your own explorer, mapping the uncharted borderlands of your natural resources; and your own alchemist, discovering, through art, what is in your own heart.

> **MANTRA:** "How do I know what I think until I see what I say?" —E.M. Forster

THE NEED TO BOTH SHOW AND TELL

Although the personal essay shares many techniques with fiction, the personal essay refutes what is possibly the most oft-used (and abused) dictum of writing wisdoms: In fiction you need to show, illustrate, depict (that is, *craft*) a believable fictional world; in nonfiction, you need to construct a persuasive realm through skillful storytelling, but you can also interrupt it by interlarding commentary, analysis, reflections, opinions, and viewpoints. Readers of the essay don't just want to feel the struggling creature in the sack; they want to be told what it is. To re-work a couple of clichés on this point: The story sells a pig in a poke—you have to suspend your disbelief and trust your imagination about what's in that sack; an essay plays things more out front—it lets the cat out of the bag. In the essay, then, you must give a reader context, a structure of engagement, a framework within which to understand both *why* you are looking at a particular thing, and *what* you are coming to realize from that.

In Harriet R. Goren's essay "I Feel a Spell Coming On," the author details her life as someone prone to fainting at inopportune moments. If all she did in the essay was simply string together incidences of fainting, pretty soon the reader would swoon into inattention as well. In the excerpt below, she ponders, albeit briefly, what she realizes from incidents like these, and thus she provides a context for the reader. Not only can the reader enjoy the anecdotes, but he can see what the writer makes of them.

After graduation, a friend's roommate invited me over for his first attempt at preparing Italian cuisine. We had salad with garlic dressing and, for the main course, garlic eggplant parmagiana, followed by an interesting soup made from a garlic stock in which I almost drowned as my body attempted to come to terms with the pungent bulb. It failed, and only my friend's quick reflexes saved me from being scalded as the room faded away and my head dropped precipitously into the bowl. Later that month my boyfriend and I found ourselves in a passionate embrace in his shower. I told him not to turn up the hot water, but he did anyway. This proved to be one too many bits of input for my sensitive bloodstream. Down from his arms I crumpled, an inelegant wet ball on the porcelain. He gathered me up and whispered into my ear, quite pleased. I didn't have the heart to tell him that my swoon had nothing to do with his prowess.

Amidst all these years of momentary excitement, I never did go to a doctor to learn the whole story, if any. In truth, I didn't want to put a name to my condition. It was much more interesting to wait to expire unexpectedly like my cousin Eugene, seventy-two, who died in bed while making love to his twenty-five-year-old girlfriend. I didn't want to know it if something dull and long-lasting was brewing in my body.

She goes on with more incidents and her responses to them, and the reasons behind those responses. And, as she regularly loses consciousness, we by contrast are made conscious of what it is to live on the edge of a swoon.

Stepping out of narrative and providing a context for things is an important principle in nonfiction writing. So here's another example, from Lydie Raschka's "Biking in the Rain," in which the author tries to come to terms with her husband's lackadaisical attitude to the dangers inherent in bicycle riding. What should her position be, given the possibilities for catastrophe that she begins to discover, and especially after a friend's husband is struck by lightning on the beach after ignoring admonitions against going out? What is love in such situations—gentle prodding, or something else?

On a Web site for cyclists you can find this topic: *Getting hit by a car, is it just a matter of time?* People describe in detail the accidents they've had and the injuries they've received. On BicycleSafe.com there is a ten-page article with the title "How to Not Get Hit by

Cars." Collision Type #3 is called the "Red Light of Death." This is a collision where a driver doesn't see the biker waiting to the right of his vehicle. When the light changes, he turns directly into the cyclist. An Austrian was crushed this way under the wheels of a truck. My husband is half Austrian, which makes this fact particularly disturbing to me. I print out the article and leave it on the table where he will see it. I do not give it to him directly because it feels wrong to love someone this way. But there's been thunder all fall, and almost nonstop rain; it's found a leak in our building and trickled down the elevator shaft; it's flooded the choir room at church. At the moment, I can't think how else to go about it.

The only actions here are the reading of the Web site and the leaving out of the warning article, which are mere mundane events unless connected to something of import to the author. And they are connected, via her reflections about loving in this insistent and cautious way, and about her fear of protecting those she loves from what they love. The author's concern is heightened by the church flood (and the thunder, which brings rain and slick roadways where bicycles may crash), another unexpected calamity emphasizing the frightening entropy of the universe. The real drama isn't in any biking mishap, but in the collision of the writer's anxieties with her husband's refusal to see the world as dangerous as does she. And so her mind spins throughout the essay like the wheel of an overturned bicycle.

> **TIP:** If you're relaying a long anecdote, make sure the reader knows why up front. Often, in early drafts, an author details incidents and events, but fails to provide a context. Answer this question when you look at your own essay: *Where is the author (where am I) in all this?*

> **MANTRA:** "What happened to the writer is not what matters; what matters is the large sense that the writer is able to make of what happened." —Vivian Gornick

VERACITY/AUTHENTICITY

I'd be lying to you if I said that accuracy isn't important. (See the section on memoirs on page 113 for further discussion of this topic.) But we're not talking accuracy in terms of letter-of-the-law fact here, but a reasonable insistence, a habitual tendency to make sure that whatever is presented as true and accurate is just so: true and accurate. Which sounds like fact-checking, but is simply being responsibly fair to whatever memory of events one might have; faithful to the characteristics of action and speech that one has experienced; authentic, as far as one can be, in representations of the self. And without suggesting that we're all a frightening batch of multiple personalities, we have to agree that each one of us is a walking, talking (hopefully, thinking) house of horrors, a multiplicity of shading and contradiction. Our sense of who we are comprises an array of selves that we proffer in everyday life, seen in the different hats we wear or the faces we present or the masks we hide behind, and even in those we shun. Acknowledging this, it's clear there's no one self to be entirely true to, but an aggregate of quirky selfhood from which we draw as nonfiction writers; we live and write with this comfortably loose adherence to a sense of authenticity.

Whether writing in first person or third, there's a narrator to a nonfiction piece. And because it's nonfiction, that narrator is essentially you, the author, but you in a particular guise or mood or hat. In other words, the voice of the essay, *your* voice, becomes almost a character in the piece—or a persona, a version of the self. But if this feels like a drift toward fiction, toward making things up, then where is the veracity? Writers play up particular characteristics in certain pieces in order to play off of this character, but unlike fiction, where unreliable narrators abound (this is why you never lend money to a fiction writer), in nonfiction, we rest easy knowing that the persona relating things for us is essentially our author, to which literary license allows only a slight distortion, the lattitude of minor exaggeration, if necessary for a particular piece.

In the extreme, it is even possible, for satiric reasons, to utilize a persona that is not the author at all. Jonathan Swift provides a classic example in *A Modest Proposal*: A supposedly patriotic and concerned citizen—the voice of the essay—suggests that perhaps the babies of the poor could be sold and eaten to alleviate poverty. For Swift, this is abhorrent, but using the persona allows him to make the point that the landlords, by exacerbating the abject poverty of eighteenth-century Ireland, were metaphorically eating the children anyway. Swift is being truthful to his beliefs and his sense of the injustice of the situation; he's merely employing a guise to strike his target with greater efficacy. The personas in most essays tend to be far less extreme, though they certainly can be outrageous in their own ways (see the references to the two Lopate essays in this chapter). The point is that an authorial presence is felt as a persona, a temperament, a disposition—a whiff of charm, integrity, spirit, or individuality. Beginning essayists tend to forget every essay has its own imprint of the author.

> **TIP:** Many people waste needless energy fretting over definitions of what is or isn't nonfiction, pacing out the property line to the inch. Use this broad yardstick and you'll not go far wrong: Don't make up what didn't happen; recreate what did happen in a way faithful to your sense of the emotional terrain.

> **MANTRA:** "Art is a lie that makes us realize truth." —Pablo Picasso

THE MUTABILITY OF FORM

The essay is a form supposedly so formless that it encompasses every ugly rhetorical mode you ever had the misfortune to meet in a dark and dreary college textbook. It's also the book review, the reportorial article, the op-ed piece, the diatribe, the paean, the case study, the travelogue. It has countless forms of narrative, as in George Orwell's descriptively persuasive essay "A Hanging" or Annie Dillard's lyrical reflection "Living Like Weasels" or Richard Selzer's "The Discus Thrower," which in its stripped-down taciturnity is almost a short story in disguise. It has its more unconventional forms, such as arrangement in segments or organization around a random pattern, (tarot cards or the rules for the use of a swimming pool). Or, like short stories, the essay can spin several narrative threads in parallel at once (noncontiguous sections on the Catholic Church and polar exploration), or take the form of a list (the contents of one writer's desk drawer; the reasons why another writes at all), or use numbered or subheaded components or fragments. The essay's multi-tasking amorphousness makes a hopeless exercise out of trying to limn its structural borders. It's the user-friendliest hydra you're ever liable to come across. Enjoy it, feed it, ride it; it won't bite you.

While in the realm of monsters, here's a mini-quiz and a brief word on digression. Who was it who said, "Not all those who wander are lost"? (Answer to follow.) Many people think the essay blithely wanders wherever it will, given its prerogative to closely follow the twists and turns of a writer's thought. While it certainly has this freedom and any veering off can have its place, a reader trusts a divergence from the point is never beside the point. A detour on your bus route is at first a delay and a tedium, but it also brings the freshness of different streets, and whatever streets are taken, you know that the destination is still the same. In any digression, the writer has an eye on the narrative arc of the piece and the through-line of theme and keeps an eye out along the way for extra or subsidiary meanings that may become apparent in this diversion, so the whole forward movement becomes stronger, even though the piece may appear to be edging sideways. Back to our quiz: The answer is J.R.R. Tolkien. And if we think of Frodo wandering, lost but always with a direction toward Mordor (and wisely not taking public transport), it's clear that detours are not digressions at all if they keep putting one large hairy foot forward, toward where the narrative intent must take us.

> **TIP:** You find a form through your early drafts. Commit your ideas to paper, no matter how fragmentary, even if you can't see all the connections or the overall direction. This creates a rough guide for you to follow and/or diverge from as you rework. As you do this, connections will suggest themselves to you and, draft by draft, a form will gradually emerge.

> **MANTRA:** "The hero of the essay is its author in the act of thinking things out, feeling and finding a way; it is the mind in the marvels and miseries of its makings, in the *work* of the imagination, the search for form." —William H. Gass

A SENSE OF INTELLECTUAL PLOT, QUEST, ENGAGEMENT, OR PAYOFF

An essay strives to reach a deeper comprehension of things at the end than was apparent at the beginning, and that may not be deep at all. It's not reaching a judgment that's essential, but the process of attempting to reach one. Solutions don't necessarily have to be found; insights don't have to be had; profundities ... well they're nice, but not obligatory. Stumble over one, then pick it up. As an essayist, you're a beachcomber: You wander, you get your feet wet, you try not to stand on a jellyfish; if you find something interesting you might carry it home. There's no test to pass. Even if all you've ever managed in life is attempts to get square pegs in round holes, you're still college material, still a potential essayist, as long as you can laugh at yourself, reflect on it, or put a framework of meaning around your experience in an interesting, emotive, engaging way.

Anne Fadiman's wry essay "Marrying Libraries" deals with domestic trivia. She describes the mounting tensions and decisions that occur when her new husband moves into her apartment. Both avid booklovers, she with Felix Ungar neatness, he with Oscar Madison slobbery, they now face a dilemma: how to merge their books and their disparate modes of being. Do they order alphabetically (her), chronologically (him), by subject? What to do with books by their friends, what to do with dual copies of classics they both have—especially when those coming-apart, retro covers also house the notes of a younger self in the margin, or endearments from past lovers on the flyleaf? For bibliophiles, these are no small matters. And there's no real solution. But what we get from the essayist is an appraisal of the problems and how this one couple resolves them, and further, the author and her audience come to appreciate something—something not articulated in any bon mot of profound epiphany anywhere in the piece. The reader comes to see the subtle mesh of bonding that two people, in marrying, come to weave, and enjoys a rewarding reading experience. Deeply cerebral, no; warmly human, ah yes.

So if an essay in some sense kicks around an idea, there's the intellectual plot. If it shows the writer on a voyage of discovery, there's a quest. And if there's insight on the part of the author—or if it's just what the reader is led to intuit by a writer who doesn't actually pin it down in language—there's a thematic payoff. All of these represent an intellectual component, however insubstantial, however gossamer light, and that *frisson* of thought or theme a reader can carry away in his own head.

> **TIP:** If you have an idea of what your essay is about before you begin, expect and trust that it will change and morph. And remember that you don't have to reach great conclusions or profound insights in an essay. If your reader comes out with a sense of things larger or fresher than he originally had, that can be enough.

> **MANTRA:** "What I like in a good author isn't what he says, but what he whispers." —Logan Pearsall Smith

> "To learn to write is to learn to have ideas." —Robert Frost

Rubbing Ideas Together

Okay, you might say, I'm not to know where I'm going, but I'm supposed to have a damn good idea. How do essayists kick start their ideas? It's simple. None of us can go through a day without reflecting on something in the world—right now I'm fuming at the treachery of the washing machine that refused to rinse or drain my wash, which now hangs like banners, like facile art everywhere in my apartment. (Gee, I wonder if I can rent Central Park and get a grant?) We worry about things, we exult, we find ourselves amused or bemused or abused or obtuse. We question things. And questions are at the heart of essay writing. Often we have an idea or an anecdote that seems like a sweet little story, but that's not enough—it has no context, no *raison d'être*, there's nothing compelling the writer to explore, to journey inside the self for some sort of meaning. A student of min, Darryl Graff, recently brought an anecdote to class sparked by a writing prompt, and he came up with this beginning:

> The synagogue sat in the middle of Rivington Street, worn and broken looking. It had been raining all afternoon, and I wasn't sure if I could go in with my wet umbrella. Did it violate some kind of synagogue rule? I couldn't remember, because it had been twenty years since I'd been in one, except for the time my wife and I took an impromptu tour of the Eldridge Street Synagogue in our neighborhood, and all I remember from that is the man who had to be ninety-years-old showing us photo albums. His one shaking hand would turn the pages slowly, one by one. His other hand was darting towards my head in a futile attempt at keeping my plastic disposable yarmulke centered. He moved it to the right; it would slide to the left. He moved it to the left; it would slide to the right. This time would be different. It was not idle curiosity that drew me here. It was more specific, more personal.

It's a good opening. We're located in a particular time and place, specific images from the past are sliding into the present, and the last line suggests that something is about to be revealed. Darryl's piece then goes on to mention briefly the stories of family immigrants from Russia, his parents, and then tells us of what happened when he entered and met the rabbi in this synagogue. After asking if Darryl was Jewish and told yes, the rabbi was welcoming; asking if Darryl's wife was Jewish and told no, the rabbi was dismissive. The brief anecdote is disturbing, but in and of itself that shock isn't sufficient for an essay. There's simply not enough substance, not enough intellectual fare for the reader. As yet, the writer isn't making enough connections, isn't quite yet exploring his own emotional terrain, and so the piece is static—five minutes on a rainy afternoon. Darryl had an idea, but he needed another, or maybe just half an idea, to run against it and engender sparks.

Fiction writer Grace Paley talks about knowing she has a story not when she has one thread, but when a second intersects with the first. The same is true in the essay. If the essay is an attempt to understand or come to terms with something, then clearly that indicates that there must be questions in the air, that things are unstable or imperfectly understood. (Otherwise, why would we be puzzling over them?) These attempts to come to terms with issues of the self in relation to a wider world are where friction, internal to the individual and/or in the outer social world, occurs—like two sticks creating a spark. Questions—or just simply evaluating the significance and meaning of something—are tinder. What's needed to convert (no pun intended) Darryl's piece to something beyond an anecdote of a memory is to connect this scene of the rainy afternoon with those earlier stories of the photo albums and the family lore of his parents and his own relationship to Judaism, thrown into high relief by the comments of the rabbi about his wife. Because then, elements are clashing just as the rain is crashing on the roof, and the writer is not only entering the synagogue, but also his own sacred ground—his own head. Writers come to realize what to do, what it is they're actually exploring, even if they weren't sure they were doing it, by asking questions and looking for an edge, an angle. Ask yourself the following questions (some of which were inspired by Donald M. Murray's "Letter to a Young Article Writer").

- What is surprising?
- Is there tension? And if so where?
- What should be and what actually is?
- Is there conflict? Is its true nature known?
- Where do these ideas/issues/opinions/interests/people collide?
- Does the beginning set up a context, a conundrum, a search?
- Are there problems, dilemmas? Where do they lie?

- What's unusual, different from what might be expected?
- Are there ramifications for the writer in particular and the wider world in general?
- What contradicts with what? And how?

All of these lead to the overriding questions: What's the idea? What's the purpose? What is the essay about? What is it trying to say? As a sophomore class recently whined to me, "Does everything have to be about something? Can't it just be funny?" Well, no, even the now-classic *Seinfeld*, the show about nothing is about something. (It's hilarious, certainly, but it's also showing the nature of the cast's characters; playing with the joyful imprecision of language and the who's-on-first confusions of dialogue; revealing the inability of television moguls to understand unusual concepts; and dramatizing that art, whether television or even Samuel Beckett's work where "nothing" happens, has a *raison d'être*, and that the best humor is to a point.)

And while we're on the *Seinfeld* theme, here's another way of answering that can't-it-just-be-funny question: Yes, it can. But the piece is probably still doing something with the humor. "Cancer Becomes Me," a piece by one-time *Seinfeld* writer Marjorie Gross, appeared in *The New Yorker* two weeks before the author died of the same cancer that had killed her mother, and it's funny—Gross wryly tells us what it's like to get the diagnosis and enthusiastically details many of the social benefits of cancer: People no longer ask you to help them move; everyone returns your call immediately, and you're never put on hold for long. The tone is resolutely humorous; even in the situation she's in, the author manages to laugh at the unexpected absurdities caused by her condition, and she helps her readers laugh, too. It's brave; it's laughing at doom and our trepidation and inadequacy in the face of it, at human absurdity itself. There's no great epiphany, for the essay reads like stand-up comedy, but implicit in the attitude, the voice, the tone is a way to look at the abyss and smile. So, okay, sometimes you can just be funny, except this, in the *Seinfeld* tradition, has a *soupçon* of social satire. Writers write for readers. Their medium is language, and deftly used language communicates. Writing worth its salt carries *meaning*. And thus it spices all our lives.

The Fiction in Nonfiction

The essay, indeed all modern creative nonfiction, including and even especially the personal narrative, has a greater tendency than ever before to move beyond the rhetorical to the filmic, from abstraction to image-making. We've all read recent articles beginning with scenes or anecdotes involving dialogue as a way to draw readers in with human interest. The modern literary essay is applying many of the techniques we normally associate with fiction. Given that you've read about characterization, dialogue, voice, description, and so on in detail earlier in this book, I need not address those topics here, but let me add a few useful tips equally applicable to fiction and nonfiction.

SCENES. Use a scene for a reason. The reader's understanding of things should be different by the end of a scene than it was at the beginning, otherwise the scene has no purpose. It has to do work to earn its place in your masterpiece. Also be aware that scenes are slow, they put individuals "on stage" (right there in front of the reader in a particular moment), and that is a different pace entirely from narration, which can move a lot faster.

NARRATION. Scenes lead to other scenes, like dominos falling in a long line, but variety is important. If you find your essay isn't engaging or feels almost weightless—one thing no more differentiated in terms of magnitude and importance than another—it may be because it's too dependent on exposition. Look to see where there are key moments that might be dramatized in scenes and break the narrative up. Conversely, if you're plodding through one scene after another and your narrator and other characters won't shut up and seem to be taking forever to get to the point, perform a little triage—make decisions about what of those scenes is essential and what cries out for excision. Think about using narrative to provide some threads between those moments of drama, as well as some context and overview.

IMAGES. You've always wanted to be in motion pictures, so now's your chance: Give visuals, pictures, images. And to do that, pay careful attention to the words you choose and the associative meanings those words carry. Readers want specifics that count for something, that do work for the piece in question: You must seek them and choose them on that basis.

Here's a lyrical example of description from Annie Dillard's "Living Like Weasels." She has just seen a weasel in the wild for the first time.

> He was ten inches long, thin as a curve, a muscled ribbon, brown as
> fruitwood, soft-furred, alert. His face was fierce, small and pointed
> as a lizard's; he would have made a good arrowhead. There was just
> a dot of chin, maybe two brown hairs' worth, and then the pure
> white fur began that spread down his underside. He had two black
> eyes I didn't see, any more than you see a window.

What's wonderful about this description is its economy and delicacy of
implication. Nothing is wasted. Words like *curve* and *ribbon* illustrate the
essential litheness of the creature, and though it is *soft-furred*, it is no cud-
dly toy—one comma away, the word *alert* reminds us of how present and
living in the moment the creature is. *Muscled* takes any lightness out of the
word *ribbon*, also; we're made aware here of a long body, and a resilient
one at that. In the choice of *fruitwood*, a wood not dense like mahogany
nor as inconsequentially light as, say, balsa, there's a suggestion of pliability,
flexibility, and strength. *Arrowhead* gives a sense of size and shape, and the
connotations, the associated meanings, also add to our sense of something
found, discovered, older than time, primitive—all associations Dillard wants
to present. *Dot of chin* is fresh and thus surprising, as is the appearance
of this weasel, and along with the two brown hairs, a minute attention to
detail brings the moment alive in its specificity and quickness. Even then
she's measuring in a glance; it's only *maybe*. The rest of that sentence, un-
broken by commas, slides long and smooth, like the very white underside
it describes. And finally, eye color, which, though cited so much by writers,
is often a wash of inconsequential hue one tends to immediately forget. But
not here: These eyes are black and opaque, a mirror-skinned glass, apropos
yet again. One cannot read the eyes of this creature, for behind them is an
otherworldly knowledge. Throughout, Dillard avoids stale, obvious, facile
choices. Did Dillard consciously think this through to this degree? I trust
not. In writing about the instinct so present in nature, what she did was trust
her writer's instinct to capture it.

MISE-EN-SCÈNE. This is the environment, the surroundings to the story.
Don't just think of this as some sort of chore—"oh, no, my character's entering a room and now I'm going to have to describe it." Oftentimes beginning
writers don't choose well, and their description doesn't really do much work
for their cause. Description needs to carry more than mere placement of
stage props. And description needs to be intelligent. Here's a paragraph from

Richard Selzer's essay "The Discus Thrower," particularly marvelous for the unusual choice he makes to describe what's *not* there.

> The room in which he dwells is empty of all possessions—no get-well cards, small, private caches of food, day-old flowers, slippers, all the usual kickshaws of the sickroom. There is only a bed, a chair, a nightstand, and a tray on wheels that can be swung across his lap for meals.

Part of Selzer's narrative intent in this paragraph is to establish the patient's room, but he's providing more than location. By describing what's *not* there, specifically itemizing what's absent, he establishes very clearly in the reader's mind just how lonely and alone in the world the patient is. These are items one does expect there on display, and their absence is profound. Selzer then describes what *is* there with a plain declarative sentence and a deliberate lack of embellishment: There's a chair, but like everything else it's functionally nondescript; he notes its presence rather than detailing its particulars because in the spare one line of what is there, he further captures the Spartan sterility of the hospital room.

Students are often unsure how much description they need. Glorious descriptions of a lawn running to ten pages, no matter how verdant and lush, drive me to distraction and to the garden shed. How much scene-setting do you need? Less than a lawn, and just enough to address narrative needs. Cut that lawn.

DIALOGUE. Muddy it. Break the language, as the French say; resist perfection (though I aspire to perfection, I nevertheless find resisting it particularly easy). People don't talk in perfect sentences, and they talk across each other. We're lazy and thus economical when we speak. We cut corners. We tend not to use *that*, for example, or address people we know well with their names again and again. Nor do we repeat the question or statement someone has just put to us. And in the essay, as much as in fiction, the snips of dialogue that do get in need to be judicious and efficacious. Don't forget to paraphrase if need be, and keep in mind that in a scene with dialogue, a writer has at his disposal (1) the words spoken, (2) the thoughts thunk, (3) the interactions paraphrased, (4) the tags (almost always *said*, the default choice; unless you're very very very good, words like *hurrumphed, guffawed, averred, chortled,* and *pshawed* are going to mark you as an amateur), and (5) the pauses. Any of these options can be (and often are) combined, depending on the peculiar needs and demands of the text and the author's intuitive choices.

So, dialogue at its best will be less than eloquent; at its worst, it is unspeakable.

PAUSES. Load them. Don't just state that a pause is taking place (e.g. "She took a drink and paused for several seconds") or, for that matter, measure the length of the pause. (And absolutely no sweating palms, brows, or following the alcohol as it surges through her veins.) What I as a reader care about is what is going on in the person's head during the pause. Is she looking at the way the wallpaper seems to reel kaleidoscopically as her drinks kick in? Is she flashing on a memory of debauchery past? Is she phrasing a reply she doesn't speak? Is that loose button becoming looser than herself at that moment? In other words, there's a possibility for making the moment more vital or significant. A pause isn't just a lull to be gotten through. Silences can often speak.

TITLES. The title is the writer's first chance (before even the first line) to direct the reader toward theme. It can tell you flatly what the piece is about, but why not use it further? Striking and original is good, but it doesn't have to be gaudy. Think about the title of Selzer's essay "The Discus Thrower" and the weight of work it does. A man's dying in a hospital bed; his doctor is spying on him because his patient daily flings his plate of food at the wall. Hence the title of the essay. But this title is of more significance to the watching writer (and to the reader), a clue to human spirit. When do we throw the discus? In sports—most notably in the Olympics, whose athletes are regarded as paragons of health and aptitude and spirit. But our patient, the discus thrower of the title, is decrepit and terminal, hardly a paragon. Yet Selzer's essay shows us that, in his action of flinging his plate with finesse and intention and laughing in triumph when it hits the wall, the patient is very much worthy of a kind of admiration and awe. And yet nowhere in the piece but the title does Selzer draw a comparison between the patient and the respected athlete. Consider the theme of your essay when thinking of titles. Long or short, literal or metaphoric, the title is often a valuable clue to meaning and theme.

DETAILS. Avoid untethered abstractions, unintended vagueness, and the numbness of thoughtless language by grounding your readers in the particulars of life as we all know it. How many times have you heard that it's all in the details?

He asked me to marry him, but I had to laugh. I was just a confused girl flailing about the duvet, sweating with him to the sounds of car alarms on the street right outside his bedroom. In no fantasy could I imagine anything permanent about this arrangement, even though I expected that it would never end. He once called me at work to tell me that he had looked at his alarm clock before going to sleep: 11:27. He woke up at dawn and looked at the clock again: still 11:27. He sat up bolt upright, he told me, and realized the horrible truth: time had stopped. Well, I laughed, but it was true. I knew we were too rooted in the present to make any agreement that would march forward beyond next Tuesday. I was pretty certain we were in love, but after all these years I didn't even have a drawer in his bedroom for my underwear and, besides, I had never learned to cook. I assumed the situation would change over time, and that I'd wake up one morning to find breakfast, a vegetarian omelet, perhaps, made with too much garlic the way Alan used to, waiting by the TV instead of the usual Rice Krispies on the plastic kitchen tablecloth. He'd get down on one knee and explain how much he needed me, and then we'd go out to new restaurants, new vacation spots, listen to music written after 1967, and finally open the mini-blinds.

HARRIET R. GOREN, "THE MUSICIAN"

Let me recast the essence of the above example in the way a writer not paying attention might construe it: "He wanted it to be serious, but it really wasn't. I kinda wanted it to last, but didn't see it happening. Not that we weren't in love. It's just we were still kind of separate in our lives. But things would change one day, and he'd really propose, and then we'd act like grown-ups."

What do details do? They particularize. They add color. They transmute abstractions to evoke human dimension. Flat fact gains inflection and feeling. The details are parts to a whole world. Note also how this passage is not one particular day or moment—apart from one very brief anecdote about the alarm, which is compressed to only that amount of space its function earns—but a concise composite of what was typical and telling from many mornings, ungrounded detail but irresistibly specific. Detail is excessive when it is extraneous, when it has no role to play. Choose your details on the basis of need and the work they do for you.

NARRATIVE DRIVE. Make sure there's a through-line of meaning, a direction, a purpose to your piece. And note that essays may start with the particular and individual, but they open out, search for a universality that any reader can, to some degree, relate to or be drawn along to consider, even if what's there is antithetical to their knowledge and beliefs. Essays open out, but in a curious way; to use Phillip Lopate's metaphor, like Russian dolls in reverse. Such dolls open to reveal a smaller one inside, and then inside that, a still smaller one, but the essay works in the opposite and more magical way. It reveals something that, once considered or explored, opens to display something even bigger, which in its turn opens to an even bigger something. The essay, like any art, achieves a little magic. One piece by my student Barry Ramus opens with a discussion of René Magritte's surrealist painting *The Treachery of Images* (*La trahison des images*), which is a painting of a pipe over the words "Ceci n'est pas une pipe" ("This is not a pipe"). Following that illogic, his essay goes on to explore the arbitrary nature of words and names; reality TV; TV news; and then a video showing two American technicians killed in Kuwait City, which was broadcast first unedited, violent and bloody, then half an hour later sanitized by the television network—thus calling into question what realities are acceptable and what not, and suggesting that the realities behind the war itself were and are manipulated in order to create a reality deemed advisable and acceptable. We start from Barry's personal look at a piece of art, and the essay opens to wider implications and deepens to something of consequence and urgency. We have an enhanced understanding of things by the end; we're in a different place. Author Jessamyn West says that "fiction reveals truths that reality obscures." I'd argue that nonfiction also—indeed, all good writing—strives to do that.

What we think of as fiction techniques are simply ways to represent reality in language—how we speak, how we paint a picture, how we show inner thought—techniques, in other words, to reveal the truths about our lives and ourselves. Abstractions are often hard, amorphous, unyielding. Your readers want an idea somewhere, but they require those ideas to be living and breathing, warm and pulsing with life. Whenever your readers contemplate a scene or hear an individual speak or vividly see what's described in sensuous, fresh detail, they are convinced of that reality, and thus, in the essay, are caught up in whatever narrative there might be. They are drawn more irresistibly toward your themes and meanings because they are reading about people in a recognizable world.

A Good Beginning Means a Good Book

The heading for this section comes from John Braine talking about the novel, and though I can certainly think of a few novels that begin dazzlingly and devolve into foot-dragging, the idea is worth considering, and for nonfiction too. Call it what you will—a hook, a lead—the reader wants to be convinced that the writer is not going to waste his time, or that the perhaps initially unprepossessing subject is worth attention, or that the viewpoint will have verve rather than vapidity, *élan* rather than the ersatz. If, as in fiction, a writer must create a world that blocks out all other realities—and clearly, listening attentively to the voice of an essayist does just that—then writers need to give thought to their opening choices. I call this a gambit, which in chess is the opening move or moves by which one seeks to gain an advantage. Certainly, in schools I don't see all that much attention paid to where works begin and why, and yet it is one of the most important aspects of writing anything. With a false start you might find yourself with a piece lacking direction, your reader left wondering about the long anecdote that doesn't seem to have any discernible purpose, or whether the author is really trying to be wry and amusing or is just hamfooted (and that foot is in his mouth). And successful openings are not about sensationalism either. Shock value carries very little, and even less far.

In the essay, the first line is crucial. For one thing, it's the first time the reader meets the writer, and the writer would be wise to make that opening not just interesting, but arresting. In fiction, we all know to expect conflict, something to kick-start the action. In the nonfiction first line or first paragraph(s), the writer has an opportunity to angle his piece, to point his reader in the direction the essay will take and toward the thematic thread he wants that reader to follow. In my classes, one of the most common problems I've encountered is that writers have not really thought about the throughline of theme/meaning, the potential energy in their piece; they simply have a narrative in which things happen. Clarifying what that opening might do often magically reveals what the theme might be. A first line can be a seed; it often holds the DNA of the essay, and in the opening paragraph(s) you can often see that seed sprouting. For example:

I spy on my patients.

RICHARD SELZER, "THE DISCUS THROWER"

What can be so fabulous about five simple words? It's that one of them is unexpected. *Spy.* Since when do people who have patients—doctors, therapists, dentists, nurses—spy on them? The word brings up connotations of furtiveness that don't seem relevant. But in this wonderful essay, Selzer makes us look at this patient not to observe *how* he's doing (this is a terminal ward and it's made amply clear that the man is deteriorating rapidly), but for *what* he's doing (he's tossing his daily eggs at the wall and laughing with indescribable triumph). More importantly, Selzer wants us to look at *why* the patient is doing this, at what we can learn about dying, about the tenacity of the human spirit in the face of extinction. Selzer provides little authorial commentary throughout the piece: We simply watch—spy—over his shoulder, and he guides us with the choices he makes to see beyond the obvious (the ornery dying patient) to an implicit meaning. Note too that the first line isn't all fireworks and sensationalism. The surprise is quiet and unassuming, but it is directive—the rest of the essay follows from that one simple but unusual word choice.

Let's look at how a few of my students got going. What's most of interest here is how right from the first line or a few lines in, there's a tone of authority, suggesting the writer knows the way to the heart of the essay, and the tour that will take us there is just beginning.

> Head lice are back and not in style. Each generation discovers them anew, and the problem becomes the family's secret disgrace. Even in private schools. During the last school year, I knocked on my next-door neighbor's door. She slipped out of her apartment and said, "I'm busy. I can't talk now." She blushed. Then she sighed and said, "Oh, come in. It's just that the picker is here."
>
> Guitar, cotton, berries—what were they picking?
>
> ARLENE BENSAM, "NIT ONE, KWELL TWO"

This example begins not only by giving us the topic—head lice—right at the top, so to speak, but also by playing on a sentence we've seen before in many a fashion piece, *X is back and stylish* being the usual tack; but here, there's a variation on the expected—we're talking stigma rather than style—which draws us further in. Bensam follows it up with the human interaction that drew her to the topic in the first place, and pretty soon we're about to meet a fifty-dollar-an-hour lice-picker (note to self: possible alternate career here

if writing thing doesn't pan out) and look at an age-old scourge through
the eyes of a woman who, in remembering it from way back, brings a fresh
perspective on an itchy social problem.

In the next piece, there's again an excellent opening sentence—do we ever
think of ourselves as having a relationship with our underwear? But once the
possibility is raised, don't we all wonder what it entails—and read on?

> I have never had a good relationship with underwear. My body has had
> brief encounters with girdles, padded bras, garter belts, corsets, baby-
> dolls, itsy-bitsy things, and even the famous merry widow brassiere
> and waist-cincher combo, and I didn't fit into any one of them.
>
> My first recognition of the problem occurred not with a specific
> item, but with its X-ray. When I started school in 1940, my mother
> dressed me in a two-piece cotton garment fastened by buttons. I
> didn't know what other children wore, but, because of an outbreak
> of tuberculosis in the first grade, we all had to have chest X-rays.
> The buttons on my little top, fashioned carefully of bone, registered
> as huge spots on my little lungs, and required the confused doctors
> to perform a differential diagnosis on the two symmetrical lesions.
> I was humiliated when the other kids found out that I wore baby
> underclothes.
>
> Things only got worse. ...
>
> ARLENE BENSAM, "CUT ME LOOSE"

After that fine opening line, we're drawn by a list of items that, with its
somewhat outmoded undergarments, is intriguing enough, even without the
author's admission that she never fit into them. Notice then how the essay
starts swelling outward—no stays hold it in; it starts breathing right away.
We get a paragraph of humorous anecdote explaining when the problem
was first diagnosed, and in the beginning of the next paragraph, theme and
conflict are developing, snapping into place like elastic you can trust.

One more variation on the successful opening gambit: Here the author
captures her readers with a pronoun.

> It usually happens when I'm trying to schedule a get-together with a
> friend. We'll keep clashing on date availability until my friend says
> in frustration, "What are you doing on that day, anyway?" That's
> when it comes out: I do a little volunteer work.

"That's so great," she exclaims. "How do you find the time? I'm impressed—I don't do anything like that."

I've usually shrugged it off as no big deal. Not because I'm modest, but because I know the truth. Yes, I'm a volunteer. But with a guilty conscience.

Deborah Ungar, "Volunteer"

What is the *it* referring to in the first line? The reader is dropped directly into the small drama of a brief conversation, and sure enough, we experience the author's reluctance to admit to volunteering. But why? Perhaps, like the friend quoted, we also feel we'd love to do some gratuitous civic good but haven't the time, but the answer isn't quite so simple—we also don't expect to feel that we benefit from it, too. The essay is going to give us a sense of being a volunteer, but with an unexpected twist—a guilty conscience. It's that confluence of doing admirable social works and yet feeling guilty that provides the grist for the writer and draws the reader along. The guilt and internal conflict stems from generously volunteering (in such ways as participating in Parkinson's walkathons and recording a regular radio show for the blind) and yet inadvertently benefiting along the way.

And as we have seen in all the examples above, guilt, anger, curiosity, and oddness are all rich raw material for essays. And the best opening—a line of dialogue, an image, an incident that set the writer thinking, or whatever—will emerge in the writing process. Whatever begins the final draft will not necessarily be the chronologically earliest event in the story, but will be dictated by its thematic importance or its ability to draw the reader in.

A few final points to ponder for the opening section of your essay:

- What's new in your essay worth paying attention to?
- What's the idea?
- Does the beginning set up a context, a search?

The Muddle of the Middle

All the points raised in this chapter—developing an idea, using fictional techniques, reflecting on experience, developing theme—have relevance to the muddle of the middle, the place where the essay needs to open out, to grow in possibility and richness, to find and refine what it is saying. As the writer, you need to look for the controlling idea.

> Until two years ago, I didn't know the color of my own eyes. It was not as if I was blind in the usual sense, just blinded to myself.

Rosie Blitchington, "Chameleon"

When the writer first brought this essay to my class, all she had was a few anecdotes that really didn't cohere. There was something about a photographer boyfriend who'd taken her picture and won a national competition with it, an event that had, to her dismay, led to her image touring the country, proclaiming her eye color everywhere it went. (But why the dismay?) There was much talk of what color her eyes actually were—one minute blue, the next, seemingly green. (Why would we care?) There was a reference to being adopted, but it was overshadowed by something her current boyfriend said about her beautiful eyes. Clearly, there was something we were just not seeing. Successive drafts included a section about a closet full of dresses from different periods of her life—her hippy period, her corporate wear, her homemaker days, her disco nights. There was a reference to her stepmother, who had wanted the author to go to veterinary school as she herself had wanted to do, despite her daughter's desire to be a writer. But what was this essay about? I suspected the adoption had something to do with it, which the writer denied—until, in one draft, she described herself as a chameleon, a creature that changes its hue, its body tone, in order to blend with any environment it finds itself in. Suddenly everything started to fit. She had found a key word, a controlling idea. As an adopted child, she had experienced conflict over her eye color—the stepmom had wanted to see her as having the eye color that matched her own and fit in with the family, just as she'd wanted her to be the vet she had wanted to be—but the author could only be herself. Who was she, then, in the boyfriend's picture? And those dresses in that closet, were they not skins to fit a variety of worlds? When she found her title—"Chameleon"—it gave her the wherewithal to shape the random anecdotes and ideas into the substantive core of her essay. What an essay is about, what goes in the middle, is often found by the trial and error of the writing process.

The middle of an essay is where the story unfolds, the themes are revealed, the arguments laid out, the examples marshaled, the anecdotes deployed, the evidence sorted, the questions explored, the analysis sifted, the ideas weighed, the fictional techniques utilized, the reflections engendered. It is where understanding is chased, but not necessarily captured. It is where the early promise of the beginning is fulfilled. It is where you, the writer, most have to trust yourself to fumble a way forward, toward a meaning and an understanding that is only inchoate when you start.

Points to ponder for the middle section:

- Does the middle build and grow, broadening a context? Is each piece of evidence or illustration essential?

- Is the evidence and illustration in service to the main idea, and does each piece support the idea in a different way?

- Is the narrative providing smooth links—transitions between scenes, illustrations, and evidence?

- Is there enough reflection? Is the writer putting things in a framework, a context? Are the connections logical, emotional, or associative?

Ending It All

Endgame, another term from chess, to me signifies finding the strategy to swiftly and successfully conclude your campaign to capture (and enrapture) your reader. The ending is something of a flourish, for most of the work of the essay should be done by this point. Just as coffee and dessert can put a final sweet and stimulating touch on a good meal, the endgame leaves the reader with a sense of satiety and completeness. A really good ending—the final paragraph, sentence, even only a word or two—can sometimes save a mediocre essay, and it certainly adds a touch of class and a high sheen to a good one. It's the last thing the reader sees, and it's also the last chance for the writer to underline or emphasize meaning. A good ending is like the final chord of a symphony, diminishing, hovering in the air and the mind before sinking into (one hopes) tremulous, beautiful memory. What you don't want, metaphorically, is the sound of the garbage can clanking or the smoke alarm going off. Here are a few examples:

> To bring the reader full circle (and to end this tale of misery and woe), let me return to my initial questions—what is it about the simple life that so attracts modern man? What is that force that compels us to

return to our primitive roots? Honestly, I have no idea. I do have a theory, though—it is the same force that compels lemmings to leap from high cliffs into the sea and certain death. It is the magnetic pull that whales must feel just prior to beaching themselves. In short, it is the inability to leave well enough alone and be happy with what you've got. At least, that is my opinion. To be quite honest with you, I have decided that I am much better off not thinking about these things anymore. Instead, I will leave you with one final quote (from that deceitful Thoreau) that sums up my feelings about the "simple life" quite nicely: "Thank Heaven, here is not all the world."

KATHLEEN LOCKE, "WALDEN II: THE REVENGE"

As this excerpt suggests, the writer opens her essay on the "joys" of country house ownership with a battery of highfalutin questions about the simple life, and an invocation of "Henry David Thoreau, the naturalist from Hell." Opening an essay with a question is—90 percent of the time—a poor choice. The writer appears to be opening with something substantive and directed, but so often the writer doesn't even bother to address her own question. But here, it's appropriate. Kathleen Locke really is going to address the maddening nature of Nature, of country house ownership in all its overstated ingloriousness. Trees thrust through her foundations, creatures cause havoc inside, unwelcome family members invite themselves and leave their beer cans, and the "professional" help that she foolishly flees to is maniacally quirky and a sure road to penury. Note the title, which clues you in to the wry ironic dudgeon that flavors the author's humorous tone. Along the way, she works in quotes from Thoreau as high contrast against her far more down-to-earth experiences.

The author wasn't supposed to use questions, but did; she pretends to answer them, but doesn't. She invokes the gravity of Thoreau's name, but then maintains a plainspoken tone that holds no truck with grand pronouncements, and she turns Thoreau's own words against him one final time to emphasize how off-the-point her experience showed her he was. The reader is indeed brought full circle.

Let's revisit two of the essays we saw earlier. You'll remember Arlene Bensam's underwear issues. At the end of the essay, she's realized that certain pieces of the anatomy aren't where they used to be, and that "Pert and perky [are] no longer applicable terms. Now, we are talking low and mournful." And a sheer sweater, gravity, and aging don't go together. She's tried to make her peace with the fractious nature of underwear, but remembering the central anecdote of her essay—a story of a friend, Rosie, who had to be cut out of her "living girdle" with shears—she must acknowledge that her attempt at reconciliation is almost certainly over. Early on in the essay, she relates that when, as a girl, she asked her mother for a bra well before she needed one, her mother's response was "What for?" At the end of the essay, Arlene wisely uses this phrase again, but with a wry ironic twist: Now, *what for?* feels a lot more friendly and comfortable. She sums up thus:

> I ran out and bought a brassiere—no trying on—just one that looked right. It fit, sort of, but it chafed and rubbed and looked more un-comfortable than I felt. So I did the only thing I could, as images of Rosie's mother cutting her out of the girdle flashed in and out of my brain. I took the brassiere off, before it grew too close, and wore a discreet black blouse.
>
> Someday, I may attempt to get all of us together—me, the bra, the sweater, and my acceptance of the aging process. For now, we are all safely tucked away, knowing that a day of reconciliation could be at hand. Although I keep hearing my mother asking in that sensible tone of hers, "What for?"
>
> ARLENE BENSAM, "CUT ME LOOSE"

Finally, here's Deborah Ungar's quick, no-nonsense ending to her piece about volunteering.

> So I'm giving up my guilt. Sure, there'll be a twinge or two from time to time. But I'll cope. My volunteering may be a form of barter. But I've learned it works well for all concerned.
>
> DEBORAH UNGAR, "VOLUNTEER"

Note how the guilty conscience referred to in the opening has become only a twinge. She's come to consider volunteering as a kind of barter, a view-point that the friend in her opening paragraph or a reader might not have thought of before, which in itself is interesting. Her guilt is on the verge of being assuaged because volunteering is working for everyone; the writer has a different frame of mind at the end than she had originally, and the reader, too, has been given a view of things he might not previously have had. And note the *but*s. There's a twinge—*but*; it's a form of barter—*but*. Doubt is at the core of the essay, and with it, a weighing of things and a change in perspective. There's more than enough for an engaging essay.

In all these endings, there's a sense of finality and completion, or at least an illusion of it, and obvious thoughtfulness on the part of the writers about what note to end on and how to play it. There might be a sense of the end of a journey or the conclusion of a process of thought or inquiry or rumination, and this might be achieved by the repetition of a key word or a telling image, by articulation of an earned insight, through dialogue that rounds things out, or the metaphor that holds everything together—the options are manifold. You, the writer, find them in the process of construction as you discover what exactly it was you didn't know you were thinking or feeling or articulating in your earliest drafts. As a writer, you are always listening to your essay as it develops, to its themes and potentialities; you are looking to end with the strategies and notes that best serve, underscore, enhance, or complete these.

Points to ponder in the last section:

- What has changed?

- Is that the change understood by the end?

- Do the reader and/or writer come to be in a slightly different emotional place, or have an altered understanding of things by the end?

Ideas Into Drafts Into Essays

Writing begets writing. Or as Gertrude Stein put it, "To write is to write is to write is to write is to write is to write is to write." Once you ease yourself into it regularly, ideas will come to you more easily. With scheduled writing (and when taking a class), you'll cultivate a sharper critical sense of which ideas have more promise and how you might develop them. In the meantime, here are a few observations that will help you develop ideas into drafts into essays.

- Essays often contain within them the moment of their own conception, the catalyst event or word or thing or question or conflict that causes the writer to muse on the subject (within himself, in relation to the world) and put down a first draft. Dillard's essay about the weasel comes from one brief frozen moment of encounter with the creature, which sends her to research and read about them. Nancy Mairs begins her essay "Carnal Acts" when she is invited to talk at a symposium of librarians about both surviving the depredations of MS and being a woman writer. Mairs, at that point, sees no connection between them. But she starts writing right there, and in the process finds a fascinating connection.

- Essay writers contain within themselves many quirks and peccadilloes and endearing or downright disgusting oddnesses; for material, you have only to mine the self (stealing from oneself is not narcissism, nor is it illegal, and it is actually quite fun). Here's my friend Jessica Treat talking about how she gets some of her ideas for stories, but substitute *personas* or *narrators* for *characters*, and what she says applies equally to the essay: "Here's how it works (for me). My characters often begin with some small aspect or quirk of my personality. It is then magnified one-hundred- or three-hundred-fold. Then comes the question: What would it be like to be out in the world if one were like that?" And so begins a voyage of discovery. No one's too boring or too twisted to write nonfiction. All right, maybe *you* are, if you insist. But, really, write about how infinitely more boring your life is than anyone else's, write about how much more twisted than your sister you are, and I'll bet you'll dig up the start to something worth reading.

- Resistance to anything will give you a workable stance. You can oppose things—the denuding of the rain forests or illegal wars or the erosion of civil liberties—that many would agree with. Those are easy. But what if you take a more contrary view? Take umbrage with the majority—do people with cell phones who blather in the middle of the sidewalk have a right to live? Maybe you don't think so, and you've got a level of surprise there that, with wit and humor, can carry far. I'd say the essay is a contrarian form, but no doubt someone would disagree.

- There are many ways to be interesting—lively language being the most preeminent—but here are two useful ideas from Joseph Epstein:
  1. Tell readers things they already know in their hearts but have never been able to formulate for themselves.
  2. Tell readers things they do not know and perhaps have never imagined.

Both involve originality of vision and expression. The point is, though, that everyone's interesting if he will only engage in the process, dip into the self, and relate what he finds to a wider world. I recently had an avowed slacker hand in his essay on being a slacker (reluctantly and late), and it was fascinating to see how much effort and pride he took in doing his work, barely, at the last minute, and ... inadvertently insightfully. Hey, whatever. You never know until you start writing.

Publishing Collections of Essays and Personal Narratives

Collections of essays are difficult to publish, despite the resurgence of nonfiction categories in recent years. I'd say they are about as hard to place as story collections, which is to say nigh impossible, unless you're a blazing new talent or well connected. The advice is always to publish a novel first, or a book-length work. Or, alternatively, you can try, like story writers, to publish your essays piece by piece in literary magazines—most nowadays are interested in nonfiction—and gradually shape a collection together. A list of publications will enhance your chances of finding a publisher, but it will still be challenging. Obviously, if you've got a pundit pulpit on something like NPR, publishers will be interested because you've got a degree of celebrity—which, as we all know these days, is highly marketable. But don't despair. Celebrity is not what being a successful essayist is about. Better to work at your craft. Find something worth saying and say it well. You'll find your venue with application and persistence.

To publish essays:

- Look at the list of magazines cited in *The Best American Essays* and *The Pushcart Prize: Best of the Small Presses* (annual anthologies you'll find in your bookstore and library). Use this as a basis for finding magazines that might be interested in your work.

- Look up the magazines in publications like *The International Directory of Little Magazines and Small Presses* and *Writer's Market* (annual directories you'll find in a bookstore or a library). Under each publication you will find information on the magazines—how large, how frequently published, readership, size, whether and what they pay, etc.—and on the editorial bent, what kinds of work they are looking for and have recently published.

- Start reading these magazines in the library. Better yet, in the case of literary magazines, subscribe to a range of them (they are a lot cheaper than hardcover books, and this support is vital to their continuing existence). This will give you a sense of what's getting published these days, what particular magazines really go for, how much the level of quality varies, and what forms the essay can take.

- When you feel you are ready, these are the magazines you will send your work to. But before you do, learn your craft. Competition is fierce, and you want to be confident when you begin submitting work, because rejection, no matter how stoic and optimistic you are, hurts and disappoints. Persisting with the writing and the submissions is the key.

Reading Others' Essays

Certainly you should look at the essays in the national magazines, such as *Harper's Magazine* and *The New Yorker*. But a writer's first home in print is much more likely to be a literary magazine, of which there are hundreds across the country, either university-based or run independently. Learn this market. Sample it as much as you can. The range is immense, from the outstanding Canadian magazine *Brick* that focuses on the literary nonfiction essay to *Fourth Genre*, a magazine devoted to innovative work in creative nonfiction. But there's there's also a range from *The Sun* to *The Utne Reader*, and, with its mix of photograph and essay, *DoubleTake*, and essay magazines with a journalistic bent such as *Creative Nonfiction*. Many literary magazines that take fiction include sections for essays, reviews, and other nonfiction pieces. You can also look online, where magazines such as *Epiphany* and *Brevity* (which, true to its name, looks for very short nonfiction narratives) can be found. And for a Web site that will give you a long list of literary magazines, check out www.newpages.com. The following is a list off the top of my head of some other literary magazines taking essays (personal or critical), memoir extracts or both. Following the list of magazines are lists of essayists and essay anthologies that you should familiarize yourself with. It is a scurrilously incomplete list, just to give you names to look for when brain-freeze strikes in the library or the bookstore and you can't think of a single writer. The full list is blissfully endless.

THE ESSAY: RECOMMENDED READINGS

MAGAZINES

Chelsea
Colorado Review
The Florida Review
Gulf Coast
Manoa
Michigan Quarterly Review
New England Review
PRISM International
Santa Monica Review

ESSAYISTS

Baldwin, James
Didion, Joan
Diski, Jenny
Hoagland, Edward
Kingsolver, Barbara
Mairs, Nancy
Orwell, George
Selzer, Richard
Steingarten, Jeffrey
Walker, Alice

ESSAY ANTHOLOGIES

Arana, Marie, ed. *The Writing Life: Writers on How They Think and Work.* New York: Public Affairs, 2003.

Atwan, Robert, series ed. Orlean, Susan, ed. *The Best American Essays.* Boston: Houghton Mifflin Company, 2005.

Writers on Writing. 2 vols. New York: Times Books, 2001 and 2003.

Longer Nonfiction:
The Personal Narrative or Literary Memoir

The term *memoir,* for me at least, has unfortunate associations with gin-drinking retired colonels in the tropics bloviating about their pathetic histories. I prefer a term like *personal narrative,* which seems at least to suggest that one doesn't have to have reached a ripe (and soused) old age before one reflects on one's life. A personal narrative, unlike the essay (which can be analytic or endlessly reflective), is just what the term suggests—a narrative, an ongoing story. But again, we're discussing nomenclature. It doesn't really matter what we call it. Either of these terms indicates that a whole or a part of a life is being recounted—not necessarily in chronological order (a pattern which older memoirs certainly tended to follow)—and that, just as in the essay, the author will be a specific presence and a guide to the insights into the self and the world that this longer story will reveal. So the memoir is open to anyone. You don't need an exciting or important life, just a fresh and intelligent way of framing your experiences. If you like, the memoir's a life story—not just the life, but the story buried in it, a story with some inherent meaning, which the writer brings out.

The book-length nonfiction work can use all the elements of the essay, though it tends toward more elaborate and deeply explored stories and themes. The longer work of nonfiction doesn't necessarily have to deal with a whole life. Many book-length nonfiction narratives these days deal with a much smaller section of a life—the years the writer was a volunteer fireman (*On Fire*, Larry Brown) or worked in the oil business as a geologist (*Oil Notes*, Rick Bass) or owned a beach house with no plumbing, power, or telephone, living on lichen (*Drinking the Rain*, Alix Kates Shulman). A young woman's coming-of-age in the beat generation (*Minor Characters: A Beat Memoir*, Joyce Johnson), or a writer traveling to Patagonia (*In Patagonia*, Bruce Chatwin), or the author's father or mother seen through the author's eyes (*A Man's Place* and *A Woman's Story*, Annie Ernaux). Or there's the love stories of a life as backdrop to the passion of an old man for a young woman (*Montauk*, Max Frisch, a classic work of personal narrative that reads like autobiographical fiction). The list is as varied as it is unending, and just as versatile. Such a wide range is far more alluring than the dustiness of the much-maligned term *memoir* suggests. Though there are trace elements of glamour or drama to some of these books—hanging out with the beats, fighting fires—that isn't at all where the focus lies. They are essentially personal visions of particular times, places, people, and events. They attempt the ultimately unanswerable question: *How to live?* They give one answer: how they tried, what they experienced. Forget the nomenclature; just think of what the story is.

The most important thing is not what we call the genre, but that we distinguish it from fiction and that we know why. An essentially "true" narrative that claims the genus of fiction has to be judged differently—in fictional terms, for a reader goes to fiction expecting certain things and not others. In fiction we reach a dream state; in nonfiction we inhabit a clearheaded state of mind. Readers of fiction expect theme to distill through character and event, and expect to be directed subtly to insight via the masks and veils and other subterfuges of fiction. The illusion is broken if they feel prodded to the point, or if they are too directly told. Readers of the nonfiction work expect to experience more directly the mind of the author, who will frame the meaning of things for herself and tell the readers. In fiction, the writer can become other people; in nonfiction, she becomes more of herself. In fiction, the reader must step into a believable fictional realm; in nonfiction, the writer speaks intimately, from the heart, directly addressing the reader's sympathies. In fiction, the narrator is generally not the author; in nonfiction—barring special one-off personas as encountered in Jonathan Swift's *A Modest Proposal*—the writer and narrator are essentially the same. In fiction, the narrator can lie; the expectation in nonfiction is that the writer won't. There's an assumption that the story is, to as great an extent as possible, true; that the tale and its narrator are reliable.

What astounds in fiction can confound in nonfiction, and vice versa: In fiction, if a man falls from an airliner and lands on his own house, the result is too pat, too neat to be believed—the delicate illusion of the fictional world shatters because (forgive me) the credibility plummets; if the same event is told by a writer of nonfiction, the reader is amazed by the ability of life to be wilder than fiction. Fiction and nonfiction are different genders; they share many similarities of form, but like men and women, there are unignorable divergences that, after all, we are only too pleased to acknowledge. *Vive la différence!*

Truth, Lies, and the Videotape of Your Own Life

TRUTH AND LIES

Truthfulness in literary nonfiction is not the fact-based, verifiable truth of journalism; neither is it the source-ridden influence-parsing synthesis of scholarship. It's veracity, an adherence to the code of truthfulness, which is measured by emotional authenticity rather than replicability; it's art, not science. Thoreau's masterpiece, *Walden*, encapsulates one year of living in nature, but in reality, Thoreau spent two years in the woods and compressed his material. One might argue—I hear some muttering about that deceitful Thoreau—this goes too far along the continuum toward pure fiction, but surely the prevailing notion is that *in essence* he's being truthful. What happened, happened. What insights he has on those matters are real and felt and true. What he's done is what any writer worth her eraser would do: He's cut out the inessential to keep the flow of significance coming and the narrative impetus unimpeded. In essence, in emotional terms, he's not made anything up, and he's stayed true to the impact those experiences—over one year or two—had on him. He's used compression to tighten his story. He's taken a liberty, used a little artistic license, but he has not out-and-out lied, thereby breaking the code of veracity that nonfiction has, by definition, with the reader.

Think of *Angela's Ashes* by Frank McCourt as another example. It's a fine book, but no one is going to tell me that the author remembers all that dialogue—pages of it. Indeed, one might say he pushes a little beyond the boundary of what can reasonably be re-created from memory. But, that said, even if the conversations in real life didn't go exactly that way, were they in essence—in tone and timbre and sweep and sentiment—somewhat close to what's on the page? If so, then the writer's been as faithful as one can reasonably expect him to be; he's represented reality as he remembers it. The issue is intent—intent to present an essentially and reasonably honest representation, as opposed to the intent to fictionalize to such a degree that the reality one started with is left far behind.

Without wishing to join the fray, I would be remiss if I didn't use the James Frey controversy as an example here. As you probably recall, James Frey is the author of the memoir *A Million Little Pieces*, which was an Oprah

Book Club pick. As I understand it, Frey altered many of the facts of his life because he believed it made for a better story. For example, he maintained he was imprisoned for a significant length of time (months), when in fact he was simply booked and then released—detained for only a matter of hours. If Frey were writing an autobiographical novel here—i.e., representing it as fiction—these changes in the actual occurrences would be fine. A reader would understand and accept that changes were made to facilitate the themes and dramas of the fictional world that Frey-the-novelist was creating. Equally, as a novelist, he'd be perfectly free to make up everything—that's the extent of the fictional realm. But at the other side of the dividing line between the genres, lies memoir, where essentially the reader expects the honesty of self-revelation, the thrill of being privy to self-exploration, and a personal framing of events. Some small recreation is acceptable and inevitable, given memory's wiles, but that isn't *carte blanche* to make things up that didn't happen. In doing just that, Frey undermines the authority of the genre. As a nonfiction writer he is deliberately misleading by intentionally misrepresenting significant, essence-changing facts in order to make the story more dramatic than it was. This is very different than merely "misremembering" or claiming this is *his* truth, his memory of it. His intent is clear; it's his justifications that are murky. If it's argued that this is how he remembers things, then clearly we've got a different story—a man who has delusions about serving time when he doesn't serve it. But that's not the book he's representing either. Fiction proceeds on the notion of *what if?* Nonfiction proceeds on the notion of *what was?* There is no *if* in nonfiction.

But what if you've got a brain like mine and you simply don't remember? What if your memories are impressionistic, maybe even pointillistic—nay, positively cubist? How do you get the details right? Do you stick a microphone under Gran's wheezing mouth, dig up the family grave, clean out the skeleton closet? Well, yeah, some research can be helpful. But research is flat fact. Those fragmentary and vague impressions are where you start. You can start with remembering an object or a snippet of dialogue or a room or a particular summer or an intense feeling or a typical image—anything can get you going. And if you allow your thoughts to be transformed into language on the page, other ideas will gradually come, and you'll find that you don't so much have to pull things from your memory, that they come at their own behest; when fishing, you don't will the fish out of the water—you throw your hopeful line in, cast around a little, and wait.

I remember a time when I lived at my grandmother's and I would try to be helpful by dusting a dressing table that sat in an unused bedroom. I'd move the ornaments, dust, put them back. I also recall an old upright gramophone which, when you lifted the lid, revealed a cache of tinned goods. (Our family was always ready for the next war—and having been through two, who could blame them?) The food was a trove, the dressing table was a shrine, and as now I think about it, the room may have been as well—grandfather's picture as a young man appeared prominently in a frame. The point is not that I remember the simple cleaning, but that I also recall, perhaps more poignantly, the sense of dust and loss and the aspiration to retain respectability. (Did I forget to say there were two probably fake crystal cookie-type jars filled with dusty, long-odorless, dried roses? As I write, I'm thinking that I recall that they were from my grandfather's grave, but I can't swear to it.) I could try to describe the little glass vials of jewelry, the knickknacks and baubles, but they've all gone from memory, except for what I've noted. What I've retained is the sheen of dust on the dark, unscratched, polished wood and the smell of polish; I don't actually have a smell—cherry? lemon?—but I do have the brand: Pledge. I could go do the research on that, but really, doesn't my flaky remembrance of something oaken, chestnut, something redolently rich and brown—emotive and filtered by a self and the senses—do the job more effectively than a scent-as-product-fact? I recall, and as I recall, as I allow myself to go there in my head, where truly I don't want to go this morning. I recall more; detail and texture become miraculously available, emerging out of the murk of my mind, if not distinct, at least discernible. And in recounting, clearly I'm re-creating, but I'm doing that from a half-buried blueprint of the past, torn and faded and crackling with my own neglect, its colors faded but its imprint, however gnawed by time, as true as anything can be for me.

You'll find it easier as a writer of nonfiction to view representations of experience as malleable. You will fare better to see literary truth as distinct from legalistic hard fact, to strive for ballpark accuracy rather than box-score statistical precision, to acknowledge memories as comprising endlessly interpretable packages of emotional re-creation. But you will save yourself endless second guessing if you remember that you can't intentionally or even unintentionally fabricate sections of a memoir. Novelists have options that memoirists don't. For nonfiction to have any validity at all, it must be as true as can be, by definition, otherwise it's fiction.

It is in the emotional landscape that a reader seeks truths, and you the writer unearth them. But which ones, and how do you polish them up? There's the rub. The Chinese proverb has it thus: There are three truths—my truth, your truth, and the truth. We know the first, what we remember of it; we may have been told some of the second, though we may not believe it; we aspire to the third, the objective one, though we can never achieve it.

EDITING THE VIDEOTAPE

Tolstoy wrote, "Happy families are all alike, and every unhappy family is unhappy in its own way." Well, every home movie is execrable in exactly the same way: It's unedited. It assumes its very existence is of interest. It falsely assumes the captive audience of family will find it entertaining. But bring out the family videotape of interchangeable babies petting kittens to death, and Grandma hot in her bathing suit, and I'm going off to find some exciting surfaces to dust. Life needs editing. Writing needs life. And this brings us to another principle: All writing, and perhaps particularly nonfiction, depends on selection, magnification, and compression in order to transform the flat fact of raw data to the vivacity of emotive truth.

If you're going to tell the story of your life—or more accurately, an account from a part of your life—then obviously you don't relate that tale day by day by day. That would simply be interminably boring because of the large percentage of utter banality in any life. A life doesn't have a theme until someone finds the underlying patterns to it and, using literary craft and artistic vision, shapes the elements of experience and directs them toward significance. Selection involves choosing the words we use for the work they will do for us: We select the scenes of importance; we select a period of the life we're dealing with; we select what, within that period, is and is not relevant to the themes that we choose from the possibilities that emerge in the process of writing our tentative drafts, our stabs at "getting something down," at understanding as best we can. Like understanding what a good story is, these semiconfident choices come from the practice of writing and more writing, and even more rewriting.

Now imagine that you've narrowed down the elements of life experience that you are shaping to become your personal narrative—growing up in a extremely wacky family, say, or surviving any from the gamut of physical and emotional disasters. There are going to be moments to which you want to allocate significance and reader attention—to descriptions, snatches of dialogue, or crucial pauses and such. Magnification is simply the bestowing of emphasis or significance by the writer: choosing to slow the pace of the narrative by giving space to greater detail or, if you like, creating something of a close-up. Not everything in a narrative carries equal weight. As the writer, you need to direct your reader to where such emphases lie.

Even if a writer is only dealing with a part of a life—a few difficult years as a sentient grunt in a merciless war, say, or driving around Europe in search of gastronomic delights—quite obviously not every second is important. Just as you might choose to give some small segment of experience the space and time for close-up detail, so you might decide that other fractions or even whole swathes of time and events don't have the required significance to merit the space it would take to render them—thus you omit them or cover them in a broad brushstroke of narrative. By compressing—omitting gratuitous detail—we acknowledge the experience, cover the ground, but don't wear out our reader's attention on narrative elements that are of lesser or passing note.

Essay or memoir, all nonfiction writing depends on the writer using selection, magnification, and compression in order to shape, allot significance, and control the material. Put ridiculously simply, you can ask these questions of your manuscript draft:

- What goes in this section?
- What specifics are important?
- What needs emphasis? Why?
- What parts/moments/scenes/images/dialogue do I need to highlight for my reader? How?
- What is extraneous to the themes of the piece? What can be summarized? What can be omitted?
- Draft by draft by draft, what am I saying and how is that developing or being refined or deepened? With that in mind, do I need to revisit some of these questions again to refine the slant or reshuffle the emphases?

In the following examples of extracts from personal narratives, I've tried to illustrate what sort of writerly decisions are behind the words that eventually come to be on the page. You will develop the ability to make these decisions with intuition through the constant and enduring practice of writing and engaging with language.

This passage below—from J.R. Roessl's *Salao*, which in Portuguese means that everything that can go wrong, does—is about an obsessive father who builds his own boat with the slave-like labor of his several young daughters and takes to the sea following his dream. This section details simply enough how things were done in the house in the many years it took before the boat was eventually ready. The pregnancy mentioned here would interrupt the launch yet again for several more years, causing distress among the daughters, who are already trying to negotiate difficult high school years.

> During the summer of 1964 and on the eve of finally moving out of our small, cramped apartment in Alameda and onto the boat, my mother discovered she was pregnant. At the time, my sisters and I had no idea she was or why our parents suddenly decided to delay moving. We were simply informed that our mother, who never went anywhere without us, was suddenly thinking of taking a trip by herself to visit long-lost relatives in Sweden.
>
> "What relatives?" we all asked.
>
> "On your Grandpa Alfred's side," mom said, hurriedly. I didn't like the sound of this. None of us could remember our mother's father, as he had died when Pam was three and I was still a baby. Why would she want to go now and visit relatives of his she had never met?
>
> "Can I go with you?" I asked. This sudden trip sounded suspiciously like Dad's "camping trip" years before, when he just disappeared and we all feared he would never come back. There was no way I was going to let my mom leave us without the guarantee she would return; if I went with her, she would have to come home.
>
> "Actually, your mother needs to go there for a little operation," Dad said.
>
> "Operation?!" we all shouted.
>
> "Jim!" Mom turned to Dad and gave him a searing look.
>
> "Mommy, are you sick?" Gayle asked.

"No dear, it's nothing really. Your father's just joking. I'm fine." Then she addressed our anxious expressions by abruptly changing the subject. "Listen, how about Dad taking us all out for ice cream?"

I looked at my mother's rosy complection, unable to detect any of the sallowness that had been evident in my father's when he was sick with hepatitis. Convinced that she looked the picture of health in her pretty blue-flowered dress and red lipstick, I let go of the nagging thought that something was wrong and happily thought of the drive over to the Tastee-Freeze.

Neither Mom nor Dad mentioned the trip again, and a few months later we began to notice that Mom, who had acquired a habit of humming and smiling to herself as she made dinner or folded the laundry, was gaining weight and mostly around her middle. Finally, we three were told that we would soon be getting a little sister or, hopefully, a brother.

Nancy was born in February, 1965.

J.R. Roessl, *Salao*

SELECTION. This takes place here in deciding to use this material regarding the pregnancy for a scene, rather than some other material. Obviously, not everything has the same significance or usefulness, and writers must weigh those options and choose. What stays out is just as important a choice as what goes in. Why a scene where the pregnancy is first noticed? Why not the birth? Why not a scene as the girls all sit around in a bedroom a few months earlier, discussing it, or the private ruminations of the main character as she walks to school and knows something's up? All these other possibilities aren't chosen because the one that was has a drama and assists the narrative intent: to give us another setback that delays departure, while illustrating how the family dynamics are playing out. This scene also shows how the daughter penning the story is being affected by the sequence of as yet mild disasters, and also sketches who these individuals are and what shapes their various enmities and needs and dynamics on shore, all of which will be intensified when this ship of fools finds their timbers shivered and themselves, in more ways than one, deeply at sea.

MAGNIFICATION. The scene gets space, we gear-change down, and time is slowed. This allows the reader to see and intuit more and be closer to the characters than exposition alone allows. We see how clumsy the father is in dealing with any topic involving emotion or sex (this is the man, for example, who will finally go to sea without an inkling that a boat of pubescent daughters will need tampons); we experience the mother as essentially avoiding conflict, meekly acceding to but not entirely in accord with the husband; the pair demonstrates the poor parenting and leadership skills that lead to much conflict elsewhere in the chapter and on the voyage. The writer chooses to use the dialogue to show the parents' evasiveness, the tensions within the family, and, in passing, to give dimension and presence to the characters.

COMPRESSION. After the Tastee-Freeze, a gear is changed upward, the pace ups from the step-by-step of a scene to the glide of narrative, and time is sketched in much more generally. Compressing the nonessential into a swifter section drives the narrative forward. In a phrase, we cover months of a beatific humming mother and all manner of suspicion on the part of the daughters, but all else other than that is deemed too insignificant to specify. This compression doesn't just mean summing up; notice how the exposition here gives us that *hopefully* in front of *a brother*, telling us so much about what the father really would have wanted, as well as being thematically significant: One thread to the book is the author often being treated as a son while enduring the constraints of a daughter. And then the selection of that simple fact of Nancy's birth: another delay, another daughter, the parental deceit underlined. The writer has compacted a swathe of life story into one brief, solid piece of the narrative puzzle that she's assembling.

Let's examine another section from early in the second chapter of the same book in terms of selection, magnification, and compression. The father has just returned from a secret mission and the family awaits him, but the narrative is about to go into a flashback, further in the past.

> 1960. A record-breaking temperature for May at Edwards Air Force Base. My sisters and I burned the backs of our necks and legs in the hot afternoon desert sun as we stood dressed in our Sunday best watching the big transport planes land. One of them was carrying my father, who was returning from Enewetak, a tiny atoll in Micronesia and the site of Operation Hardtack—the last nuclear testing performed in the Pacific. We hadn't seen him in a year and a half and, at seven, I was nervous about the change our household was going to undertake upon his return. My other sisters didn't share my anxiety. Pam, at nine, was excited about the new development, eager to have Dad back, and four-year-old Gayle, who didn't remember him, was

just plain excited. Everybody but me seemed to forget that this was the second time he had left us.

The first time he had disappeared for three weeks. One night he didn't come home. I waited and waited for him on the front steps, anxiously scanning the street for our blue-and-white station wagon to appear around the corner. Mom came out with Pam and Gayle and sat down beside me. "Sweetie, your Dad needed a vacation, so he's going to be away for a little while," she said.

"Why isn't he taking us with him?" I asked.

"Well, he needed some time ... alone."

I couldn't believe he was going by himself. I pictured him in Disneyland—my idea of a perfect vacation—and riding all the rides, like Dumbo and the Matterhorn Mountain roller coaster, without us. I was furious.

Three weeks later he walked through the front door. His unshaven face had a yellow tinge like the old lampshade in Grandma's room, and his eyes were glazed like he had eaten too much cotton candy and soda pop. Now Pam and I were certain that he had rubbed elbows with Mickey and Goofy. When Grandma took us there for the first time, we had felt then just like he looked now.

He told us he had gone on a camping trip.

Wherever he had gone, he had contracted hepatitis B, and would have to stay in the hospital a long time. And since all of us had been exposed, we would have to stay inside, quarantined for two weeks. Not only had Dad gone on a vacation without us, but now we were prisoners in our own house, staring out our windows while the rest of the neighborhood kids played. I was doubly mad.

When our quarantine lifted and we visited Dad at the hospital, he looked stick-like, sporting matching saffron-colored skin and eyeballs. Two different colored bags, one filled with bright green liquid and the other with orange, were hanging on hooks. Thin tubes, sprouting like tentacles from the bottom of each bag, were attached to his forearm. Slender ribbons of green and orange flowed through them and into his arm.

"Hey, Dad, is that stuff your food?"

"How come you're yellow?"

"When are you coming home?"

"Is your skin gonna stay that color?"

"How come you're so skinny?"

"When do they change the bags?"

Overwhelmed by our barrage of questions, he shouted, "Get out, get out, GET OUT!" His rage, like a spray of buckshot, left tiny but deep impressions as the three of us fled the room. "This virus makes him very crabby," Mom said, trying to console us.

Seven weeks later he came home, weak but recovered. There were no more outbursts. He even gave each of us a quick squeeze and said he was glad to be home. But sometimes I would watch him as he looked out the window from his chair in the living room. What he saw always made him sad, but when I peeked through the curtains to catch a glimpse, all I saw out there was the lawn.

A month later a shiny cherry-red MG sports car sat in the driveway, its gleaming paint matching the happy glint in my father's eyes. For the next two months, we resembled the perfect nuclear fifties' family as Dad took us out for a nightly joyride on the Seven Sisters—a series of roller-coaster hills in the Livermore countryside. While Mom sat in the passenger seat, we three girls scrunched together in the rumble seat, screaming with glee as the little car bounced along. Then, as if there was something sinful about having too good a time, Dad announced he was going away again. Determined that I wouldn't miss out on another vacation, I insisted on accompanying him. "I'm going away to work, Sport," he said.

SELECTION. What to include and what not? The father's return is obviously important, but what's also important is to find a way to work in a previous leaving and return to put even more gravitas on this one where, we are to find, he's changed even more. The writer chooses to establish the physicality of waiting in the hot sun because waiting at an enforced distance behind a fence also establishes metaphorically how distanced the family is at this point from this absent father. The obvious elation of the children isn't just idly recorded—what do we care about something so obvious unless, as it does, it holds greater significance: The one child with misgivings about this event is the one telling the story. One of the threads of that story is going to be the battle between the writer and her father, both with tempers, and both shown in this passage, the former's being one that grows steadily over the years as she passes through adolescence, the latter's showing the man's trademark short fuse.

The writer is also choosing to establish the significance of the past leaving, and needs to do that quickly so that the thread of the present moment—they're waiting for him in that sun—isn't lost. With this in mind, what to put in? The significant things: that last time, his return resulted in the discomfort of quarantine for all, and that he'd left on a lie and left them confused. We get just enough dialogue to feel that past moment by the father's bedside, see the children as they are, and show that fatherly rage erupting. But there's also the writer's noticing something extra, a father's sadness that seems to be dispersed only when the red car arrives—perhaps cluing us in to a certain yearning for a less drab existence, explaining perhaps why he soon leaves again, and showing the wanderlust still within him that, after he comes back this time, will entangle all the family: a dream project of ten years that will have an even greater impact on them.

MAGNIFICATION. What would be the moments to foreground? Obviously the kicker is when the father so blithely announces in the car on the joyride that he's going away again—we hear that line and can feel what it means to the kids, especially the writer, after all that has gone before. Three other details to magnify are the hot sun (to establish scene and to ground the reader), the sickbed scene (to allow for interaction and character portrayal), and the snippet of dialogue from the mother (to answer why he first goes away; that he needed time "alone" suggests so much about the marriage and the mother's feelings at that time). The line about a camping trip is foregrounded because it is a one-line paragraph. That the writer sets it apart underlines the pain that comes from the obvious lie that it is. Even the detail that Grandma's lamp is the color of the father's jaundiced face establishes her importance to the children and the role she plays in the story elsewhere.

COMPRESSION. The passage itself is backstory designed to fill in what's happened in the past of significance to this particular moment in time; by going back there and seeing for ourselves in sufficient detail, we will return to the wait in the sun with far more understanding and trepidation that we would have had otherwise. There's also the compression of time in the phrases *seven weeks later* and *for two months*. Clearly much may have happened whilst the father was recuperating, much too in the brief halcyon months of the family being "the perfect nuclear family" (an irony in itself, given the father's work on the radioactive atoll) and joyriding in the car, but that's established just enough to tear down—the happiness was snatched away, with what pain we can imagine, leaving us crisply aware of what issues are simmering in the baking sun as the family members try to recognize their father and husband walking across the tarmac, but, as the next section will show us, can't even be sure which of the men disembarking he might be.

Selection, magnification, and compression are merely the strategies that writers employ in bringing their vision to bear on raw experience. They are the words I use to delineate the choices, the thinking involved in a writer's decision-making when constructing a narrative. Using these techniques is a little like driving. When driving, you look in the mirror, regulate the pressure on the accelerator, signal, remain aware of unexpected possibilities—suicidal pedestrians, cabs that screech across three lanes for a fare, road signs that don't tally with your sense of the universe—and remain alert in several directions at once, even as you fiddle with the radio dial for a station that befits your age, and curse out the morons who invariably presume to drive on the same road as you. You are not consciously thinking about these different elements, but you are monitoring each factor even as you deliberately yet nonchalantly exceed the speed limit. So, in writing, we monitor several components at once and strive for a harmony that drives our narrative and keeps us on the road, however much we fishtail. The more you handle the responsibility of the wheel and experience the consciousness required on the road, the more successfully you handle and adapt to road conditions, the better you drive. Writing is about mileage: putting in the miles/minutes/pages, logging the decision-making experience, applying the subconscious concentration that splices the building blocks of your writing together.

The more thought you can give to how writers achieve their effects, the better you can apply these principles to your own work. So let's evaluate selection, magnification, and compression once more in another personal narrative, *Habit Forming* by Nicole Quinn. In this chapter, "We Killed a Nun," we see a black family determinedly integrating a stolidly white area, the children only partially aware of the racism of a wider world until this incident.

> We were enrolled in a local parochial school, and fared well there, academically at least, despite the school bus that refused to stop until Mama stood in the middle of the road daring the driver to hit her. The dog feces hurled at our cars, the dead animals in the mailbox, the garbage cans heaved at our front windows, the cold shoulders and muffled expletives from our white neighbors we took as an element of being different. We accepted it all as part and parcel of changing entrenched attitudes and racial stereotypes, because Mama said that's what we

were doing, and she had a knack for making terror fun. For months we only walked along the edges of the rooms facing the street of that new house. I thought it was to maximize the number of footsteps, thereby increasing your chances of winning her "footstep game." It was only later that I realized she had invented this ruse to keep us from being easy targets for any rock throwers who showed up during that first year. We were surprisingly unafraid, unscarred by the hate of those around us. At least I was until that Valentine's card was presented to me, amid a chorus of snickers, by a ruddy-faced thug who regularly taunted my sister and myself on the school bus.

"Happy Valentines Day Nigger" was scrawled in number 2 pencil across pink card stock liberally ornamented with red hearts and silver glitter.

SELECTION. The long paragraph details several incidents of racism and what the mother does to diffuse them. Each in itself would make a good scene, but the writer has realized that they are all a buildup to one that eludes the mother's protective shield. To stop and describe how there was a thud against the window and they went outside to find feces in the window box, or how brave her mother had looked, hands-on-hips, facing down the bus driver in the street would give an emphasis to *those* scenes and not the one that the author rightly deems the most significant—the Valentine's card, which is to result in the children going to a very exclusive Catholic school. All those incidents, then, are examples leading to the writer's comment on their surprising innocence.

MAGNIFICATION. The shock of the card gets a tad more detail in order to foreground it and establish both its importance and its reality. There's not a lot of detail, but there's enough to establish it as very real for the reader: the banality of evil in the scrawl, a particular quality of pencil, the hearts and glitter. By heightening what it looks like in the hand, the unignorable fact of its ugly existence is underlined.

COMPRESSION. Ten lines of description would dilute the shock value of the Valentine and its ugly racial epithet. The few, effective details need to come fast; hence they're all in one sentence. There's compression in the long paragraph too, not only in the choice made to keep the anecdotes in a list-like series, but also in the amount of commentary this elicits—the one sentence ending "she had a knack for making terror fun." This allows for the action to keep building toward the incident that will finally breach the mother's defenses.

Why You Should Happily Write About Your Unhappy Family

One of the most common excuses for people not writing the book they want to write—usually involving their family—is that it would hurt someone. Writing a book always hurts someone—preeminently the writer, who grows poorer and more alienated. And banging the head on the desk and devouring the contents of the refrigerator don't do a lot for self-esteem. Writing is hard work, and we always want to avoid it unless it's absolutely necessary. Obviously, though, you need to apply common sense and compassionate empathy. If someone is dying or suicidal or clearly deeply vulnerable, then human decency dictates you should be extra careful about what you write about them. But this carefulness has to be separated from using the potentially-hurtful-to-others argument as a perfect rationale for not embarking on a project that is going to flay every ounce of your own skin in the process. Flaying should not be an aspect of things at all. Whatever we do, we must avoid playing the hard-done-by victim, the innocent on whom all wrong is heaped and thus for whom all manner of revenge is fair. Do not write if you are Mr. or Ms. Perfect. If you are not flawed, then those you are writing about aren't either, and the joke's on you. It's a bad bad memoir, a very dull and unfinished one, in which readers must follow the flapping, squalking self-righteous cries of "look what they did to me, look how bad they were, look how I've suffered." No one cares, because everyone knows they're flawed ten times over, and even the most self-doubting among us is aware that nobody's even close to perfect; we don't relish being in the company of someone who sees the world in such simplistic, foolish terms, either.

But what if the book has to say things that will deeply trouble or offend or wound others close to you? Well, conflicting views on events are simply a part of literature and of life. Writing must take on difficult subjects and seek to fairly express hard, buried, denied, painful truths, but in so doing it contributes to our mutual benefit, to a wider social, human good. As author Dawn Powell tells us, "The truth is not so shameful it cannot be recorded." It's your truth; others can write their own. So long as you're not distorting for sensationalism, so long as you reach for whatever modulation is possible in any given situation, so long as you strive for compassion and empathy, you've treated the subject fairly.

Yet several of my students have said they could not—absolutely not, heaven forbid, perish the thought—alienate, say, their sister by writing about her. Even if she was twisted. This was for her protection, you understand, out of decency. And, to my mind, not a little bit of residual anger too. But as I've pointed out, they couldn't write the book they needed to write without including said sister. Or that brother that, until then, they hadn't mentioned to me they even had. No wonder there was a black hole of an absence in what they'd written, and the story warped into it.

That said, anger is energy, and writers need to tap it. Let me give you a story of one of my students, who had this problem, wrote through it, and published a fine book. My student's story dealt in part with how her mother had incarcerated her in a psychiatric facility as an adolescent because she couldn't cope with, among other things, the daughter's wildness. From the daughter's perspective, of course, her mother didn't understand that she was a free spirit and that it was the 1960's (and who understood those years at the time?) and that a few relatively harmless drugs were cool. But half a lifetime later, the pain was still there for the daughter, and she believed that she couldn't write her book because of it.

Except that pain can be fuel—it's emotion—and that's reason enough to write. You write despite the pain, you write in the face of it, you write until you can face it more honestly than you may initially be doing. As my brave student attempted her tale in all its gradations of complex complicity, she belatedly came to acknowledge she probably *was* a little wild, that she surely was difficult to handle—especially given the mother's situation, largely on her own as she was at that time. So no longer was it a story of a cruel heartless mother or of the writer as hard-done-by victim. The story had real people trying to be good, thinking they were, even as they partially failed each other. Real is flawed. Real is forgiving and not forgiving at the same time. Now that the excuse of not writing out of kindness had seeped away, the story was actually getting written.

So there's discussions between mother and daughter, there's lots of scribbling on the daughter's part (read: ravaging self-doubt, months of blocked despair, mounting credit card debt, back pain enough to send a chiropractor's kid to private school), there's a hundred pages that have to be cut out of the final manuscript. (You're lucky if the necrotic tissue comes out in chunks; the editing is more like hand-to-hand phrase-by-phrase combat, trench warfare on the sentence level.) The book's completed. Mom is sent the not-always flattering sections featuring herself; the writer bites her nails, curses her old writing teacher for ever having led her into this mess. Mom likes it? Well, she doesn't read much of it before she buries the manuscript in her closet (where family skeletons always go). Denial still coats everything, and even now, bitterness stings. But what she has read has surreptitiously wrought a pocketful of change within. It has stirred her considerable courage, matching that of her daughter, for whom, of course, she has always wanted the best. She doesn't see the past the way her daughter does; there are some factual things she corrects; there's some further explanation and background she gives to clarify some of the decisions and the prevailing winds of that past time. But now their rationales are taking on a tone more understanding than damning. They're both rediscovering enough generosity of spirit to begin to support each other in this. They cry, really, they do, but it's not that the writing brings them together in a genetically modified saccharine blob of forgiveness. It's that they've straightened out some things that have gotten twisted through being buried. Also, being part of an attempt to put words to things, they've come to appreciate a lot more about the past and each other. Mom is no longer the wicked witch of the west. And ten-foot-tall Alice admits to more than a mushroom or two. Aw.

So the book comes out, our writer now has readings to do, and lo, Mom is coming to Manhattan all the way from the back of beyond for one of them. What should the writer read? "The Mom section," I whisper innocently. Hey, ask the oracle advice, it doesn't always say what you want to hear, does it? The writer demurs—no, the writer writhes in great and understandable discomfort ... but does it. It's a lively, fabulous reading. Not only is there a long line to buy a signed book from the beaming author, there's a whorl around Mom, as our writer pointed her out in the audience. Mom's a part of the moment too, people are flocking to congratulate her on her daughter's achievement and to commiserate with the difficulties she herself must have gone through. And she is proud. (This is the bit where I cry.)

That chapter was better than it could ever have hoped to be had the writer not embarked on the long, sorry, painful process of wrestling with the demons, of facing one's fears while still scared. Rapprochement complete, our mom and daughter/author are happier, interact more—and a lot more sweetly than they would have had they not engaged the twin ugly horrors of the unspeakable past and the stony blank page. Yeah, real tears were shed and pain felt. So maybe law school was a better option? But I'd rather take the risk of hurting and being hurt—as we do in love—than playing it so predictably safe no one could ever hurt me again. I'd rather feel enough to cry rather than never feel anything. That's why we write. That's why we read.

Seeing the Light of Day

Learning craft and compassion isn't all it takes to bring your book to the world, though. Alas, you need an agent. One of my students found hers at a meet-the-agents event for women, approaching with both temerity and timorousness at the end, when everyone gets about a minute to make a pitch. From that she was invited to send a proposal, and from that got a book contract. Others have found them through friends, their writing instructors, or simply by looking in the various agents guides. The key to finding an agent, though, is being a writer in the first place, knowing one's craft and having good work to show.

Unlike fiction, where you have to write the book before you can find an agent (gone are the days when Nelson Algren could hop the boxcars from the Midwest to New York, improvise in the office of an editor, and leave with an advance on a spurious idea), in nonfiction you can still sell the book beforehand. Why? Well, because it can be accurately described as a concept. You will still have to produce at least one chapter—probably several—and submit it (or them) to the agent with a book proposal, which may or may not need to include a table of contents or chapter outline. Don't worry about the latter, because you are as beholden to it as Nelson Algren was to his pitch (he wrote the novel he wanted, not the idea he'd sold). A chapter outline is a sketch, so the agent and publishers can get a good sense of what the book might contain. Some can be extensive and go to pages and pages in great depth. But my feeling is that if you are going to put that much energy into writing about what the story is, you might as well put the same energy to actually writing the chapters. Even though the extended proposal has brought some people big advances, I wouldn't undertake it lightly. All that work and it might not sell (and you've still got to write the book). That's not a good way to work. There's a much more sensible way to go, which I'll outline in a moment, but one more thing about the chapter outline: Don't sweat it. If writing is a process, then how can you possibly know yet how you are going to break up the story line into sections or even chapters until you get to writing them? How can you really know what goes in yet, beyond a general idea? How can you know what you're exactly saying until you, as the writing process dictates, actually discover it? Just do it as best you can. You are the author, and if the form demands a shuffling or eradicating or a separating or a combining of chapters down the road, then you'll do that. An outline is a simple listing of chapters (sometimes with a paragraph of description under each heading), not a legal contract.

WRITING A BOOK PROPOSAL

Your success will depend on how well you can represent your book and its possibilities and yourself in the four stages I've outlined below. And, of course, on the quality of your sample chapters, submitted, in all likelihood, with it.

THE OVERVIEW

Describe the book. What's it about? How is it structured? You don't need every detail; you want the essence. You are representing the tone of the book (if it's humorous, does your proposal catch that flavor?), the reach, the depth, a fair limning of the subject matter. It doesn't matter what the book's structure is, but if you've got a sense of how you will tell the story (alternate chapters featuring two different parts of your experience, say; or it starts in the present and then moves backward in time to bring us up-to-date chronologically; or it intersperses diary entries or hospital records), include it. This helps agents and publishers garner a more accurate sense of things, and tells them how well you know your own book at this point (and that's useful to you, too).

THE MARKETS

Describe who will buy the book and why. A book about a sailing voyage may or may not appeal to sailing types, depending on how much (or what kind of) boating lore it encompasses. But it might also be of interest to armchair adventurers, or appeal to people who don't sail but might be interested in a theme. Is it about searching for a dream and achieving it, say? And if it entails a family, then maybe there's a general audience there—but a family very much out of the norm, then maybe we're talking about a specialized (book-buying) subset. A ship full of women, well, there's another market; a female narrator who's treated essentially as a son and has to find herself, another subset; that character an adolescent when she sets to sea, a subset there. And if there's some stuff about the father's involvement in atomic testing on pacific atolls, yet another swathe of the book-buying public may be interested. You won't know who it will sell to when you first sit down. Don't worry about that. Just keep pondering what of the book might appeal in a loose way with different factions of the book-buying public. Start with general categories (women), and try to narrow that vast abstraction to more specific subsets (adolescent girls, feminists, older baby boomers), and so on. Gradually you'll create what might seem a ridiculous picture of the commercial possibilities of the book you're writing out of love and interest rather than desire for fame and money. But phrased smoothly and thoughtfully, your thinking things through is putting ideas in the publishers' heads, ideas that they might not have thought of, and thus you're helping to sell your book.

THE COMPETITION

Describe books similar to yours and in what ways your book differs from them. Is it dealing with a subject that seems currently popular? Is it sufficiently different that your book won't be seen as duplicating that already popular book? If that type of memoir is seen to be outré, then how is yours not? You're trying to be sufficiently like something that has found an audience that it speaks well of your book, and yet sufficiently different from that so that you are offering something new. Of course, your book may be totally different from the field. But you can still locate what that field is and then emphasize your book's uniqueness. Don't make the comparisons ridiculously superficial. Yours might be about suffering abuse, but that doesn't mean you can claim it's going to be a bestseller like Kathryn Harrison's *The Kiss*. Plenty of others of that ilk didn't make it. Speak of apt and significant similarities, otherwise you'll just sound self-aggrandizing and silly. If it's our sailing book and it's humorous and lightly rueful rather than technically specific and adventure laden—then it's perhaps more akin to the family portrait of Augusten Burroughs's *Running With Scissors* than to Sebastian Junger's *The Perfect Storm*. Your memoir might deal with being in a mental facility; you might point out, like my student did, that while Susanna Kaysen's hugely successful *Girl, Interrupted* took place in a private facility for the well-to-do, her memoir presented an entirely different version of the experience, that of a state facility. Thus, in a crowded field, you gain connection with the successful book and yet distinguish your book from it in an interesting and alluring way.

THE BIO

Describe the author (yourself) and illustrate your ability to write this book. This is where past publishing is useful. If you've had essays or extracts or other things published in literary magazines or local newspapers, these now count for something; it might be a little something, but they are at least in your favor. They say that you have a working relationship with language, that you're not just a schlub who had half an idea over a beer and thinks he can write a book as easy as downing his next beer. Again, you don't need to fluff yourself up to look important here; if you have any publications to cite, then fine; any experience relevant to the work at hand is admissible, too. But if you're new to the literary world, that's okay—maybe you've lived in various interesting places or done other things worthy of note. You're writing the briefest of thumbnail sketches of yourself in a flattering but not garish light.

How long should the proposal be? An agent might ask you to flesh out a longer one for a particular publishing contact he has, or maybe not. I've seen sharp book proposals that whetted my appetite in four pages; I've seen entries on each chapter around a page; I've seen obscenely detailed and long examples. My Zen answer: How long is a piece of string? That is, if the agent/publisher is intrigued by your story and senses your capability to write it, you're in business: It's long enough. And I would always choose concision before overexplained, overdramatized, overwrought hucksterism, and editors and agents appreciate that too. But if you're submitting directly to a publisher without an agent, make sure you check that publisher's guidelines for what they want in a proposal first.

PUBLISHING PERSONAL NARRATIVES AND MEMOIRS

Memoirs or personal narratives are more the equivalent of novels in terms of the market. Publishers will buy them, they're selling—in a world of ersatz reality shows, people retaining the ability to think want intellectual sustenance, not an idiot's spectacle—and you have much more of a chance with them than essays, stories, or poems. Celebrity still helps publication, but not the writing quality; if you can tell your story with élan, you've a chance of finding a literary home. Again, if you've published an extract or two, a chapter here or there in a national magazine or a literary one, that's a testament to quality (usually) and ups your chances. The main thing is not to think overly much about publication or publishers or agents. It's too upsetting. Learn your craft, and in so doing you may well embark on writing a good, worthy book. And that's the best first step to publishing there is.

Reading to Improve Your Own Work

This chapter contains references to a number of fine memoirs and personal narratives well worth reading. The following is a list of notable memoirs and personal narratives, brought together here because of their style, originality, humanity.

If you seriously intend to write a book-length nonfiction work, read as many books as you can in the genre. You need to see the variety of form and style and topic that is open to you. You need to examine the choices writers make and the ways they shape the materials of their lives—selection, magnification, and compression. And you want to have a sense of your narrative too, how it compares, how it stacks up. Learn from the works that are out there, as all writers do.

LONGER NONFICTION: RECOMMENDED READING

Allison, Dorothy. *Two or Three Things I Know for Sure.* New York: Dutton, 1995.

Bradbury, Ray. *Dandelion Wine.* Thorndike, ME: G.K. Hall, 1999.

Burroughs, Augusten. *Dry.* New York: St. Martin's Press, 2003.

Coetzee, J.M. *Boyhood: Scenes From Provincial Life.* New York: Viking, 1997.

Eighner, Lars. *Travels With Lizbeth.* New York: St. Martin's Press, 1993.

Hamper, Ben. *Rivethead: Tales From the Assembly Line.* New York: Warner Books, 1991.

Knipfel, Jim. *Quitting the Nairobi Trio.* New York: J.P. Tarcher/ Putnam, 2000.

Lewis, Mindy. *Life Inside: A Memoir.* New York: Atria Books, 2002.

Millett, Kate. *The Loony-Bin Trip.* Urbana: University of Illinois Press, 2000.

Rose, Phyllis. *The Year of Reading Proust: A Memoir in Real Time.* New York: Scribner, 1997.

Magazine Writing
by CHARLES SALZBERG

CHARLES SALZBERG has written for *New York* magazine, *Esquire*, *GQ*, *Elle*, *Redbook*, *Good Housekeeping*, *The New York Times* Arts and Leisure section, *Travel & Leisure*, and various other periodicals. He has written over twenty nonfiction books, including *From Set Shot to Slam Dunk: The Glory Days of Basketball in the Words of Those Who Played It*. His novel, *Swann's Last Song*, will be published in 2006. He has been a visiting professor of magazine at the S.I. Newhouse School of Public Communications at Syracuse University, is a founding member of the New York Writers Workshop, and teaches writing at Sarah Lawrence College.

Introduction

When I graduated college, living the life of a magazine journalist was the last thing on my mind. In fact, I didn't even know what the life of a magazine journalist was. I wanted to be a "serious" writer, a novelist. My heroes were Saul Bellow, Philip Roth, Vladimir Nabokov, and Bernard Malamud, not Gay Talese, Hunter S. Thompson, Tom Wolfe, or Joseph Mitchell. And though I was an avid reader of magazines and newspapers, the idea of researching, interviewing, observing, then putting it all together and crafting a magazine article bordered on the absurd. That wasn't *real* writing. It was *reporting*, a totally uncreative endeavor, requiring little if any imagination. It was the difference between taking a snapshot with a Brownie Instamatic and painting Picasso's *Guernica*. Besides, I was much too lazy to do research—I had coasted through college as an English major, reading novels and short stories, which was hardly work, after all—and I was much too shy to actually approach a stranger and start asking questions, some of them personal enough to make me blush just thinking about them. No, it was much easier to simply sit at my typewriter and, to paraphrase the literary critic and author John Bardin, lie like crazy. And that's exactly what I wanted to do: sit alone at my desk and make up stories.

But I soon found out that the real world doesn't pay most writers a living wage to do that. In the real world, you have to pay rent, buy groceries, and pay for utilities, and the kind of fiction I was interested in writing, as I soon found out, was something publishers called *mid-list*, which was really just a code phrase for "very few copies sold."

I had to make a living, and as I was casting about for some way to do that, a friend suggested I try to get a job as a magazine editor. "After all," he reasoned, "you were an English major. You know how to write, and presumably you know good writing when you see it."

That made sense, but of course I had no idea how to get a job like that, and even if I was lucky enough to find one, I had no idea how to perform it. What did I know about journalism?

The answer was, absolutely nothing. In four years as an undergraduate at Syracuse University, I had never even set foot on the hallowed grounds of the S.I. Newhouse School of Public Communications, one of the finest journalism schools in the country. (Ironically, almost thirty years after graduating from Syracuse, I actually found myself a visiting professor in the magazine department at Newhouse.) I hated writing papers in high school and college, and frankly, I wasn't very good at it. I was much better at making up facts, rather than digging them out and reporting them. And I was far more adept at making up conversations than reconstructing them. Besides, I had no J-school connections, which meant I knew no one in the business, a business I was completely in the dark about. How did it work? How did those wonderfully articulate, entertaining, and informative articles that I read in *Esquire*, *New York*, or *The New Yorker* actually get written? The sad truth was, I had absolutely no idea.

Fortunately, however, a family friend happened to work at *New York* magazine, which was in its heyday, under the leadership of the legendary Clay Felker, the inventor of the city magazine. The family friend casually mentioned an opening in the mailroom and that the path to the editorial department led through that very small (albeit strategically located) room through which all mail was collected, sorted, and dispensed. My ears perked up. In my inexperienced and naive mind, that meant I would spend a few weeks in the mailroom, learn how magazines worked, and then I'd be an editor.

Of course, it didn't actually work that way. I did get the job—it wasn't all that difficult if you had a college education and were willing to work for embarrassingly low wages—but after a few days watching what editors actually did to earn their keep, I decided that the last thing in the world I wanted to be was a magazine editor. They looked, for the most part, wan, dejected, and harried. Most of their time was spent hunched over their desks editing other people's work, cajoling—sometimes threatening—writers to get their pieces in on time, or attending meetings where ideas that someone else would actually execute were lobbed around like grenades, most of which had the firing pins removed.

But the writers. Ah, well, that was something altogether different. They would wander into the office around ten, ten-thirty. They'd drink coffee, smoke cigarettes, talk on the phone, shoot the breeze with other writers or editors, and then, at noon, they'd disappear for two, sometimes three hours, inevitably arriving back in the office, the smell of whisky preceding them by a few milliseconds. They'd get on the phone, smoke cigarettes, drink coffee, swap stories with other writers and editors. At four-thirty or so, they'd disappear again until the next day, or maybe we wouldn't see them for two or three days.

Now that, I thought, was a job I could do.

But how?

I was the "boy" in the mailroom. I knew nothing about journalism. But I did know how to tell a story, and I did know a little about how a magazine worked from my strategic vantage point, sorting and delivering mail. And so, with more than a little hesitation, I approached senior editor Elizabeth Crow and mumbled that I had three article ideas for *New York*; what should I do?

"Write them up and give them to me," she said.

I smiled, but I had no idea what she was talking about. Write them up? What, exactly, did she mean?

I was going to find out, not by taking a class or enrolling in an MFA program, but by trial and error, and by observing what went on around me. And in finding out, I was able to piece together, quickly at first and then frustratingly more slowly, a career as a magazine writer and author of more than twenty nonfiction books.

What follows is what I hope is a clear and concise examination of the life of a magazine article—and of a magazine writer. Along the way, using my own experiences and the experiences of many of my friends and colleagues (both writers and editors), you'll find out how most magazines work, which will help you break that mysterious code that allows you to get your foot in the door. You'll also learn how to write a query letter—which is what I had to do with those first three ideas, although I had no idea that's what I was doing—how to research and interview, and how to craft a magazine article.

What I learned about magazine writing came from being in the trenches. I learned most from my own missteps, mistakes, and successes. Today, few MFA programs focus on magazine writing—it's mostly taught in journalism schools—and yet with the explosion of that hybrid called creative nonfiction (God knows what that actually means) more and more universities that offer MFA programs are including courses in magazine journalism—basically, courses on how to write a magazine article. What I hope to offer here is much more than that: a practical guide to magazine journalism with tips you can only get from working magazine journalists. In truth, there's so much more to being a magazine journalist than actually writing the article. In fact, many freelance writers will tell you that's the easy part. What they don't tell you in most MFA and journalism programs is all the other stuff: ways to come up with saleable ideas, how to pitch them, how to deal with editors, how to deal with rejection, and a host of other things that come with the territory.

One caveat, though. In the end, no matter how much training and how much advice you get, you're going to have to figure out a lot of things yourself. In my experience, there is no right way or wrong way to do something. Instead, there's the way that works best for you—this goes both for writing and selling your articles. Know the rules first, and then figure out how you can bend or even break them in a way that gets the job done. And so, rather than take this as a precise blueprint as to how to write for magazines, think of it as a sketch that you can fill in yourself. What worked for me and my colleagues might not work for you. But knowing what worked for us will, I think, help you to avoid some of the pitfalls and allow you to create your own path, a path that isn't always a straight line.

By the way, of those first three ideas I had, two of them sold—one to *New York* magazine and the other to the *New York Daily News Sunday Magazine*. In total, I made almost $2,000 for what amounted to a couple of weeks' work. I thought I had it made. I quit the mailroom to make it as a freelance writer. I was in for a rude awakening. In the next six months, I made a grand total of an additional $1,000, but what I learned during that time was priceless.

How The Business Works

READ, READ, READ: LEARNING THE MARKETS

When I teach a magazine journalism class, one of the first things I do is find out something about the people taking my class. Most have been out in the working world for a while, which is a plus, because it means they've had time to develop interests and hobbies (and quirks). I ask them what they do or have done for a living and, most importantly, what magazines they read.

While performing this routine in one of the early classes I taught, I came to Sean, a man in his late thirties, perhaps, who said he was a musician. I asked him what magazines he read.

"Uh," he mumbled, "I don't read magazines."

"Well," I said, "what books do you read?"

"I don't read books."

"How about newspapers?"

He shook his head no.

Reaching for straws, I asked, "Well, have you done any writing?"

"Nope," he said.

Leaving class that night, I would have bet my meager wages that Sean would never return, but he did, though I never did find out why. He didn't say two words in class for the rest of the semester, and I'm pretty sure he never tried writing a magazine article. But I know that he couldn't have been successful, no matter how hard he tried, unless he started reading magazines.

The reason for this is simple: In order to write for magazines, you have to read magazines. That seems fairly obvious, but it always surprises me how many people want to write for magazines without actually reading them.

Why bother? The answer is simple.

- You can't know what kinds of stories magazines publish without reading them.

- You can't know who the audience is for a magazine if you don't read it.

- You can't know that your article idea hasn't been done before by the magazine you're pitching it to unless you read that magazine.

- And, most importantly, you can't possibly know what a good magazine article is if you don't read magazines.

So, the first advice I give anyone who wants to write for magazines is, *read* them. *Voraciously. Indiscriminately. Religiously.*

After a while, even without being aware of it, you'll be able to tell a good article from a bad one; good writing from bad writing; a well-structured article from one that's not. And, most importantly, you'll be able to recognize that all articles—all writing, in fact—is about telling a story. And a story (fiction or nonfiction) has three parts: a beginning, a middle, and an end. And every magazine article, no matter how long or how short, no matter what the subject is, no matter where it appears, has just that: a beginning, a middle and an end.

One of the things I learned early in my career is that there is a very close connection between writing fiction and writing nonfiction, that form I had previously scoffed at. And I'm not sure they teach that connection in journalism schools. Fiction-writing techniques—creating scenes, using dialogue, things you've learned from earlier chapters in this book—will serve you well when you're writing nonfiction.

Another important thing I learned writing magazine articles was how to write concisely and economically. Concision is important not only because magazine articles have strict word limits, but because good editors don't like flabby writing. Good writers don't give good editors the opportunity to cut their work for that reason.

So, if you want to know how to write well, read. And then read some more. Because no matter how helpful how-to books might be, the real key to good writing is reading and then writing, and then reading and writing some more.

YOU *CAN* JUDGE A BOOK BY ITS COVER: KNOWING YOUR AUDIENCE

Most MFA programs are craft oriented. Certainly, there's nothing wrong with that. Craft is extremely important. But what these programs often neglect to teach is the practical aspect of trying to make your living as a magazine writer.

In order to write for magazines, you have to know what they are, who they cater to, and why they exist.

Magazines are about fantasy. They play to the lives we want to lead, not necessarily to the lives we do lead. People read Martha Stewart's magazine because they want to be Martha Stewart, and they read *O* because they want to be Oprah Winfrey. (At the very least, they want to live like these two icons of pop culture.) They read travel magazines because they'd like to travel if they could afford it and if they had the time. People read magazines that chronicle the lives of the rich and famous because that's what they'd like to be: They fantasize about rubbing shoulders with Brad and Tom and Angelina and Jennifer and Madonna on St. Bart's over the Christmas holidays. People read magazines so they can learn how to knit, conquer depression, lose weight, look beautiful, feel better about themselves, dress to impress, find a lover, be a better parent, live a life of adventure. People read consumer magazines because they want to consume, which explains the recent upsurge of magazines like *Lucky* and *Cargo*. You can tell an awful lot about a person simply by asking him what magazines he reads regularly.

And if, as a writer, you know this about people and can understand their relationship to magazines, you've taken the first step in learning how to write for them.

Any aspiring magazine writer must know the markets. Knowing the markets means knowing what magazines are out there—and there are plenty of them, for all kinds of interests and tastes—and, perhaps most important, who reads them.

In the magazine business, the study of who reads a particular magazine is called demographics. Demographics identify who the ideal (or average or prototypical) reader is of each magazine. This is the reader the advertisers in the magazine want to reach. Unless you, as a writer, know who the typical reader of a particular magazine is, you can't possibly know what kinds of articles that magazine runs. Finding out, however, is as easy as examining the cover of a magazine.

For instance, take an issue of *Good Housekeeping* featuring Goldie Hawn on the cover. Goldie is sitting on the grass and wearing a lavender tank top and white slacks. The cover lines that surround her are:

- Take-It-Off Tips From 200 Successful Dieters

- Steal These Ideas! Great Decorating Makeovers

- Beauty Clinic—How to Get Gorgeous Eyes, Pretty Lips … and That Glow!

- 10 Things You Should Never Do With Your Husband

- So Good, So Fast—5-Ingredient Dinners

- Stop Suffering—Allergy Drugs That Really Work

- Too Little Sleep? 9 Ways to Feel Alive and Stay Sharp

- Girl Talk With Goldie—On the Joy of Crying, Outfoxing Age, and Keeping It Hot With Kurt. Plus: Her Exercises to Wake Up the Soul.

Now, using these clues like a detective would, create a profile of the prototypical reader of *Good Housekeeping*. What is her age? Marital status? Household income?

Here's what you should have come up with.

Simply by who's featured on the cover, you can tell this is a magazine for women in their early thirties to late forties or early fifties. Why? Because Goldie Hawn, though she might look to be in her late thirties, is well into her fifties. The fact that she looks much younger than her age makes her appeal to an older audience than would, let's say, Britney Spears, who (at least until she puts on another ten or twenty years) would never be on the cover of *GH*.

From "Tips From Successful Dieters" you should be able to deduce that the reader probably struggles with her weight. She probably doesn't have a lot of disposable income ("Steal These Ideas") but is interested in upgrading her life. She's still interested in her appearance. She is married ("10 Things

You Should Never Do With Your Husband"), she has kids, and she's working either full- or part-time ("So Good, So Fast—5-Ingredient Dinners" and "Too Little Sleep?"). She's concerned about aging and keeping her sex life active, and she's interested in spirituality ("Exercises to Wake Up the Soul").

Now consider a past issue of *New York*. The cover features two models—one man, one woman—on a cover that reads, "What It Costs to Live in New York at 25, 35, 45, 55." The woman, dressed very fashionably, has a debt of $20,000 in student loans, $7,000 in credit cards, and pays $1,400 rent; the man, dressed in a well-tailored suit, is a publishing executive with $20,000 in credit-card debt, a $500,000 mortgage, savings of $25,000, and a retirement account of $200,000. She's twenty-four, he's forty-five. Other stories touted on the cover are "Heavyweight Bout: Harvey Weinstein vs. Scott Rudin," "Tina Brown Is Stealing My Shtick!" and "Beyond Anthrax, How Prepared Are NYC's Hospitals for Bioterrorism?"

Now, create a profile of the typical *New York* reader.

Here's what you should have come up with.

You can tell this is a magazine for men *and* women because both genders are displayed on the cover. And the age range is much wider than for *GH*, from the early to mid-twenties all the way up to sixty. From the figures on the cover—the $500,000 mortgage, for instance—it's obvious that the average household income of the *New York* reader is higher than that of the average reader of *GH*.

You also know that the typical *New York* reader is upscale, quite literate, and media savvy—he recognizes Harvey Weinstein (the former head of Miramax Films) and Tina Brown (the former editor of *The New Yorker* and the now-defunct *Talk* magazine). These are not the kinds of stories that would interest the typical reader of *GH*, who probably wouldn't even know (or care) who Harvey Weinstein and Tina Brown are.

Once you've assessed the demographic of a magazine, you can use your knowledge to determine whether the magazine is a match with your idea. For instance, if you've got a great idea for an article on dating for women over the age of forty, *GH* is definitely not the right magazine; married women, the core readers of *GH*, are not supposed to be dating. On the other hand, if your idea is how to prepare gourmet meals for your family on a tight budget, *Good Housekeeping* might well be the right place to pitch.

If you want to do a story on the hippest night spots in New York, or the hot young novelist about to hit the best-seller lists, *New York* might be the right magazine. A true crime story? Probably not *Redbook* (unless it involves a woman, married with kids, who lives in the suburbs), but very possibly *Rolling Stone* (if it involves music or nightlife) or *New York* (if it took place in New York's Diamond District) or *Esquire* or *GQ* (if it has a political, social, entertainment, or adventure aspect to it).

The First Step

THE COIN OF THE REALM: IDEAS

Becoming a successful magazine writer starts with the idea. No matter how good a writer you might be, if you're not adept at coming up with article ideas, you have little or no chance of making it as a magazine writer. In part, this is a practical matter. You can't simply approach a magazine editor and say, "Look, I'm a great writer. Come up with an idea for me and I'll prove it to you." It just doesn't work that way.

The process is simple: You come up with an idea. You make sure it's focused. You match it up with the appropriate magazine. You write a query letter. You send it to the appropriate editor. You wait for the answer.

For some people, ideas come easy. I have a writer friend who could walk into any room and, within five minutes, come up with four or five ideas for magazine articles. For others (and I was one of them), coming up with exciting and appropriate ideas is a little more difficult. (It's not that I didn't have ideas. I did. And I thought they were brilliant and fascinating. And maybe they were. But that didn't mean that I could sell them to a magazine. I tended to come up with quirky, out-of-the-mainstream ideas that interested me, but that didn't mean they would interest readers of a popular magazine.)

The trick is this: You can't be too much ahead of the curve, and you can't be too far behind the curve. Most magazines want article ideas about subjects their readers are already interested in; they don't necessarily want ideas about subjects their readers have never heard of, even if you think they should know about them.

For instance, years ago I went to a prerelease screening of a movie called *Urban Cowboy*. The lead actress, whom I'd never seen before, gave a terrific performance. Her name was Debra Winger. I knew she'd become a star, and so I pitched a profile of her to *Mademoiselle*, figuring that was the right magazine because Debra Winger was well within their demographic group and young, attractive, talented. I sent in a query. The answer came back very quickly: no. Why not? Because, the editor said, although they loved my clips, they didn't think any of their readers would know who Debra Winger was. *Wasn't that the point?* I thought. Wouldn't they be doing their readers a service, introducing them to the next hot Hollywood star? Evidently not. Instead, they assigned me a profile of Timothy Hutton, who was all over the media because he'd just won the Academy Award for *Ordinary People*. However, if I'd found a magazine that ran short profiles of up-and-coming movie stars, I might have been able to sell the story. Or maybe I should have tried a magazine devoted solely to movies, like *Premiere*. But a mainstream, general interest magazine like *Mademoiselle* wasn't interested in being ahead of the curve.

One of the best ways to get ideas is to indulge your own curiosity. Sometimes a good idea is right in front of you. Is there something particularly interesting about your job, the people you work with, your friends, your hobbies, your obsessions? Have you spotted some cool, interesting trend?

Recently, a woman who worked the door at a men's strip club took my class. When I asked her questions about what her job was like, she told me how terribly the women behaved in the club—"worse than men," she said. I asked her about the men who stripped and about the women who came to the club. The idea for a potentially fun and interesting story began to form. That was something she could certainly write about, though she'd never even thought of it.

Of course, you've also got to take into consideration whether or not your idea will interest other people. The more general interest it holds, the easier it will be to sell the story. But that doesn't mean that, if you have an esoteric idea, you can't find a specialty magazine that will publish it.

Several years ago, a man named Rodger took one of my classes. He was a musician by night, but by day he was a toll booth clerk in the New York City transit system. One of the exercises I use in class is to invite someone, usually a friend, in to be interviewed by the students. This time, I thought Rodger might make an interesting interview subject, but he didn't think so.

"Why would anyone want to hear about what I do all day?" he said. "It's pretty boring."

I finally convinced him to do it, and his fellow students had all kinds of questions for him: Since he was often alone in the booth, what did he do if he had to go to the bathroom while he was on duty? Had he ever been robbed? What was the most ridiculous question he'd ever been asked?

After the mock interview was over, Rodger came up to me and said, "You know, I think they really were interested. Maybe I should write something up."

He did, sent it to *Long Island Newsday*, and a month later, there he was, on the front page of section two. The paper featured a full-body shot of him jauntily leaning against a subway pole, with the headline, "One Day in the Life of a Toll Booth Clerk." This led to him getting other assignments from the newspaper.

There are plenty of ways to get ideas, but there are also ways not to get them. You can't pick up on an idea that you read in the latest issue of *People* and think you can sell it to another national magazine. Once an idea is in any national media outlet, especially television, it's just about dead for any major magazine—unless, that is, you can put a new spin on it. For instance, reading the *New York Daily News* one day, I spotted an item about an artist whose van was stolen, along with a good deal of his work. Nothing special—robberies occur every day in New York City—but buried in the story was the fact that this particular artist, Morris Katz, was in *Guinness World Records* as the most prolific painter in the world. *Now that*, I thought, *might be a good story*. I did a little more research and found that Katz could complete a painting in under ten minutes, using only a palette knife and toilet paper—no brushes—and that he took his show on the road, appearing in all sorts of public venues, like the Catskills. And so I pitched it to *New York* for a section called "Brief Lives," and they bought it as a profile of a man I called "The King of Shlock Art."

Sometimes, an idea might seem too foolish to pitch to a magazine, but in the hands of a skilled writer, that same idea might turn out to be a real winner. When I was first starting out, a friend of mine, an advertising copywriter—ad people and PR people are great sources for ideas, because they think very creatively—said he had a terrific idea for a story having to do with the lottery, which had just introduced scratch-off tickets. "Ask *New York* to give you some money, and go all over the city buying up tickets and see what happens." I thought it was the dumbest idea I'd ever heard. What was the story? And why would the editors give me money to go out and spend on lottery tickets? So, I did nothing with it.

Three months later, *New York* ran a cover story based on just this idea. Editor Byron Dobell had given Jon Bradshaw, a wonderfully creative writer who'd written a book of profiles of notorious gamblers, $500 under the condition that Jon go out and spend it all on scratch-off lottery tickets. And here's the kicker—whatever he won would be his fee for the article. Jon wrote a wonderful article—a far better one than I ever could have written, in large part because he had the imagination and insight to make this into a real story. He went all over the city, throughout all five boroughs, to the smallest store that sold lottery tickets to the largest. Sometimes he went alone, sometimes he went accompanied by the luckiest person he knew, or by a psychic who would guide him as to which ticket he should buy. He wound up "winning" $200 (which really meant he lost $300) and writing an article for the least amount of money he'd ever received.

Certainly, journalism schools assign their students various kinds of magazine articles to write. But they don't necessarily inspire students to use their imagination when choosing topics. I like my students to push the envelope and challenge themselves. For instance, one student asked if she could do a profile of a horse. I saw no reason why not, and she wound up writing a wonderful piece. Another student wanted to profile the fraternity bong. He wound up writing a terrific profile that he later successfully used as a writing sample when he applied for a job as a writer in a computer company. I've had students write service pieces about where the best water fountains are on campus and where the best places on campus are to take a nap. For a participatory piece, one of my students fulfilled a lifelong (admittedly warped) dream and spent a day as a used car salesman, while another wrote about a typical day in her sorority house.

Selecting unusual topics allows you to take chances, and forces you to experiment with different writing styles, something that's very important if you're going to write for a number of different kinds of magazines. Often, the best ideas come from something you do for a living, from something you enjoy doing (like a hobby), or from a particular field that interests you—science, perhaps, or sports. So, before going out shopping for ideas, take a look in your own closet. You might be surprised what you'll find.

MAKE AND MATCH IDEAS

Come up with three story ideas and try to explain them in no more than two sentences. Then, try to match each idea with a magazine that would most likely publish it.

Finding the Angle: The Hook

No matter how good your idea is, you need what editors call a hook. Simply put, the hook explains why readers would be interested in the story. It's up to the writer to come up with the hook. Sometimes, as in the profile of Daria, the hook is within the genre of the story: Woman struggles against tremendous odds and becomes a success. Other times, the hook is relevant to something that's in the news at the moment. For instance, after the tsunami in Asia in December 2004, it was easier to place a story that had to do with floods, tidal waves, or other natural disasters. Other hooks have to do with anniversaries. I have a writer friend who's been waiting for years for Paul McCartney to turn sixty-four. Why? Because he knows he can come up with an essay or article based on the Beatles song "When I'm Sixty-Four." Perhaps you've got a great story that has to do with Christmas or Easter (or spring, summer, fall, or winter). If you do, that's your hook, but you have to make sure that you pitch the story at the right time, because magazines usually work several issues ahead. Monthly magazines, for example, are working at least three or four months ahead of the issue currently on the stands. So, in January, monthly magazines are probably working on their May or June issues. The moment the article is assigned to the time when the issue is actually published is called lead time. To accommodate lead time, writers have to think way ahead and send out their ideas at the appropriate time.

CREATE A HOOK

Try to figure out the hook for each of the three story ideas you came up with in the last exercise. Then decide upon at least two magazines for which each of the stories might be appropriate.

Getting That Assignment: The Query Letter

In order to get an assignment, you've got to present your idea to an editor in a query letter or proposal. The query letter is really nothing more than a sales tool. You're trying to convince an editor that you have a good story for her magazine and that you're the right person to do the job. Seasoned writers can sometimes get away with sketchier query letters because they've got clips (samples) of their work; but for beginning writers, the query letter must be very strong because it is the only weapon in your arsenal. The query letter is the first impression you'll make on an editor. Most magazine editors will tell you that the majority of query letters they receive are just plain bad, so a well-written, well-researched, well-shaped query letter will certainly get an editor's attention. Here are some requisites of a good query letter:

- Query letters must be well focused. In other words, your idea must be well defined. You can't simply suggest an area that you'd like to write about. In my classes, I have students come up with one or two ideas for a magazine article, then identify the particular magazine(s) they would pitch to. Then we have a mock editorial meeting, in which the idea is discussed by the rest of the class. Recently, someone said, "I live on the Upper West Side and there are an awful lot of dogs around, so I think I'd like to write an article about that." Well, about what exactly? That there are lots of dogs and dog owners on the Upper West Side of Manhattan. So what? That's not a story idea, that's an observation. And observations aren't article ideas. But if you're creative, you can use an observation to come up with a story idea that might interest a magazine editor. How about matching dogs with their owners? Why do people gravitate toward certain breeds of dogs? What can you tell about a person by the kind of dog she owns? Or, thinking in terms of a woman's magazine, what can you learn about a man by the way he treats his dog? *Now* you've got the beginnings of a focused query letter.

- Query letters must be well written and well structured. As an editor, if I saw a query letter that rambled on and on or that contained grammatical mistakes, misspellings, or poor sentence structure, there was no way I would make that assignment. Though all the seasoned writers I know hate writing query letters—they're time consuming and you don't get paid for them—they take them very seriously and spend an inordinate amount of time working on them. You will be judged as a writer by the quality of your query letter, no matter what kinds of clips you have (editors know that published articles don't necessarily reflect the talent of the writer so much as they reflect the talent of the editor).

- Query letters should be written in the style of the magazine to which they're addressed. This is the only way you can show that you're familiar with the magazine and that you can adapt your own writing style to that magazine. Writing for magazines is a little bit like being a chameleon: Often, you must adapt your writing style to a particular magazine, rather than write in your own style, if you have one. While you're struggling to establish yourself as a reliable magazine writer, you will probably have to write for a lot of periodicals you would normally never read, on subjects that don't particularly interest you. This is not necessarily a bad thing. In fact, it teaches you about craft and how to change voice and tone, something we'll address later.

- Query letters shouldn't leave much to the imagination. One of the biggest mistakes beginning writers make in query letters is withholding critical information from the editor. A query letter is not like a mystery story—you can't say something like, *I've got some really good stuff that you'll read when I get the assignment.* Yeah, right. This is your one chance, and you can't expect an editor who doesn't know you to take it on faith that you've got great information and great anecdotes. Use them in the query.

- Don't make promises; deliver. If you say you're going to write a humorous piece, you'd better give examples of the kind of humor you're capable of. I've read some deadly serious query letters that then end with: *and I'm going to handle this subject with wit and humor.* Sure. And if it's a story that must be heavily researched, show the editor in your query that you're capable of that kind of research.

- Don't make mistakes of fact. I can't think of anything that will get a query letter tossed faster than factual errors. I have a friend who's been a magazine editor for years, and he told me that if someone spells his name wrong in a query letter, he immediately throws it in the trash. And for good reason. He figures if someone who wants to get an assignment can't even research how to spell his name—and it's an easy one—then she can't be trusted to research an entire article.

- Generally speaking, query letters should be no longer than a page and a half, single-spaced. If you need a thousand words to describe what your article's about, how could you possibly write an article of fifteen hundred words on the subject?

- Don't bother suggesting word counts and delivery dates. Many of the books and articles I've seen on the subject of writing for magazines suggest offering a word count or telling the editor when you can deliver the finished article, but frankly I don't see the point. The editors of the magazine are going to decide how many words they think your article is worth, and they're going to tell you when they want it.

- Find the right editor to send the query to. This is something I think most journalism schools tend to neglect to teach their students. You can waste an awful lot of time by sending your letter to the wrong department or the wrong editor. Check out the masthead of the magazine and you'll probably find the proper editor to submit to—many mastheads list the editors for particular sections. If the masthead doesn't list a likely candidate, call the magazine, ask for the editorial department, and then ask who would handle, say, a profile query, or a query on health matters.

How to Write a Query Letter

Basically, there are two ways to approach writing a query letter. The first is very straightforward—you get right into what the subject of your article is. For instance, if you were pitching an article on where the jobs are in the twenty-first century, you might start off with something like, "Since the dot-com bubble burst five years ago, the unemployment rate has dropped significantly and X number of jobs have disappeared from the economy. But if you know the right places to look, there are jobs available. ..."

The second way to begin a query letter is far more artful and, I think, better showcases your ability as a writer. Start the query off the way you're actually going to begin the article. In other words, use a possible lead for the article as your lead-in to the query letter, thus giving the editor a peek at what she might expect.

Although I don't believe in setting out a template for query letters (or for anything else, for that matter), you should at least know what to include in your query letter and how the letter can be structured. But, as with anything else, once you know the rules, you can figure out ways to bend them to your advantage. I think some of the most successful, interesting, and imaginative query letters do just that. Query letters should contain:

1. The lead, which introduces the editor to your idea—preferably in a creative, active way, often using an anecdote or even dialogue.

2. The intended content of the article. After you introduce the idea in a general way with your lead, focus on telling the editor precisely what your article is going to be about.

3. Specifics—exactly what will be in the article, and how you're going to research it: who you'll interview, where you'll get your information, what your point of view will be. Point of view is very important in magazine writing, unlike in newspapers, where reporting is supposed to be objective. But just because you are writing from a particular point of view and sharing a specific opinion doesn't mean that you're not going to be fair. You're not going to step up on a soap box. The best articles can often be rather subtle, but a close reader can almost always tell how the author feels about a subject.

4. Your credentials—why you're qualified to write on this subject.

This is all of the information that should be in the query letter, but it doesn't necessarily have to be in this particular order. Use this list as a good jumping off point.

Following are a couple of effective example queries from former students.

SAMPLE QUERY TO *GENTLEMAN'S QUARTERLY* MAGAZINE

Dear _____:

I thought you might be interested in the following article idea for *GQ*.

YOUR SUIT IS TALKING ...
IS IT SAYING WHAT YOU WANT IT TO SAY?

Some women will drop their eyes to the gluteals before they'll give a guy the time of day. Others live by the law of the hands and feet. Me, I go for the gorge. That's right, the gorge. Next, I size up the silhouette and eyeball the besoms—or their lack. If I like what I see, I may even try to estimate the drop. Rest assured that if you should happen to meet me at your local watering hole after work, I will smile politely (and quite possibly flirt outrageously) while I read your suit. And it will tell me more than you might think about the man inside.

Is men's fashion still a bit of an oxymoron? Despite the best efforts of Calvin, Ralph, and Giorgio, yes. Not because men aren't interested in making a statement with their clothes, but because most men and their clothes don't speak the same language, particularly when it comes to suits. Most guys don't know a poplin from a popover. That ignorance doesn't stop them from buying, but it does tend to dampen their enjoyment of the process. And it definitely puts them at a disadvantage when the babe at the bar tweaks a lapel and purrs, "*Nice*. Is that a nailhead or a bird's-eye?"

I propose a feature on decoding the language of men's clothing—a regular-Joe's guide, from the point of view of a regular Jill who happens to know a thing or two about suits. While light and humorous in tone, this piece would serve the reader by letting him know both what his clothes are really saying about him and how to look for the suits and furnishings that might take his "statement" to the next level ... without risking the cardinal guy-sin, overstatement.

Since my days as PR manager for the Greif Companies—the now-defunct manufacturer of tailored clothing for Ralph Lauren and Perry Ellis, among others—I have been a devout suit watcher, a perpetual grad student in the venerable old school of men's tailoring. And I have been casually educating grateful male friends—as well as unsuspecting men in bars—in the language of suits and furnishings. Not just about what the gorge is, mind you, but about what it stands for ... and what it says about you when it stands too high or too low on your shoulder. The language of suits has history, sex appeal, and the totally random irrelevance of the best trivia. It also has practical applications. Knowledge of it will not turn men into virtual women on the subject of fashion, but it might just make them look twice at that double-breasted blazer, or walk a little taller in their brogues.

One possible sidebar would be a glossary of terms with which to impress the salesmen at Barney's—not to mention women in bars. Another could provide diagrams of basic silhouettes or a brief interview with a designer, merchandiser, or buyer about men's shopping styles and levels of suit awareness.

This piece could accompany a tailored-fashion story with photographs, but would also be effective with illustrations. And, needless to say, it's tailor-made for *GQ*.

I am enclosing a couple of clips of articles I've written for _____ and _____. [If you don't have any clips, just leave this sentence out.] If you have any questions, please don't hesitate to contact me.

Sincerely,
Shannon Barr

Why is this query effective? First of all, the lead is humorous and mysterious enough to make the editor want to read more. Second, it is filled with information that only someone with a good knowledge of the subject would possess. Third, it's written in an accessible style, one that could easily work for *GQ* or *Details* or *Esquire*.

Here's part of another very effective query letter.

SAMPLE QUERY TO *FAMILY CIRCLE*

Dear _____:

"Mommy! What I really want for Christmas is this flying sparkle doll—see, Mommy, there she is, with glitter, see? But if I can't get her, I want a baby that drinks from a toy bottle and comes with her own diapers, or else I want a kitchen baking set with a real oven and cake mix, like Emily has, Mommy, please, please, please!"

And so the song begins in the aisles of toy stores and shopping malls: the "I want" serenade. It is a theme with infinite variations—"What I really want is Nintendo ... Air Jordans ... Gap overalls, size 10 ... a life-size walking fashion doll complete with her own wardrobe and hair accessories." But the point remains constant: Whether your family celebrates Christmas, Hanukkah, or Kwanzaa—and whether your kids are into diapers or grunge rock—the holiday season often means long wish lists, piles of presents, and a frantic parental effort to stay at least in sight of financial reality.

Families have to work hard to resist the multicolored, spangled "buy-me" blitz and kindle the spirit of the holiday season. I propose writing an article that would offer a dozen practical, inexpensive strategies to bring wonder and meaning back to the holidays. These strategies include activities in the home and in the community, and involve the whole family. Here are a few examples:

Recycle your own good fortune. With your kids, sift through outgrown or castoff playthings. Give your found treasures a spruce-up. Add a fresh ribbon to a teddy bear; wash and dry wooden blocks; treat that old, tired toy train to a fresh coat of paint (nontoxic, of course). Once the gifts are wrapped and ready, take them—and your kids—to a family shelter in your community. Many shelters host Christmas parties and are grateful for presents for their clients' children. Your family will see firsthand that kids can help other kids in trouble, and that you don't have to be a grown-up to give from the heart.

[*The writer gave three other examples so that the editor could see exactly what she had in mind for the article, a tactic that went a long way in getting her the assignment.*]

I would be glad to provide clips, or you can visit my Web site, www._____.

Sincerely,
Helen Zelon

WRITE A QUERY LETTER

Match one of the ideas you thought of in the previous exercises with the magazine for which it's appropriate, then do some research on the subject. Write a query letter of no more than 250 words. Pepper the query letter with facts and anecdotes, and don't be afraid to include some quotes, which will not only spice up the query letter but will also prove to the editor that you can get a good quote and that you know how to use one.

Submitting Queries and Following Up

Most magazines and books I've seen about magazine writing suggest sending along a self-addressed, stamped envelope (SASE) with your query letter. But I've never received an assignment through the mail. Instead, assignments always come when an editor calls.

One of the most common questions I get is *How long should I wait before I follow up on a query submission?* Most editors will tell you that they answer query letters within two or three weeks. All I can say is that I've got queries that have been out there for ten years without an answer, and I'm not holding my breath to hear back on them now. The truth is, query letters sometimes fall through the cracks, or never reach their destination, or are simply ignored. It's part of your job as a writer to follow up on your query letters. If you haven't gotten a response within a couple of weeks, send an e-mail to the editor asking if she received your query. If you don't hear after another two weeks, try again. (But, at the same time, I'd probably send the query off to another magazine.)

Today, many magazines prefer to get query letters via e-mail. Check the magazine's submission guidelines. Most magazines today have Web sites that include this kind of information, but if you find one that doesn't, just call the magazine, ask for the editorial department, and either request the guidelines or ask if the editor accepts e-mail queries. Send the query as an attachment, but also include it pasted into the body of the message, in case the magazine doesn't open attachments.

What to Do When You Get the Assignment

When you get an assignment, there are several questions you ought to ask:

1. Make sure the assignment is the same as the story that was in your query. Sometimes, a magazine editor will tweak your story without informing you. By verifying the assignment, you'll guarantee that the story you give her will be the one she wants. Just ask the editor if she wants you to do the story just the way you presented it in your query letter.

2. Find out what the due date is. If it's unreasonable, say so. Don't just let the deadline come and go without handing in the piece, thinking the editor might forget. Editors like to work with writers who deliver

well-written, well-researched, clean articles that are on time. These are the writers they tend to use over and over.

3. Find out what the word count is. You may think the article is worth 2,500 words, but the editor knows what she wants. This is usually nonnegotiable. Here's something they don't tell you in MFA programs: Editors usually assign more words than they need, because it's easier to cut an article than it is to pad it. Overwrite at your own peril. Generally speaking, providing anything more than 10 percent of the requested word count is asking for trouble. Either you will be asked to make cuts or, even worse, the editor will make the cuts for you, and they won't always be to your liking.

4. Find out if you're getting a contract. The contract will tell you the word count, the due date, and how much you're getting paid (as well as the amount of the kill fee, which is what you'll be paid if the article isn't used, usually 25 percent of the original fee). It will also put in writing exactly what you're expected to deliver in terms of the story. The contract will tell you if the magazine is buying all rights or first North American serial rights, under which ownership of the article returns to the writer after a certain amount of time (often ninety days from the time the article is published). First North American serial rights benefit the writer, so if the magazine wants all rights, try to negotiate them down to first serial rights. The contract will also tell you when you're getting paid: on acceptance (much preferred), or on publication (to be avoided—what if the article isn't published for two years?).

5. If you aren't offered a contract, ask for a letter of agreement, which will include all the above items.

Getting Started

RESEARCHING THE ARTICLE

Once you've gotten the assignment, the first thing you should do is determine what kind of information you'll need. To do this, you've got to have a pretty good handle on what the article is going to look like and what kind of information it's going to contain. Your assigning editor should be able to guide you in this regard.

It's a good idea to decide how much information you think you're going to need before you start the project. For instance, if you're writing a relatively short article (a thousand words or less), you don't need mountains and mountains of research. Over-research will only bog you down and make writing that much harder. I know one writer who did so much research for her first article that by the time she had to write it she was virtually paralyzed by the sheer volume of information in front of her.

Nevertheless, research is key to producing a good article, and only you can decide how much of it you need before you feel confident enough to tackle writing the article. Veteran writers have a feel for how much research they need to do, and this sense is keyed to not only the size of the article, but also to how much they're being paid to write it.

There are a number of ways to research an article, but you can rely on the resources discussed below to get you started.

- LexisNexis is an online service that has a comprehensive databank of articles on practically every subject in major magazines and newspapers. Unfortunately, you have to subscribe to the service, and it's quite costly. Universities connected to LexisNexis may grant students access, and if you have friends whose companies subscribe to the service (law firms usually do), you may be able to prevail upon them to let you sneak in and use it (or perhaps they can do it for you).

- The Internet, of course, has become a great source of information for journalists. In fact, the search-engine Google (www.google.com) has revolutionized researching. The search engine https://vivisimo.com also clusters subjects. But other sites are also good for journalists, including www.expertclick.com and www.profnet.com, both of which can help you find experts on a variety of subjects.

  Individual Web sites can also be very helpful. When I was researching a story on baseball umpires, I came across a host of sites devoted to that subject and was able to pick up a good deal of useful background information. When I was working on a project with a soap opera director and he couldn't remember particular plotlines, I was able to find a Web site that included every plotline the show had done.

  Practically every major corporation and government agency has a Web site from which information can be obtained. The U.S. Department of Labor, the Department of Agriculture, the Census Bureau, and the Department of Health and Human Services all have useful Web sites.

But beware: There is a lot of misinformation floating out in cyberspace. Check and double-check anything you find on the Internet.

• The library, as old-fashioned as it might be, is still a major source of information. The old standby *The Readers' Guide to Periodical Literature* offers a comprehensive list of articles written on virtually every subject. And there's also the *Encyclopedia of Associations*, which is extremely helpful. I first ran across this source when I was doing a series of articles on collectibles, and I found that practically every subject has an association. You would expect to find listings for the American Psychiatric Association (APA), the American Medical Association (AMA), and the American Bar Association (ABA), but you can also find listings for every interest, no matter how small. For instance, there's an association (and museums, to boot) for people who collect barbed wire, or bottles. Somewhere out there in the heartland, someone with an all-abiding interest in bottles has set up a museum in his garage, and if you contact him, he'll be more than willing to help you out with any information you might need. And he'll probably make a great interview subject, too.

• The white and yellow pages are two of the most obvious tools of research, yet they are also the most neglected. You'd be amazed what you can find in the white or yellow pages. For instance, while writing an article on collecting old trains, I opened to the hobby section, found a store that sold vintage toy trains, called it up, and got great leads to collectors.

For a survey assignment from *Travel & Leisure* (these always turn out to be much tougher than you'd think, primarily because you have to contact so many people), I was commissioned to find ten famous people, from all walks of life, and ask them to tell me about the best vacation they'd had in the past three years. Politicians are always easy to contact because they love getting into print. I decided to include former New York City mayor Ed Koch, but how would I get in touch with him? Easy. I picked up the white pages and found that his office number was listed. I called, left a message with his secretary telling her what I needed, and within a day he was back to me.

- Corporate communications or press and public relations departments are common to every large and most small businesses. They disseminate information and set up interviews for journalists. Remember, of course, that going through these departments means that you're going to get the party line, and if you're doing an investigative piece, this is not exactly what you want. But whatever kind of article you're writing, it's also good to get both sides. Going through the press relations department is a good start and can point you toward other information you might need.

- Six degrees of separation can be a useful concept when you're researching. As soon as you get an assignment, tell everyone you know what you're writing about. I guarantee that someone will know someone who's an expert in the field or who has some information you need. This technique worked for me when I was researching a story for *Rolling Stone* on film pirates—those people who find prints of films before they're even released, duplicate them, and sell them on the black market. I had done most of the research, but was having absolutely no success finding an actual film pirate to interview. I happened to be in the office of a friend one day, and she asked me what I was working on. I told her, and an assistant in the office overhead us and said, "I know a guy who does that." I asked if he'd talk to me, she said yes, and so I had a very important piece of the story.

Researching Around a Subject

Sometimes you just have to go the indirect route by researching around a subject: Perhaps your subject is uncooperative; or you simply can't find a good firsthand source for information. For instance, I was once assigned a cover story on Brooke Shields by a major women's magazine. Unfortunately, Shields was angling for a cover story in a different magazine, and didn't want to cooperate with the magazine I was working for. To get around this, the magazine assigned what's called a *write-around* or *cut-and-paste job*. Writers don't usually like these kinds of assignments—and I didn't—but since they were going to allow me to use a pseudonym, and the article was not intended to be mean-spirited, I agreed. But they didn't want a piece taken entirely from previously published stories, so I had to get some firsthand interviews. For starters, I got the magazine to pay for me to go to a Broadway performance of *Grease*, in which Shields was starring. I wanted to see her performance, but even more than that, I wanted to get some "color" for the piece by seeing how she behaved with her fans. So, after the performance, I parked myself at the stage door and waited, along with two dozen fans, for her to come out. When she did, I watched as she happily signed autographs for everyone there, stopping to chat with each one of them. It was a nice and very usable moment, but I needed more—I needed anecdotes, stories about her in different situations.

I combed the gossip columns and found she'd recently done a photo shoot with a famous photographer. I called him up—he was listed in the white pages—and he told me a delightful story about her. Then, still needing more, I remembered that up and down the Upper East Side, in delis, pizza joints, and Chinese take-out restaurants, I would often see Shields's autographed photograph hanging on the walls. I figured she must do an awful lot of eating out, so I trekked all over the Upper East Side, looking for someone who could tell me something about her. I found someone who could in a bagel joint on East Eighty-Third Street. He told me she was in there all the time, and that when her show opened, she came in and offered everyone who worked there comp tickets.

Another time, when I was doing a profile of Meg Ryan for *Redbook*, there were certain aspects of her personal life Ryan didn't want to talk about. But, of course, these were the very areas the magazine insisted that I cover. I was able to track down Nora Ephron, the director of her most recent film, and she gave me the number of Ryan's sister-in-law, who spoke very freely about the subject of Ryan's relationship with her mother (which, by the way, Ryan herself spoke very freely about months later in an interview with another magazine).

FORMULATING A RESEARCH PLAN

Formulate a plan for how you would begin research for the following assignment I received. At one time, the editors at *Redbook* asked me to find and write about three women who'd recently won something for the first time in their lives. Each woman had to be a married mother between the ages of twenty-one and forty-five. I could not choose women from either New York or California. The prize had to be won totally by luck (which negated something like the Nobel Peace Prize), and not by gambling (which left out winning the jackpot slot in Atlantic City), and it couldn't have been won in a contest held by a competing magazine.

How would you go about researching this particular article? Think about it before you read on.

Here was my solution: The first thing I did was ask everyone I knew who fit the demographics if she'd recently won anything for the first time, or if she knew anyone who had. No. Then I tried Publishers Clearing House, but all the recent winners seemed to be much older than forty-five. I decided to focus my search better, toward areas where I was more likely to find young mothers. I thought I had a brilliant idea: cereal companies. I called Battle Creek, Michigan, the home of Kellogg's, and spoke to someone in corporate communications who laughed when I told her what I was looking for.

"You have to understand that most of the people who enter our contests enter hundreds of other contests—they do it professionally—so you're probably not going to find anyone who's never won before," she said.

My next attempt was with cosmetics companies, and it was there that I found someone who'd won a beauty cruise. She was a thirty-five-year-old resident of Atlanta, Georgia, a mother of two, and a former model who now worked in real estate. She had read about the beauty-cruise contest in *Redbook* while on the exercise bike at the local gym. I held my breath after I asked if she'd ever won anything before. The answer, thankfully, was no.

I found another first-time winner by calling the Mall of America and asking if they'd had any recent contests—again, I figured that the kinds of women I was looking for frequented malls, and what better mall to check than the largest in America. It just so happened that they had recently held a contest for a new house: Fortunately, a woman was the winner, and she had not won anything before.

The third woman was found from a small item in a newspaper about three women—a grandmother, her daughter, and granddaughter—who'd purchased a winning lottery ticket in Florida. I figured one of them fit the required profile and had never won anything before, and I was right.

RESEARCH GUIDELINES AND DOCUMENTATION

Many magazines offer research guidelines, which advise you to ask for transcripts, tapes, and citations for information included in the article; and for phone numbers and other contact information for any people interviewed. For instance, if you've cited figures from a Web site, make sure to include the Web site address or, if you've used quotes from a television or radio interview, make sure you provide the name of the show, as well as the day and time it was aired—and a copy of it, if possible.

Most of the larger magazines have fact-checkers on staff, who go through every article carefully, looking for possible errors. This may seem like a pain in the neck for the writer, but ultimately the writer is the beneficiary of this close scrutiny. Your name goes on the article, and you're the one who will take the heat if there are any errors. So, in order to help out the fact-checker, it's a good idea to keep all phone numbers and research material handy. I know that I tend to write phone numbers on scraps of paper and then misplace them, so keep a notebook or a file on your computer with all relevant information.

Interviewing

Before you embark on any interview, do some research on the subject of the interview and/or on the subject you're writing about. The necessary amount of preparatory research will vary from minimal to extensive, depending at least in part on the kind of person you are.

For instance, I don't do an overwhelming amount of research on a subject before the interview because I like to keep my sense of curiosity fresh—it's what fuels the interview for me. I'm afraid that if I know too much about the subject, if I know the answer before I even give the question, I'm less likely to ask it, and I run the risk of not listening closely when it's given.

On the other hand, if you do extensive research before an interview, you're more likely to know what areas to cover and what kinds of questions to ask. Research can also result in unexpected benefits, as it did with a friend of mine, Tom Seligson, in his interview with Kirk Douglas. It often happens that the writer gets very limited access to a celebrity for an interview—sometimes, an hour or less. Tom was rolling along when he asked the question, "You've made a number of movies with Burt Lancaster; what's that like?" Douglas responded, "Yes, we've made seven movies together. ..." "Excuse me," Tom said, "but you've actually made nine." Douglas thought a moment and said, "You're absolutely right." When the hour ran out and Douglas had to leave, he turned to Tom and said, "You know, you're a real professional, you've done your homework, and I appreciate that. I know there's more you have to ask me, so why don't you come over to my place tomorrow, and we'll have breakfast and finish the interview."

This is gold to a writer. Not only would Tom have more time to ask questions, but he'd also get to see how and where Douglas lived; all a benefit of his research.

It's a bad idea to go in to any interview completely cold, thinking that you can wing it. Years ago, I was assigned a piece on the women of *Saturday Night Live*: Julia Louis-Dreyfus, Mary Gross, and Robin Duke. I did the interviews with Louis-Dreyfus and Gross, and they were terrific, filled with amusing stories; but when I got to Robin Duke, she had absolutely nothing to say. No matter what question I asked, I'd get at best a one- or two-word answer. I was running out of questions and starting to get very anxious when I asked one more, desperate question, a question I never would have thought to ask if I hadn't done some research before the interview: "You went to high school with Catherine O'Hara; what was that like?" Suddenly, Duke's face lit up and she started to tell me all these stories about Catherine O'Hara and herself (in the role of sidekick), which I was able to work into the story about the three women. If I hadn't asked that question, I don't know what I would have done; the article would have been a disaster.

SETTING UP THE INTERVIEW

There are three ways to conduct an interview: by phone, in person, or via e-mail. If you possibly can, it's always better to do an interview in person, but there are circumstances in which that's not possible, either because the subject is not available or because the amount of information you need doesn't warrant a face-to-face meeting.

PHONE INTERVIEWS

It's always a good idea to tape phone interviews, if you can. When you're interviewing someone in person, you can pick up all kinds of nuances and physical movements that add to the understanding of what someone's saying. This isn't the case when you're talking to someone on the phone, and so the words themselves become even more important. But if you are taping someone, don't forget to ask permission. In some states, it's against the law to tape someone without permission. In New York state, only one person in the conversation needs to give permission for it to be taped, but if you're in New York and you're talking to someone in another state, that state might have more stringent laws. In any case, it's just polite to inform the other party that you'd like to tape the conversation.

Even if you are recording the conversation, it's still a good idea to take notes during the interview. I do so because it helps me focus on the conversation, instead of relying solely on the tape recorder. In fact, I don't even bother to record short interviews that are mostly informational in nature and you don't need to pull direct quotes from. Instead, I sit at the computer and take notes.

Don't call without warning and begin the interview. Make preliminary contact to set up a time that's convenient for the person you're interviewing. Tell him exactly what the story is, what kind of information you're looking for, and how much time you'll need. (Don't overwhelm someone by saying you need a couple of hours of phone time—she'll just roll her eyes and say no; no one wants to sit on the phone with a journalist for that length of time.) Most people want to be helpful, and your preliminary phone call gives them the opportunity to prepare. I've found that if you are considerate in this way, people will go out of their way to cooperate with you. No one wants to look stupid during an interview, and if you tell your subject the kind of information you're looking for, I guarantee that she'll spend hours before the interview trying to think of information that might be helpful to you.

E-MAIL INTERVIEWS

In my experience, e-mail interviews are rare, but they can be useful. Remember, however, that they're rather clunky; follow-up questions are difficult, unless you intend to carry out a never-ending back-and-forth stream of e-mails. If you do have to conduct an interview via e-mail, write up a list of clear and concise questions, and inform the interview subject that you're likely to send follow-up questions to clarify some of her answers.

TAPING INTERVIEWS AND TAKING NOTES

One of the first questions I get about interviews is whether they should be taped. The problem with taping interviews is transcribing them later.

Transcription is one of the most odious and tedious of the writer's jobs. Interview someone for five minutes and then spend almost half an hour trying to transcribe it, and you'll see what I mean. Nevertheless, it's always a good idea to use a tape recorder if you can. And if you are taping interviews, I advise investing in a top-of-the-line recorder. You'll appreciate it when you have to listen to the interview. Whether or not you use a recorder, always take notes. I do so for several reasons:

1. Tape recorders, no matter how sophisticated, sometimes malfunction. Several years ago, I was assigned an interview with Lynn Stalmaster, a legendary Hollywood casting director. He happened to be staying in a nearby hotel, so I walked the dozen or so blocks in the bitter cold of February. When I got there, I turned on the tape recorder, made sure the red light was on and that the reel was turning, and started the interview, taking notes the whole time. I finished the interview, went home and turned on the tape recorder. I was shocked to find that, for the first fifteen minutes of the interview, all I heard was a low humming noise. Evidently, on the way over, the recorder's condenser microphone had frozen. Fortunately, I had taken notes and was able to reconstruct that first quarter of an hour.

2. Contrary to what some might think, recorders don't have difficulty picking up sounds; they pick up *all* sounds in the vicinity. When you're talking to someone and there's a fan humming in the background or music playing, your brain eventually screens out those sounds and you're able to focus on someone's words. That's not the case with a tape recorder. It doesn't discriminate between background and foreground sounds. There is no sound filter. And so, if you're taping a conversation in a restaurant (as I have), when you play back the tape, you're bound to hear the sounds of silverware clanking, glasses clinking, people at the next table ordering, and the busboy dropping a tray. That's exactly what happened when I was interviewing Scottish director Bill Forsyth, who insisted on going to a noisy Italian restaurant in Little Italy here in New York City. After five minutes, I shut off the tape recorder and just took notes furiously.

3. Notes can verify quotes in case a tape recording is garbled or unintelligible. When interviewing Meg Ryan in a Santa Monica restaurant,

I noticed that she was uncomfortable. I said, "You don't really like being interviewed, do you?" "No," she said, "I feel like there's a giant microphone on the table and everything I say is being broadcast out to the world." I immediately knew this was a great quote, and I included it in my profile. But during the editorial process I received a call from the fact-checker saying that that quote was garbled on the tape and that they would have to take it out of the article unless I could verify it in my notes. Fortunately, I had taken notes. And when I went back and found them, there was the quote. It stayed in the story.

4. Taking notes helps you focus on what's being said. In effect, it slows down the process of the interview a little simply because you're taking notes. And if the person being interviewed talks too fast, don't be afraid to slow her down a little so that you can get everything she's saying.

Type up your notes as soon as you get home. You're probably going to be writing quickly during the interview, and there's a good chance you might have trouble deciphering your notes. If you type them up right away, you're more likely to remember what it is you wrote. Typing the notes right away will also reinforce the interview, and this will help when it comes to writing the piece.

LISTENING

The most important thing for a journalist to do during an interview is to *listen*. This may seem obvious, but many of us have a real problem listening. I have a friend who's brilliant, a wonderful writer, but he rarely *listens* to what people are saying. He'd make a terrible journalist, because many questions that journalists ask actually come directly from the answers people give. You'll never know what important follow-up question you might have missed had you not been listening.

You can train yourself to focus and actually remember what people say, and this is important because if you're not taking notes or using a tape recorder, you might have to re-create the conversation. A few years ago I had lunch with the comedian Pat Cooper. I had no intention of writing about him—we were just meeting to discuss a possible book project. But he was so amusing, so outrageous, and so quotable, that when I got home I sat down at the computer and started writing up our meeting. I had no notes. I had no tape-recording to transcribe. And yet I was able to re-create our conversation almost word for word. Why? Because I was listening to what he had to say. And that's what good journalists have to do: listen.

Listening carefully will also help you be sensitive to what the subject of your interview is going through. It's not easy being interviewed, and sometimes people get tired or frustrated. As an interviewer, you have to know when to back off. There's nothing wrong with terminating the interview and asking if you can continue it another time. One day I was interviewing actor Matthew Modine in a Greenwich Village restaurant. The interview was going great; I thought we were really connecting. But at one point he seemed to run out of steam, and his answers became monosyllabic. I asked if he'd like to end the interview and he said yes, and then, as I asked for the check, he grabbed my notebook, scribbled something on it, and pushed it back at me. He'd written, "The reason I'm starting to guard is because someone's listening to us." When we got outside, he said, "Thanks for picking up on that. There were two women sitting next to us and they recognized me and they were listening to everything we were saying. But we don't have to end the interview now. I've got some errands to run, why don't you tag along." I did, and I got some great material I wouldn't have otherwise gotten.

GETTING PEOPLE TO TALK

In my experience as a journalist, the problem isn't getting people to talk, it's getting them to shut up. This isn't necessarily true of celebrities, but it is true of just about everyone else. Think about it. How many people do you know who will sit and listen to your every word, focusing intently on your answers, taping what you have to say, taking copious notes? Not your mother or father or boyfriend or girlfriend or husband or wife, and certainly not your teacher. But here's a journalist sitting in front of you, staring you in the face, paying rapt attention to everything you have to say ... and then memorializing it in print. In some cases, interview subjects treat journalists like priests or psychiatrists, someone to tell their troubles to. Some even see it as a way to settle a grudge.

One of my first articles concerned inventor fraud. The perpetrator placed ads in various magazines aimed at inventors, promising to help them get a patent and market their inventions. Of course, all he really did was take their money and leave them high and dry. I found someone who'd been ripped off by this man and went out to Queens to interview him. I sat in the kitchen with him and his wife. Theirs was a very sad story. Not only had they lost all of their savings, but only a month earlier, their teenage son had been involved in a fireworks accident and had lost three fingers.

After the interview was over, the husband offered to drive me to the train station. In the car, he started to talk about how difficult the situation had been for his family, but especially for his wife. "You know," he said, "I've lost her services." Sliding down in my seat, I fervently hoped he meant services like cleaning and cooking. But no. He continued talking about their sex life. All I could think was *Please, stop.* Of course, I could have used this information in my story—he'd never said that it was off the record, nor would he probably have known what that meant—but I knew I wouldn't.

That incident taught me a lot about interviewing, about earning the trust of the interview subject and then not using it to betray him, and about bonding with him.

It also taught me that sometimes, when an interview subject claims he "never said that," he's not necessarily telling a deliberate lie. He may genuinely not remember saying it, or he may have blocked it out because it was so embarrassing.

INTERVIEW STRATEGIES

Here's a little secret about journalists and interviewing, something you will rarely hear in a classroom: No matter how long you've done it, no matter how many interviews you've conducted, you're still going to be nervous before (and maybe during) your next interview. And maybe that's a good thing, because it keeps you on your toes, it keeps you thinking about the interview, and it gets the adrenaline going. Most actors, especially the good ones, will tell you the same thing: that they're nervous before every performance. There's the anxiety of failure, the fear that you're not going to get good quotes, the certainty that you're not going to ask the right questions, the ever-present danger that you're going to open your mouth and nothing intelligible is going to come out.

An interview can carry the same kind of discomfort as a blind date: You don't know her and she doesn't know you, and you may not have much in common. Somehow you've got to work through that. The problem is worse if your interview subject is reluctant or hostile. Then your job is to make the interview subject comfortable, so she'll open up to you. You're trying to get specific information from her, and she's trying to make sure you get only the information she wants you to have. Here are some things you can do to smooth the way:

- **BE PREPARED.** Know at least something about the person you're interviewing or the subject you're writing about. This will help put the interview subject at ease, making her think she's in competent hands when it comes to your actually writing the piece. If you know something about the subject, it will probably help you connect with her more easily.

- **BE YOURSELF.** Don't create a persona that's not you. Instead, use your own personality to its best advantage. You don't, for instance, have to be aggressive. I'm very shy, and that often puts the interview subject at ease. For instance, when I was assigned to write the profile of actress Amanda Plummer, I was very nervous about it: I had to turn the piece around in one day, something I'd never had to do before; and Amanda Plummer had a reputation for being a little spacey and enigmatic. In any case, the interview went fine—in large part, I think, because I wasn't aggressive with her. Later, when I spoke to the editor, she asked, "How did you get her to talk about Jimmy Hayden? She's never talked about him before." (Hayden was an up-and-coming young Broadway actor who, after appearing in David Mamet's *American Buffalo*, was touted as the next James Dean.) "I didn't even ask her about him," I said. "She just started talking about him during the interview." I got those quotes simply because she felt comfortable with me. In most MFA programs, students are taught to be "professional," which all too often translates into being aggressive or unrelenting. Remember, you're dealing with other human beings who have the same insecurities that you do, and to treat them otherwise is a big mistake.

- **SET UP A STRATEGY FOR THE INTERVIEW.** For instance, it's probably a good idea to go in knowing your first question or the first topic you want to discuss. When I was assigned a profile of Kevin Kline, I knew he didn't like to be interviewed, so I tried to think of a way to put him at ease. I had read a recent profile of him in *Rolling Stone*. So I led by telling him that I'd interviewed Amanda Plummer, and then asked him what he thought of the *Rolling Stone* profile. He *hated* it. And I gave him time to vent his anger, which then led to a very interesting interview.

- **DON'T THINK OF THE INTERVIEW AS AN INTERVIEW.** Think of it as a conversation, with the other person doing most of the talking, but with you occasionally offering something of yourself. If you're able to pull off this fiction, you're likely to elicit much more information.

- **DON'T SCRIPT THE INTERVIEW.** That is, don't prepare a list of questions in the order that you're going to ask them. I've found that the best interviews are organic, in the sense that they evolve naturally. Scripting interviews makes them feel artificial and impersonal and, more importantly, there's always the danger that you'll pay too much attention to the list, and miss important follow-up questions. However, it is important that you write up a list of questions that you want to ask and areas that you want to cover. Just don't worry about putting them in a specific order.

- **SHAPE THE INTERVIEW.** A student who wanted to write an exposé on a cult came up to me after class one day and said, "I interviewed this expert on cults, and I've got ten hours on tape. What do I do with it?" I didn't quite know what to tell her, other than that if she had ten hours of tape for one interview, she probably wasn't doing a good interviewing job. She wasn't writing a book, she was writing an article. She didn't shape the interview. She let him ramble and repeat himself and tell four or five stories to make a point when one or two would have done the job. It's your job as an interviewer to make sure that the interview has limits. Sure, you let someone ramble a little bit—you never know where a good digression is going to take you—but if you see that it's irrelevant or unnecessary, get the interview back on track. How do you do this? Simple. Just inject another question that puts the conversation back where you want it.

- **SAVE THE TOUGH QUESTIONS FOR THE END.** You're not Mike Wallace or Geraldo Rivera, with a camera and plenty of backup behind you. If you ask a question that alienates your subject before you get started, you're left with nothing—just a lot of empty space on the page, which means you've got no story. Ask that tough question with one foot out the door, and ask it in a way that doesn't alienate the subject of your interview. For instance, I had to write a profile on John Travolta, and there were all these rumors swirling around about his membership in the controversial Church of Scientology and about the possibility of his being a homosexual. Although I felt it was his business and only his business, I knew the magazine wanted to know, and I knew it was my job to ask the question. I didn't want to offend or alienate him, so I had to figure out a "nice" way to ask. Finally, at the end of the interview, I asked, "John, how do you feel about all those rumors written about you in the tabloids?" He couldn't have been nicer in answering the question (by saying he didn't pay much attention to them), and I had done my job.

- **ASK IF YOU CAN RECONTACT THE SUBJECT.** When the interview's over, ask the subject if it's all right to recontact her if you have more questions (and chances are you will). Get a contact number. This way, you won't be embarrassed if you have to reach that person again.

WHAT TO LOOK FOR IN AN INTERVIEW

In any interview you're looking not only for information, but also for good quotes and anecdotes you can use in your story. In order to get good quotes and anecdotes, you can't simply accept one-word answers. It's your job to coax the interviewee to giving details. If the subject is telling a story, ask for details so you can re-create the scene. For instance, for a profile of writer/director John Sayles, who had just finished the film *Eight Men Out*, I interviewed a few members of the cast, including the actor D.B. Sweeney. I asked Sweeney what he thought of Sayles as a director and he said, "He's great." If I'd left it there, it wouldn't been much of a quote and it wouldn't have added much to my story. But when I asked, "What makes him a great director?" he said, "Well, in reality, the World Series that year took place in mid-September and it was very, very hot. But we were shooting in mid-fall in Indiana and it was freezing cold, so cold that [fog] was coming out of our mouths. But we had to act as if it were very hot. Well, in order to make us feel that it was that hot, John wore a T-shirt and shorts while he directed us."

Now I had a great answer: an anecdote I could use in the piece.

Never settle for single words or phrases instead of examples. It's the old saw: *Show, don't tell*. While writing a story on baseball trainers, I interviewed the trainer for the St. Louis Cardinals. I asked him how he felt the first time he had to go out on the field to minister to one of his injured players. He said, "Nervous." That didn't really help me much, so I asked him to describe the situation. I got this:

"It was a televised Game of the Week, and what I didn't know was that our shortstop and second baseman got together and decided to play a little joke on me because they knew how nervous I was. So, they faked an injury and I ran out there, in front of all those people, and my hands were shaking so much that I couldn't get my fingers on that little red thread that opens the Band-Aid."

Now I had a visual, an anecdote, that I could use and that the reader could identify with.

Beginning interviewers often neglect to ask follow-up questions. For one of my class exercises, I brought in a friend of mine—a television commercial producer—to be interviewed. I thought she led an interesting enough life to provide good material for the class. The first questioner asked her what she liked about her job, and she said, "Well, one day I can be traveling through Europe shooting a commercial, and the next day I can be working with Frank Sinatra."

A great start, I thought, but during the next hour, not one person asked what would have been the first question out of my mouth after her initial answer: *What was it like working with Frank Sinatra?* This question probably would have elicited a host of interesting anecdotes.

However, later in the interview, someone asked her, "What was the oddest commercial you were ever involved in?" She answered, "We did a commercial for a financial company in which we had to have three elephants walk up Wall Street." Fortunately, this time the interviewer did ask a follow-up question, "What was that like?"

"We got the wrong kind of elephants. We wanted the ones with the big, floppy ears, but we got the ones with the small ears. So we made artificial ears and pasted them onto the elephants." Now, the interviewer had the makings of a great anecdote.

Be aware of what's going on around you while you do the interview, especially if you're writing a profile. What the person says is certainly important, but so is how she behaves during the interview, and how she reacts to what happens around you while the interview is taking place. Also, the setting itself might be important if it relates to the person you're interviewing. Details are important in any article, but they're extremely important in profiles. An interview isn't just made up of questions and answers. For instance, when I was interviewing actress and comedienne Brett Butler in the restaurant of a hotel in New York City, she asked a waiter, an older gentleman, if there was anyplace she could smoke. He pointed to a little alcove and said, "Yes, over there. That's where we put Al Pacino, when he wants to smoke. He puts me in all his movies." Butler said, "I can see why, you're so handsome." He smiled. I had a nice anecdote for my story. Don't be afraid to make notes about what happens during an interview in addition to what's being said.

Off-the-Record Answers

I strongly believe that everyone has the absolute right to privacy, which translates into the right to not answer any question. That doesn't mean that as a journalist you shouldn't ask, it just means that if someone doesn't want to answer, for whatever reason, that's her right and you should just move on. (If it's vital information, you might be able to obtain it another, indirect way, either from another source or from published information.)

However, there are times when someone will answer a question off the record, meaning she doesn't want the information or the quote attributed to her. Journalists can use the information if they conceal the identity of the source. However, in most cases, an editor will need to know where the information came from so it can be checked. (This is why there was at least one other person, besides Woodward and Bernstein, who knew that Deep Throat was W. Mark Felt. That person was *Washington Post* editor Ben Bradlee.) Journalists can also use that information to lead them to other sources, which might either corroborate or add more to the information.

If someone does want to go off the record, she'll often ask to have the tape recorder turned off. If you are still taking notes (and there's no reason you ought not to), do something to make it clear to yourself that those comments were off the record, so that when you come back to them later, you won't forget that they're not supposed to be attributed. I do this by drawing a box around the notes and then labeling them *OTR*.

Structuring the Article

Several years ago, I had a fellow in my class named Harold, who made his living repairing appliances. Harold took copious notes, and one day, after a discussion on how to structure an article, Harold came up to me after class and said that he'd missed something I'd said about structure. Looking down at his yellow note pad, I noticed that he'd made a schematic drawing of how to structure an article, the kind of thing you'd see on the back of a refrigerator or washing machine. I smiled and said, "Harold, if this kind of schematic helps you understand how an article is structured, that's fine. But the truth is, it doesn't work that way. You can't simply map out how every article is structured so that you have a template. If I could do that for you, or if anyone could do that for you, writing an article would be easy, and it isn't. There is no all-purpose formula."

Every article has a structure, but it's impossible to come up with a design that fits all stories. Every article has a life of its own. It's organic, and its structure depends upon a number of things, including the facts of the story, the style the author decides to use, the tone, the magazine, the audience, and the creativity of the writer.

For her final article, one of my students decided to write about her upcoming wedding. One day, she walked into my office looking defeated. I asked what was wrong. "I have all this information and I don't know how to organize it into a story," she said.

I asked her to tell me some of the things she was going to cover in the article, and she proceeded to relate all the problems she had buying the ring, deciding who would be invited to the wedding, where they would be seated, and choosing the caterer. Listening to her rattle off all these stumbling blocks to wedded bliss, I realized she could structure the piece chronologically, using mock place settings for each part of the story, like the ring, the invitations, the seating plan, the dress. That was the breakthrough she needed, and she handed in a wonderful piece about all the problems that go along with getting married.

Another student showed me a draft of a piece she was writing on spousal abuse. She began it with the story of a woman who was badly abused by her husband: One night, while their children were sleeping upstairs, her husband severely beat her with a baseball bat. The next day, her husband visited her in the hospital and put poison in her IV, killing her. And then the writer went on describe the problem of spousal abuse in this country, citing figures and interviews with experts, along with a few other graphic examples. But her opening story was so powerful that I thought it would serve the piece better if, instead of telling the story all at once, she interspersed it throughout, thus infusing the article with suspense and holding the interest of the reader (*What's going to happen to this woman?*). That's what she did, and the article was riveting.

These examples should give you an idea of how difficult it is to define any particular structure for a magazine article. So many different things are involved in deciding how to structure an article, it almost becomes a matter of instinct or "feel."

One thing to consider when deciding on a structure is focus. As discussed in the section on query letters, focus or theme is of utmost importance in any article. You've got to know what your story is before you can tell it. The main story is the backbone or spine of your article, and without it, your article will lack cohesion, ramble all over the place, and ultimately fail. If you have that focus, that theme, that backbone, that spine, you can move away from it every so often, only to return later.

Another factor that affects article structure is voice and tone. Before you begin to write, you must decide on the voice and tone you're going to use. In large part, your voice depends upon the audience you're trying to reach and your subject material. For instance, if you're writing a piece on the latest cancer treatments, you want to use a very authoritative voice, one that reassures the reader that you've done the research and you know what you're talking about. If you're doing a piece for a young, hip magazine like *Jane* or *Rolling Stone*, you might want a voice with a little attitude.

Tailoring your voice to the audience and content of the article might seem difficult, but it isn't. Think about all the different voices you use in your daily life. You talk one way to your parents, another way to your friends, another way to your boss, another way to your boyfriend, girlfriend, or spouse. There are many voices available; you just have to choose the right one.

WRITE IN DIFFERENT VOICES

Imagine you've just broken up with your boyfriend or girlfriend. Write three separate one-page letters about this breakup: one to your father or mother, one to your best friend, and one to the person you broke up with.

When you're finished, you'll see how different the tone, language, and vocabulary is in each letter. This is because each audience is different and so, necessarily, is the point of view of the writer.

Finding Your Voice

There's a story, perhaps apocryphal (though I don't think so), about Tom Wolfe going down to North Carolina to write an article for Byron Dobell at *Esquire* on race car driver Junior Johnson. Wolfe was down there for some time researching the piece, but when it came to writing it, he was stuck. He called Dobell and told him that he was blocked, that he didn't know what to write. Dobell told him to simply write a letter containing all his research notes back to New York, and the magazine would find someone else to put the article together for him. When Dobell got the letter, he read it, took off the "Dear Byron" and the "Sincerely, Tom," and ran the story as Wolfe had written it. The story became the lead article in the book *The Kandy-Kolored Tangerine-Flake Streamline Baby*. And why was Wolfe suddenly able to shed his writer's block? Because he finally knew who his audience was: in this case, his editor, Byron Dobell.

The best way to find your voice is to figure out who your audience is, check out the voice of the magazine (every magazine has a range of voices, depending on the type of article), and then take into consideration the subject of your article. For instance, if you were writing an article about the latest medical breakthroughs in controlling pain, then you'd want to use an authoritative voice. But if you were writing an article on celebrity breakups, a snarky, sarcastic tone might be called for.

THE LEAD

The lead is perhaps the most important part of the article. It must immediately engage the reader's interest. It focuses the piece, acting as a guidepost or a road map as to where the story is going. The best leads draw a picture and actively engage the reader's mind. And once you've captured your reader's mind, once you've got him inside the story, you've won half the battle.

Because the lead is so important, writers often spend a good part of their writing time crafting it. Once you've come up with the proper lead, the rest of the article will come more easily.

The lead, which can vary in length from a sentence to a page or more, does several things:

- It sets the tone for the article.
- It focuses the reader's attention on what she is going to read about.
- It gives the reader the author's point of view.
- It brings the reader into the "world" of the article.

It's very important that the lead fit the publication for which the article is being written. No matter how good a lead might be, if it doesn't work for the magazine you're writing for, it's a failure.

When I was assigned the profile of Brett Butler, who was then playing a blue-collar, Southern, single mother in the hit ABC sitcom *Grace Under Fire*, I wasn't given much guidance from the magazine, *Redbook*, as to what the focus of the article should be. I went into the interview with a clean slate. What I found was an extremely bright, well-read, witty, urbane woman without children, who was definitely not playing herself on TV. This, I thought, would be the perfect theme of the piece, that Butler was very different from the persona she presented on television to millions of her fans. For the lead, I needed something that would show this, and I found the perfect anecdote when, after I interviewed Butler, I went to see her perform at the Westbury Music Fair.

Butler came out on stage wearing black jeans, boots, a green turtleneck sweater, and a black leather jacket. Her first line was, "I know. I look like a bouncer at a dyke bar in Mineola." With that, she took off her jacket, tossed it behind her, leaned into the audience (which mirrored her mostly middle-American, mostly female television audience), and said in a stage whisper, "I'm not Grace, you know."

Perfect, I thought. Not only could I relate this line to give the readers a sample of Butler's sense of humor, but I could use it to get right into the theme of the article, which would be that what you see is not necessarily what you get.

I handed in the piece, and a week or so later the editor called and said that the lead didn't work for them. "None of our readers are lesbians," the editor said, though how she knew that I couldn't be sure. "But what we're really interested in is her decision to get breast implants, which you mention in the piece. So, we'd like you to go back to her and get some more information about that."

And so, not without some embarrassment, I went back to Butler and sheepishly asked her more about her breast implants.

"That's okay, honey," she said. "I was on Barbara Walters a few weeks ago and she asked me and I wanted to say, 'Honey, I'm not the only one in this room with stitches.'"

My final question to her was one the editors wanted me to ask. This was a woman who had been in an abusive marriage (her husband had actually taken a shot at her with his rifle), who had abused drugs and alcohol, and who had been in a near fatal car accident—and the editors wanted me to ask her if she'd ever considered the health hazards of breast implants. When I asked her, she laughed and said, "Honey, wouldn't it be ironic with all I've been through if my tits killed me?"

I had to come up with a new lead. I remembered that Butler had been slightly late for our interview, and when she did arrive, she apologetically explained that she was going on Letterman that night and wanted desperately to impress him, so she was looking for just the right dress. "I finally found it," she gushed. "It's this polka dot number that makes me look like Jayne Mansfield raided Audrey Hepburn's closet." Boom, there it was: the perfect allusion to her new figure. I had my new lead, the editors loved it, and I presume that no one was offended by it except, perhaps, women with smaller breasts.

Once I knew what the new focus of the article was, I could write the proper lead. The lesson here is that before you can write the lead of an article, you must know exactly what the article is about, what the focus or angle of it will be. Then, you've got to come up with a lead that uses that focus or angle. Here are a few examples of what I think are wonderful and effective leads:

> Let's say you'd dropped from Mars into Palumbo's restaurant at Ninth Street near Christian in South Philly—only then would you be excused for not recognizing the paddy wagon of a man in the .38-caliber suit, bulletproof hair and shoes, plowing among the ancient tables like an icebreaker—*Jimmy! Howsa wife, Jim?! Izzat your boy? Helluva cop*

your dad was! Started on the force the same day as me, October 6, 1943! It takes Frank Rizzo exactly fourteen minutes to move the approximate nine yards that separate the bar from the Nostalgia Room at Palumbo's (dark-red lighting, framed palimpsest of Sinatra and DeNiro), to swivel slowly like a sixteen-inch gun turret in an *ack-ack* World War II movie about clearing the Japs from the skies—Frank is *solid* when he shakes hands with his fans, he *means* it when he looks at you, no wimpy liberal diffidence here, no computer-driven circumspections: *You're from the* neighborhood, *John? Whereja go to school? Vare? Southern! At last!* he says, throwing head back and flinging his arms wide: *They've sent me a live one!*

JOHN LOMBARDI, "FRANK RIZZO WITHOUT
PREJUDICE: THE RELUCTANT MELLOWING OF PHILL'S
ATTILA THE HUN," *ESQUIRE*, AUGUST 1989

Notice that Lombardi puts us right in the room with Rizzo and himself. Immediately, we are thrust into Rizzo's environment. We see how people react to him; how he reacts to people. Also, note the way Lombardi describes his subject: "paddy wagon of a man," ".38-caliber suit," "bulletproof hair." These are not random descriptions. Lombardi is very carefully building an image of a man who has always been associated with violence, who has lived and thrived in a dangerous world. As a reader, we know exactly what kind of profile we're getting here, because we know what kind of man Lombardi is writing about.

In the driving rain, 67-year-old Lucille Chasin left her first-floor rear apartment at 76 Horatio St. in the West Village. The "Mayor" of the usually quiet, tree-lined street didn't need an umbrella—she was protected from the elements by a body bag.

ADAM MILLER, "THE HORATIO STREET
MURDER," *MANHATTAN SPIRIT*, JUNE 23, 1992

Why does this lead work? Because in a mere two sentences we know exactly what kind of article we're going to be reading: true crime. Miller has cleverly and skillfully drawn us into this mystery, making us want to read more, in large part by creating a scene—something we can picture in our mind's eye.

It is New Year's Eve, and Rodney Dangerfield is down in Florida, coughing and wheezing his way through an act that—even on nights like this—is exactly fifty-seven minutes, or 325 jokes, long. It is not a pretty sight, even if you're a sucker for heavyset guys who perspire profusely. Rodney's face and scalp redden alarmingly with each strangled sneeze, setting off the gray roots in his show-biz-blond hair. His eyes, pregnant puddles under normal circumstances, now water uncontrollably. A few hours later, Rodney will check himself into a Fort Lauderdale hospital for a brief stay. But right now he makes no reference to his upper-respiratory distress. Rather, he rants on about the unfaithfulness of his wife, ("I asked her, 'Why don't you tell me when you have an orgasm? She said, 'Because you're never around'"), the stupidity of his girlfriend ("It takes her an hour and a half to watch *60 Minutes*"), and the harshness of his own childhood ("I told my father, 'I'm tired of running around in circles.' He got mad and nailed down my other foot.") He gets, he says on more than one occasion, absolutely no *reh ... reh ... respechchooo!*

Talk about your serious spritzing: Anyone seated in the first three rows of the Sunrise Theater probably could use a penicillin shot. And yet there is something riveting about the sight of Rodney, rolling with the twin punches of age and illness while firing off wicked combinations of one- and two-liners with impeccable comic timing, even if most of the jokes are shinier-with-wear than his suits. This is one guy, ladies and gentlemen, who knows how to work a rheum.

Now Rodney reaches his endearing exit line—*I can't wait to get the fuck out of here*—and the crowd is on their feet. Technically, their reaction is spontaneous. But like the fifty-seven minutes and the 325 jokes, it, too, can be depended on.

Charles Leerhsen, "Whatever Happened to
Rodney Dangerfield?" *Esquire*, May 1992

In this lead, Leerhsen leaves little doubt as to the kind of profile we're going to be reading. This is not a hagiography. Instead, it promises to be a warts-and-all picture of a man self-destructing. How can we tell? Simple. Take a look at the way Leerhsen describes Dangerfield: "It is not a pretty sight, even if you're a sucker for heavyset guys who perspire profusely." "Rodney's face and scalp redden alarmingly with each strangled sneeze, setting off the gray roots in his show-biz-blond hair." These are not the kinds of descriptions that lead readers to believe a piece is going to be laudatory.

The one thing all these leads have in common is that they're entertaining. They draw the reader in. And, in the end, that's what it's all about.

Sometimes, a lead can be as short as a sentence or two. One of the most intriguing leads I ever read was written by a student, Eugene White, and was essentially only two words: "Neon wept." This lead certainly made me want to read more, if only to find out what the piece was about. The next paragraph told me.

> The ever-growing puddle of antifreeze underneath the green four-door made it look like the little car was crying. Perhaps it was crying from the effects of the fireball that had erupted from under its hood halfway down the drag strip. Perhaps the strain of months of abuse finally made the poor compact break. No matter the cause … some soothing words and a small strip of duct tape on a radiator hose stopped the sobbing.

THE NUT GRAPH

After you've crafted your lead, the next part of your article is the nut graph. The nut graph, in essence, lets readers know exactly what the article is about (what the focus of the article is) and why they should be reading it.

For instance, you might be writing an article about the latest treatment for breast cancer, and so the lead of your article might focus on a particular patient and her experience with the disease. But your nut graph might give a brief history of breast cancer treatments, bringing the reader up-to-date on what you're going to be talking about in the rest of the article: the latest treatment.

The nut graph is perhaps the one place in the article where you can invert the old writing adage *Show, don't tell*. In the nut graph, it's *Tell, don't show*. Let the rest of the article do the showing. For instance, here's the lead of a profile I wrote of John Travolta for *Redbook*:

> John Travolta, one-time disco king, former sex symbol, star of *Saturday Night Fever*, wants to talk diapers.
>
> "I'm not as good at it as my wife, but I can do it in a pinch," he says, as he sits in the living room of his secluded rental house in the Santa Monica hills, tending to his new son. It's mid-afternoon, and in the background, there's a buzz as Travolta's household staffers—a cook, a nanny, an assistant—see to their chores. But the bleary-eyed actor, who woke up an hour or so earlier than usual today, presses on. "The diaper may be half off, but it's okay. He'll get through till the next time."
>
> Four months earlier, Travolta's wife, actress Kelly Preston, gave birth to their son, Jett. Now the proud parents are eager to offer

baby tips to anyone who will listen. In fact, for their interview with *Redbook*, they thoughtfully prepared a detailed "List of Helpful Hints." The diaper dilemma is number four.

Travolta continues reading: "'Sometimes the plastic diapers have tape that's hard or rough, and the edges can scrape the baby's leg. ...'" He stops. "We found a little red mark on Jett, near where the tape was, so we had to cover that tape with some surgical tape. And we thought, *How many other babies are being hurt by this?*"

"They didn't think of the consumer—you know, the baby who's actually wearing it," adds Preston.

Travolta jumps up, then disappears into another part of the house. A moment later, he materializes carrying a handy visual aid, then proceeds to launch into an animated, detailed demonstration of the potential dangers of disposable diapers.

I was able to use the list as the spine of the article, going back to it whenever I thought it was necessary. Now, here's the nut graph for the same article:

This is the same John Travolta who played the ultracool punk Vinnie Barbarino in the mid-seventies TV sitcom *Welcome Back, Kotter.* The same Travolta who starred in a series of megahits, including *Saturday Night Fever*, *Grease*, and *Urban Cowboy.* And he's also the same John Travolta who seemed to disappear from the face of the earth, sucked into Hollywood's black hole of lost leading men after a series of film failures like *Moment by Moment*, *Perfect*, and *Chains of Gold.* By the mid-eighties, John Travolta was a forgotten man. He stopped making films. He put on weight. His sexuality was called into question. Hollywood types mocked his interest in the cultish Church of Scientology. He seemed more interested in indulging in his favorite pastime, flying jets, than he was in his career. At least that was the word whispered by his colleagues and trumped by the tabloids.

But when Travolta "bounced back" in 1989, he did it big with *Look Who's Talking* and its sequel. "You're never out of the business," explains his friend and manager Jonathan Krane. "It wasn't as if John was missing. He was just waiting for the right picture to come along."

Travolta is set to star in *Look Who's Talking III*, but has turned down other work. The actor doesn't need the money—his films have left him very comfortable. And there's another project at hand. A labor of love. Call it "Bringing up Baby: Part I."

As you see, in this section of the article I summed up what the rest of the piece would be about: not only the resurgence of Travolta's career, but also his new role as father, which is something *Redbook* readers would be most interested in.

After the nut graph, I moved on to the heart of the article, which gave details of Travolta's life, both personal and professional. After that, I just needed an ending to the piece, and here again, I was helped by the list.

> It is nearly six o'clock, and Travolta is obviously slipping into a lower gear. Preston excuses herself to put the baby to bed. Travolta stretches out on the couch and yawns. It's okay. We're pretty much through The List now anyway, having covered everything from "natural cleansers and wipes with aloe" to "how to give your child a liquid antibiotic." But there is one "Final Note," which you can't help thinking about as you see Travolta lying there.
>
> "Try to sleep when the baby sleeps, if possible."
>
> Good night, John.

Tips on Style

As you read the following style tips, remember that there's at least one exception to every rule, and it's part of your job as a writer to find that exception and see if it works for your article.

- Be very careful about starting an article with a question. It's a mark of laziness, and it's often a waste of time and space, since such questions are usually rhetorical. If you're directing a question to the reader, the chances are *you're* going to answer it, so why not simply make a statement or, better yet, *show* it, don't *tell* it.

- Write the way you speak, but the way you speak on your best day, not your worst. Good writing is often conversational in nature, and I can always tell when a writer is using words he wouldn't use in his everyday conversation. You don't want to give the reader the sense that you're carrying a thesaurus in your hip pocket.

- Find the right word. As Mark Twain once said, "The difference between the almost right word and the right word is really a large matter—it's the difference between the lightning bug and the lightning." As a writer, it's your job to be precise, especially when it comes to language. Take the time to find the right word, not one that just approximates what you're trying to say.

- Do your research carefully. If readers or editors pick up mistakes in your work, no matter how well written it is, your conclusions won't be trusted.

- Be authentic. Readers can tell a phony, someone who puts on airs. Occasionally, I'll come across an article that makes me think the writer is either full of himself or, to put it bluntly, a pompous ass. Remember, you represent yourself in everything you write. If the reader doesn't like you, the narrator (or worse, if he mistrusts you), you'll lose all credibility.

- Don't mix metaphors. Be consistent. Take a look at the lead by John Lombardi. Notice that all his metaphors make the same aggressive, violent associations: "paddy wagon of a man," ".38-caliber suit," "bulletproof hair," "swivel slowly like a sixteen-inch gun turret in an *ack-ack* World War II movie ..."

- Be alert for words and phrases that have taken a pounding; i.e., clichés. Some clichés have now lost all meaning from overuse. In every case, there's a better, tighter, fresher way to say what you want to say. And it's your job as a writer to find that way.

A Roundup: Types of Articles

Some of the most popular article types are:

1. service pieces
2. profiles
3. participatory pieces
4. investigative pieces
5. personal essays/op-ed pieces

Personal essays and op-ed pieces are discussed in chapter two. Investigative pieces use the same skills as any of the other articles discussed in this chapter, and are structured in much the same way as any other type of article. Following is a discussion of service pieces, profiles, and participatory pieces—the kinds of articles you're most likely to work on—and a few tips on how to write them.

SERVICE PIECES

Service pieces are the easiest articles to write, primarily because they are straightforward and focused by nature. Essentially, they fall into three categories:

1. how to do something (cooking, gardening, and home improvement)
2. where to find something (shopping or travel)
3. how to deal with something (health and fitness)

Ideas for service pieces are usually plentiful, and they often come from your own experiences. For instance, students in my classes have come up with ideas like where to take a nap on campus; the best water fountains on campus; body modification, branding and scarification (the student who came up with this idea went well beyond the call of duty and actually had herself branded to see what the experience would be like); the best bars near campus; the best happy hours; the best quickly prepared meals; how to change a tire.

Service pieces are usually easy to structure. You start out with an introduction, in which you explain the service you're writing about and how you obtained your information. For instance, if you were writing a piece on how to buy a used car, you'd have to let the reader know who is acting as your expert. Then, once you've established that, go right into the heart of the piece, which is primarily informational.

Nevertheless, you still have to establish voice and tone—to me, the best service pieces are also entertaining, but not so entertaining that they lose sight of the main purpose of the article: to impart useful information.

Here are excerpts from a service piece by a former graduate student at the S.I. Newhouse School of Public Communications at Syracuse University:

BODY WASHES By Nicole Tucker

As you wander through the supermarket, trying to avoid items that are not on your shopping list, your fickle eye will probably light upon the numerous and colorful pastel bottles of body products in aisle 2A. Soap is a necessity, and many products are economically priced under five dollars—by all means, transform your routine shower into a fruity, aromatic experience. But you can easily be misled by revitalizing, herbal, fruity labels coupled with economy. Here's what you should know.

White Rain Zesty Guava and Tangerine Moisturizing Body Wash (Refreshing Formula) will probably remind you of a sugary, orange-flavored brand of Hubba Bubba (my impression on first whiff). If scent is what you're looking for, you'll have to look a little further. White Rain's scent is not very strong, which could be an advantage (I was relieved) or drawback (if you are looking for that zesty guava and tangerine fragrance). After several applications, you will detect a faint hint of the product's scent. So, the guava and tangerine scent does at least show up for the shower.

Even without a strong scent, White Rain does have its appeal, and it won't leave you disappointed. What it lacks in a strong scent it makes up for with a strong lather—creamy, silky, and smooth. The lather goes a *short* way (the entire length of my 5'2" frame) with a small application. After the first application, you won't resist lingering in the shower longer than you expected.

Eventually, you'll step out of the shower feeling positive and refreshed for a reasonable price (about $2.19).

Suave Moisturizing 2-in-1 Body Wash: Passion Flower and Rosemary with Vitamin E (Herbal Care) sounds like a passionate shower experience, and with an initial whiff you will probably believe in the product's potential. I did. (We all make mistakes.)

Unfortunately, the shower experience is ruined by the exotic and sensual union of passion flower and rosemary, which in combination is reminiscent of some type of bathroom cleaning product, not an herbal body wash. It will assault your nostrils, as it did mine, if you even attempt to have the relaxing shower. A bar of Ivory would be a more aromatic than this herbal pick. Suave's lather is not rich, creamy, or smooth. More of the product is needed to keep the lather bubbly and to achieve that "squeaky-clean" feeling. Needless to say, you won't linger over this body wash or in this shower.

The only suave characteristic about Suave is its price (about $2.39). But you can be just as suave *without* using this product.

Caress: Luscious Nectar indulges your senses with its full-bodied essences that will wrap you in this delectable aroma every time you shower.

This body wash declares it strong scent from the moment you open the bottle. Even after you get out of the shower, the scent lingers in the bathroom. The fragrance is relaxing, rejuvenating, and scores high if you want an aromatic shower experience.

Caress's lather also scores high. The gel will produce a thick lather with only a drop or two, and will indulge your skin in a foamy, silky smooth lather.

Caress's price (about $4.29), strong aroma, and silky lather make this a great pick! My suggestion: "Before you dress, Caress!"

This is a good example of a service piece. It has a short, snappy intro that leaves no doubt what the piece is about, clearly setting the parameters of the article: body washes for under five dollars. And the author delivers, giving us detailed information about each wash, including the kind of lather you can expect, the scent, and the price.

PROFILES

The biggest mistake I see in profile writing is making a piece look like an extended résumé. When I read a profile, I want to know what makes someone tick, which doesn't necessarily mean that I need a listing of everything that person has done in her life. The most interesting profiles are those featuring nonfamous people (otherwise ordinary people who have accomplished something under difficult circumstances) or people who have led an interesting, unconventional life. After reading a successful profile, you should feel like you could pick the subject out of a crowd without ever having seen her before, simply by watching and listening to her for a short time.

Several years ago, one of my Syracuse students, Ryan Van Winkle, asked if he could write a profile of a streaker. I said, "That's fine, Ryan, but if you do, I don't want it to be simply a listing of his most memorable streaks. I want to know why he streaks, what motivates him."

A few days later, Ryan said that he'd found a streaker who was willing to be profiled, under one condition: "He'll only do it if I streak with him. Is that okay?" Mentally picturing headlines in the paper that read "Prof Urges Student to Streak," I said, "Don't do anything that's against your morals."

"No, you don't understand, I want to streak with him, I just want to know if it's okay in terms of the story."

I gave him the go-ahead. He streaked, and he wrote a terrific story, which he eventually got published. The article was terrific because, in fact, the author did get into the mind of this particular streaker; by the time I finished reading the piece, I knew exactly what made him tick, and I knew whether or not I'd want to spend any time hanging out with him. (The answer, by the way, was no.)

Here are some tips for writing a good profile:

1. Pick a theme. What's special about the subject? What is most likely to interest your readers? For instance, if I had been writing the John Travolta profile for *Rolling Stone*, my theme certainly would not have been John Travolta as father, but John Travolta as movie star. The right theme will keep the profile moving forward, and can also provide the conflict or tension that keeps the reader interested. If you don't have a theme, the profile will just flop all over the page.

2. Through your research and interviews, try to get as much insight as you can into what makes your subject tick.

3. Don't forget physical description, which includes the subject's wardrobe.

4. Be sure to get input from other voices—people who know the subject and are willing to share insights with you.

Here's an example of a 600 word profile that tells you everything you'd want and need to know about the subject:

GARBAGE PICKER BOBBY By Jeffrey A. Charboneau

It's a quiet Sunday evening in suburban Syracuse, New York, and Bobby G. is on the prowl. He slowly rolls his grimy Plymouth station wagon along Cedar Street, working the brakes, casing each property, panning for gold.

But it isn't an unlocked window or open door Bobby's searching for. He wants garbage. Between the piles of Hefty Cinch Saks bulging with moldy bread, used Kleenex, and rancid chicken bones, Bobby scavenges for broken radios, busted TVs, or any other I-can-fix-it castoffs he finds. And tonight, as always, the 'burbs are ripe for the picking.

"People say we live in a throw-away society, and I can tell you that's really true," Bobby says. "But what they don't know is that for every rich guy who chucks a busted VCR in the trash, there's someone like me waiting to find it, fix it, and sell it. That's how I make my living, and I'm not doing too bad."

Bobby has been picking, as he calls his profession, for close to five years. It all began the day he came across an armchair with two broken legs sitting by the roadside. He took the chair home and repaired it, then consigned it to a local auction house. He made $34 on the sale. "I couldn't believe how easy it was," Bobby grins. "Here I am working at Wendy's for five bucks an hour, and in like ten minutes I make as much as it would take me a whole day to make flippin' friggin' burgers. After that, I started picking full time."

Bobby shares this tale, and countless others, with the pride of a new entrepreneur cashing in on something the rest of the world has missed. Scrape away the chin stubble, scrub his face, and wrestle him into pinstripes, and Bobby could reasonably pass for a mainstream businessman. Make the suggestion, however, and he flies into a rage. "I could never be one of those bastards," he fumes. "They're users and liars and can't be trusted for a second. No, I'm better off right where I am."

Maybe so, especially considering how much worse Bobby could have ended up. High school dropout, street punk, regular guest of the county juvenile hall, Bobby didn't even consider trying to straighten himself out until he'd reached his early 20s. "I was never much of a boozer or a druggy, which probably helped me see I wasn't going anywhere," he says. "Then this guy whose house I tried to rob took a shot at me; that was it. I ditched my friends after that, took any job I could find, and started getting real. Now, any time things get rough and I start losing it, I just remember the sound of that bullet whizzing by my head."

That bullet's song has not kept Bobby's straight road completely free from bumps and curves. He can recount at least a half-dozen dead-end jobs leading up to his stint at Wendy's, none lasting much more than a year. Today, at 31, he's the father of two, husband of none, and, at the moment, a filthy figure shrouded by dusk, scratching out an existence from the discards of traditional American life.

"Some people won't believe it, but I like my life," he says. "I have a place to live; I have a car; I've got money—maybe not a lot, but enough; and I make a living without having anyone telling me what to do.

"I like to think of picking as a treasure hunt. The only difference is that instead of people wanting to watch me, they try not to notice."

Notice how, in only six hundred words, Charboneau skillfully builds a detailed profile of Bobby, so much so that you could probably pick him out in a crowded room. We know that he's bitter; we know that he's easily enraged; we even know, without a detailed description, what he looks like. We know that he's been in trouble with the law, we know his marital status. Charboneau makes his theme very clear: He's writing about someone on the margins of society, someone who exists on the detritus that we hardly give a thought to, someone who may be seen but certainly isn't noticed.

PARTICIPATORY PIECES

In participatory articles, the journalist either participates in an activity and writes about it, or observes someone so closely that the reader feels like she is actually participating in the event. Participatory articles are among my favorite because they allow us, as readers, to walk in the shoes of someone else, to see how she lives. They provide us with a picture of what it would be like to perform a particular activity or job. These are the kinds of articles that George Plimpton made famous in books like *Paper Lion*, which chronicled his attempt to play quarterback for the Detroit Lions.

I've had students write about their jobs as waitresses, sales clerks at malls, used car salesmen. (Yes, one student actually convinced a used car lot owner to let him try selling cars for one day. The result was a startlingly good piece; the writer actually morphed into a salesman before our eyes—and yes, he did sell one car by the end of the day.) I've also had students who hung out at beauty parlors for a day or drove along with police officers at night. Playwright Charlie Schulman, one of the contributors to this book, wrote a wonderful piece (published in *The New York Times Magazine*) about the few months he spent working as a census taker.

Here are some tips for writing a good participatory piece:

1. Make sure you've got a storyline—a beginning, a middle, and an end. It's your job as a writer to shape your experience so that the reader doesn't just get a list of "what happened next."

2. Be sure to include detail, but not *every* detail. Detail should add understanding to the piece and work to move the story along. For instance, if you're writing about a day in the gym, it would be important to the reader to know how people at the gym—staff and patrons—were dressed.

3. Make sure you include the ups and the downs of the experience. If you're doing a piece about being a shoe salesman, include the periods of boredom (but write them, of course, in a nonboring way—you certainly don't want to put your reader to sleep).

Here are some excerpts from a participatory piece by one of my students:

A DAY AT COSMOS By Joslyn Matthews

I got to work at 10:40 A.M., which left me just enough time to put on my dirty red apron, fix my baseball cap, and remove the sweats from underneath my skirt before I punched in. In the hours before I arrived, the other three waitresses— Katie, Michelle, and Kelly—had thoroughly prepared for the morning shift. The bright yellow tables were wiped (it's hard to tell, but they were), the syrups were filled, and the prepackaged Paul de Lima coffee was poured and stacked five filters high. A safe bet says they had also served a handful of spare-change tipping customers, and had given five or six refills to Clyde, the caffeine-guzzling and often forbidding-faced cook.

After two years of employment, weekend mornings at Cosmos restaurant have become highly predictable. Each week's shifts run together, creating a composite picture of life as a waitress. But being a waitress is one thing; being a Cosmos waitress is quite another.

Today, it is manageable, even slow. It's too early for the juke box, and my co-workers are still groggy from the night before. A few customers are eating, most by themselves, reading the newspaper and drinking coffee. I tell Frankie, the other cook on today, that I like his gray T-shirt. He stretches, rubs his chest, flexes his well-defined arms, and grins wide. "I know what you like," he says. "Why don't you just say it."

I roll my eyes. My day has begun.

I have a theory: Only weird people eat at Cosmos. Even if they seem normal at first, they are really, truly strange, especially people who sit at the counter. In Cosmos, the customers and employees are only separated by the counter, so whoever sits there gets the best ear on all the gossip. They hear us grumble when someone stiffs us, they see us grab three dirty forks from the silverware bin before we find a clean one, and they watch us scrape all of the uneaten food into plastic buckets and throw the dishes in the wash bins. Sometimes, we include counter-sitters in our conversation. Other times, they jump in without an invitation. Most of the time, though, we forget they are even there.

If they listen now, they'll hear Katie complaining about the family at table six. It turns out to be a simple problem. They are Cosmos-virgins, and they don't know a few unwritten but pivotal Cosmos rules:

1. You won't get one waitress—whoever has time will bring you your food or fill your coffee cup or get you more to eat.

2. Waitresses usually don't remember who at the table ordered what, so to save time, they hold the plate in front of everyone and say, "ham and cheese omelet?" You must answer in the affirmative to receive your meal.

3. Everything you order will come at separate times, and home fries will always come at least five minutes after everything else.

I retreat to my classic response for this customer case-type: "Where do they think they are! Why don't they just go somewhere expensive?"

By 1:00 P.M., the pace picks up a bit. Kelly, Michelle, Katie, and I brush past each other with coffee pots and stacks of dirty dishes. Sometimes, in busy moments, four waitresses are two too many for the confined behind-the-counter space. The classic diner din is now in effect: chatter from the tables, the sound of dishes hitting metal bin, and a peppering of shout-outs from Frankie, Vivian, and George, the pizza maker. "Hot slices." "Order up." "Table nine; I said table nine." "Pizza for eleven." "Who has table eleven?" "Hot slices."

We take a quarter out of our tip jar to play the juke box. The usual rule applies: choose anything but the Spice Girls (no one even knows how they got on there). We decide on "Blackbird," by the Beatles, "Learning to Fly," by Tom Petty, and "Leaving Las Vegas," by Sheryl Crow. I fill drinks at the soda fountain and bop to the music.

I get home at 3:45 P.M. My clothes are heavy with the smell of grease and my pockets are light with not-enough tips. For a second, I wonder why I haven't found a cleaner, better paying, more normal job while I'm in college. But even at moments such as these, I know I won't quit.

I have another theory as sure as the one about the crazy clientele: The people who try to leave Cosmos always come back.

Joslyn has given a wonderful, bird's-eye view into what it's like to be a waitress in a greasy-spoon, college pizza joint. In details like how she's dressed, how the waitresses interact with the patrons, and even what they like to play from the juke box, we are brought into a world few of us inhabit. By chronicling a typical day from the beginning of her shift to the end, she has given the piece a beginning, a middle, and an end: The patrons come back, and so will she.

WRITE YOUR OWN ARTICLES

Practice writing different kinds of articles. First, write a 500-600 word service piece. Then try a 600-700 word profile of someone you don't know, keeping in mind that you must have a theme. Finally, write a participatory piece in 750 words or less, making sure that you've got a story line; i.e., beginning, middle, and end.

Conclusion

Like any other kind of writing, magazine writing is a craft. The more you study that craft, the more you work on that craft, the better you'll get.

In many ways, writing articles is the easy part. Selling them is the hard part. If you're faint of heart, easily discouraged, and shy about sending your work out, I can promise you one thing: You'll never get published.

Keep the ideas flowing. Keep sending them out. If your idea is rejected by one magazine, send it to two others. Persistence is the name of the game.

RECOMMENDED READING

PERIODICALS

Allure

Elle

Esquire

GQ

Glamour

Good Housekeeping

The New Yorker
Redbook
Rolling Stone

AUTHORS WORTH READING

Auletta, Ken
Gladwell, Malcolm
Jacobson, Mark
Lombardi, John
Talese, Gay ("Frank Sinatra Has a Cold")
Toobin, Jeffrey
Wolfe, Tom

USEFUL GUIDES TO WRITING AND MARKETING ARTICLES

Best American Magazine Writing, The. New York: Columbia University Press, 2005.

Brogan, Kathryn S., Robert Lee Brewer, Joanna Masterson, eds. *2006 Writer's Market.* Cincinnati, Ohio: Writer's Digest Books, 2005. An updated version of this book is published every year.

Ruberg, Michelle, ed. *Writer's Digest Handbook of Magazine Article Writing.* Ben Yagoda, intr. 2nd ed. Cincinnati, Ohio: Writer's Digest Books, 2005.

Poetry

by RITA GABIS

RITA GABIS is a poet and prose writer whose work has appeared in *Harvard Review*, *Poetry*, *The Massachusetts Review*, and other journals. Her poetry collection, *The Wild Fish*, was published by Alice James Books. A past fellowship recipient from the Fine Arts Work Center in Provincetown, Massachusetts, she is also the recipient of a grant from the Connecticut Commission on the Arts for poetry, the Peter S. Reed Foundation also for poetry, and the New York Foundation for the Arts for nonfiction. She lives and teaches in New York City.

Why Poetry?

When asked what the difference is between poetry and prose, poets will often tell you that a poem, unlike a story, can't be paraphrased or summed up. It may tell a story if it is a narrative poem, but there will always be at least one other layer to it that impacts the reader or listener in inexplicable ways. Why is this so? Perhaps, in part, the rhythm of the words in a poem creates a bodily response in the reader. We listen to or read a poem with our entire self. (This is why, at a poetry reading, you may find yourself swaying a little to the music of the poems you're hearing.) Even narrative poems that tell a story have an urgency to them that prose does not. A good poem makes us sit up and take notice. A short story or novel may take us on a roller coaster of highs and lows, but is never as immediate as a poem simply because we expect to live in the world of the novel for the long haul. We settle in. We meander through.

In a poem every word counts, no matter how small, how seemingly insignificant. There is no filler in a poem, no transitional passage that works mainly to orient the reader to a shift in time and/or a particular setting. In a memoir one might write: "It was spring in the orchard," and then go on to describe the orchard in a way that helps the reader understand why it's a meaningful place. The poem "Orchard" by H.D. (Hilda Doolittle) begins:

> I saw the first pear
> As it fell—
> The honey-seeking, golden-banded,
> The yellow swarm
> Was not more fleet than I,

The active "I saw" and the "first" in the first line give, right away, a sense of the poet as witness to an event. "First pear" evokes both seasonal time and more subtly, the speaker's age and experience. "First pear" is vaguely sexual, female. These initial lines hint at ripening and what happens after ripening. "Honey," "golden" and "yellow" resonate with heat and light and the sound of bees, of wings. It's not the pear that is important, it's what the pear means to the writer.

This is why poetry needs to be particular. You don't experience the world in a general way and it's your experience the reader is hungry for. When you step out your door on a fall day, you may say to yourself, "oh, a fall day" but you are experiencing it in a sensory, personal way. You hear a mower, the cranky one your neighbor is always saying he will replace. You smell burning leaves and also, faintly, the smell of burning plastic. It's a smell both sweet and acrid, and it makes your throat burn a little. As your foot hits the pavement you remember, suddenly, being a child and pressing a red leaf between two pieces of wax paper. That's what your reader wants and what the poem needs, not "It's a fall day."

In Sonnet XXX of her *Sonnets From the Portuguese*, Elizabeth Barrett Browning's last line is a wonderful reminder of the richness of the particular.

> I see thine image through my tears to-night,
> And yet to-day I saw thee smiling. How
> Refer the cause?—Belovèd, is it thou
> Or I , who makes me sad? The acolyte
> Amid the chanted joy and thankful rite
> May so fall flat, with pale insensate brow
> On the alter stair, I hear thy voice and vow,
> Perplexed, uncertain, since thou art out of sight,
> As he, in his swooning ears, the choir's amen.
> Belovèd, dost thou love? or did I see all
> The glory as I dreamed, and fainted when
> Too vehement light dilated my ideal,
> For my soul's eyes? Will that light come again,
> As now these tears come—falling hot and real?

If you are not used to reading sonnets and have never read any Elizabeth Barrett Browning before, think of how often your own love adventures have caused doubt and worry in your heart. Then read this poem again, using the feeling words as guideposts through the poem; "sad," "perplexed," "uncertain." The syntax Browning uses may seem foreign, but the situation of the lover in the poem is familiar. At the end of the poem, the tears that fall "hot and real" jump out at us, pull us into a moment that has dimension, heat, reality, and vitality. We feel the tears on our own cheeks. Better than any long-winded explanation could do, that particular description of the tears allows us into the heart of the poet. They are words that count.

Lyric poetry, to the ancient Greeks, meant a poem sung to the accompaniment of a lyre. A lyric could also be a poem that was spoken without music.

The main feature of the lyric is that it was and has remained a cry from the heart: personal, direct, sometimes guided by strict form, sometimes wild and raw. The Song of Solomon is a great example of this: "Let him kiss me with the kisses of his mouth: for thy love is better than wine."

The Greeks were not alone in the value they placed on poetry. All cultures, past and present, have their poems, their vehicles for capturing and expressing the history of the human heart. From the ancient Hindu Vedas in Sanskrit to the Navajo poem-stories from the Bitter Water Clan to the classical Somali poetry known as gabay, nothing represents our commonality more than the need to communicate private experience and cultural inheritance. A poem carries within it our hope and our ghosts, our individual experience and our social history. A poem does this better than any other art form because it is a moment or, in a longer poem, a collection of moments. And that is the truth of the lives we lead; we exist moment to moment.

But the simplest answer to the question *Why poetry?* might really lie within you. Poetry usually calls to the writer. Sometimes it is as simple as the feeling *I have something to say. I'm not quite sure what it is. I'm going to try and say it in a poem.* Sometimes, after reading or hearing poems that make you cry or astonish you with their beauty, you finally buy that notebook or sit down at the computer and discover that the stuff inside you that needs to come out doesn't work in a story or a novel. You may not know exactly what a poem is (and that's the beauty of poetry—it can change; it should change), but you know you must try to write one.

This chapter will guide you step by step. All through the following pages, you'll hear me urge you to immerse yourself in the study of poetry. Don't wait until the end of the chapter to get the books on the suggested reading list. Get them now. Don't wait to expand your knowledge of poetic terms. A great place to start is www.poets.org, the Web site of the Academy of American Poets. If you don't have Internet access at home, go to your local library. In addition, subscribe to *Poets & Writers* magazine, which is chock full of news about contemporary poetry, and highlights opportunities for poets at different stages in their writing careers. Finally, the most recent edition of *Poet's Market*, compiled by Writer's Digest Books, is a terrific resource as you begin the process of submitting your poems for publication. Now, sharpen your pencil, take your phone off the hook (or turn off your cell phone), and dive in.

Structure and the Portable Poetry Semester

One of the great benefits of an MFA program is that it provides an instant structure for learning. Each week you have to attend a workshop, where you are expected to present your work and to thoughtfully, intuitively critique the work of your fellow students. Each week you attend a class on the craft of writing and/or a literature class, where you are required to immerse yourself in the work of wonderful writers—a class on, say, modern poetry, where you read T.S. Eliot, Elizabeth Bishop, and Robert Frost, and have to write about them, have to read their poems over and over, read *about* their poems, read what they themselves wrote about writing. Not because you are a scholar—though if you are, fine—but because any writing program worth its salt will insist that you immerse yourself in the work of a wide range of poets so you can learn from them. Reading helps you to learn about yourself as a poet: what language moves you; which poets make you laugh and cry and feel connected to time and life and change; which poets make you remember, in a rich feeling way, particular moments in your life (a first kiss perhaps, the birth of a child or the death of a parent, a visit to the dentist's office, an encounter with a moose or skunk or bear). Which poets make you say to yourself, *How did they do that? I want to do that.*

Reading helps you set the bar for yourself as a writer. It's part of a great apprenticeship that can, if you are willing, last your entire life.

An MFA program also gives you the structure of a writing community: a ready-made group of aspiring poets you can thumb through literary journals with, share your excitement about writing with, read poems aloud to. A group you can cheer with when one of you gets a poem published for the first time, and commiserate with when the rejections come in. It's with them that you can share the poems you are too nervous and uncertain about to take to workshop. It's with them that you can talk over the instructor's commentary that you just don't understand. And it's with them that you can go to the readings of your peers and of writers you admire. Sounds great, doesn't it?

Here's the flip side. What if you're shy and don't really get to know your fellow writers, and $40,000 later have had only two or three manuscript conferences with your busy MFA advisor—who, just like you, is trying to fit writing into a life that is full of other demands? What if your financial situation necessitates that you attend an MFA program while you work full-time and perhaps even raise a child? The structure the program offers may not adapt to a shift in your work schedule or to a sick kid who needs you at home. The community of your fellow students who gather after workshops and classes to hash over poems and writing and life may be wonderful, but if you have to race from school to the library or home to work on a paper because the next day you won't have time to study, you miss out on that community.

The interesting thing is that almost every writer who goes through an MFA program learns how to create her own structure only after school is done. The structure of an MFA program does not teach you how to work independently with passion and consistency. Many graduates of these programs stop writing. Perhaps their initial drive wasn't that strong, or maybe they developed another passion. It is the poet who creates her own structure who continues to grow and write and publish and thrive. And indeed, poets like Galway Kinnell, W.S. Merwin, and James Wright didn't go to MFA programs—MFA programs didn't exist when these poets were learning their craft.

From this chapter you will learn how to create a workable, dynamic structure for yourself as a poet. The steps outlined here are a template from which you can make your own structure. A semester in an MFA program is about eight weeks long, taking into account exam weeks and holidays. This chapter presents an eight-week program that, unlike an MFA semester, can be tapped into again and again. You can mix the order up or repeat certain weeks. You can use this chapter with other aspiring poets and form a community of your own.

Week One: Beginnings

One of my poetry teachers was fond of telling us, "Don't get it right, get it written." That is your mantra for this week. This is the week you open up your writer's notebook. You can create a file on your computer or write in an actual notebook. I suggest you begin writing by hand in a notebook and then transfer your jottings onto a computer later. Doing so allows you to travel with your work.

This is the week you begin to think, feel, and live like a poet. What does that mean? In some ways, the first week in an MFA program gives you, as the student poet, a feeling of legitimacy. Now, you are really a writer. There's something about registering for classes and even paying tuition (or getting the final paperwork for a hefty student loan) that can make you feel like it's finally okay to take yourself seriously, to "waste time" fooling with words, to imagine that eventually those words will be poems, the poem a book, the first book only one of several important efforts.

This is the week you give yourself permission to write. How? By making a commitment to work through the eight weeks outlined in this chapter, no matter how frustrated, distracted, overworked, in love, out of love, old, young, successful, talented, boring, complicated, pained, or joyful you are on any given day during this time frame. The beauty of a personal commitment to engage deeply in the process of writing poems is that it challenges all the negative voices in your head, the voices that say you're really not a poet; you're fooling yourself; you're boring; no one reads poetry anyway; what if you write something your lover, father, sister is offended by and hates you for; what if no one ever reads your work; etc. All of this commentary serves one purpose—it pressures you to close the notebook and walk away from your desire to write. The antidote to those voices is commitment to action. For a poet, for you, this is what action means this week.

DAILY WRITING

This week you will "stir the pot" by spending at least forty-five minutes each day writing in your notebook. Feel free to begin in the morning by recording a dream or snippets of a dream lingering in your consciousness from the night before. Feel free also to break up the forty-five minutes into increments: fifteen minutes in the morning, fifteen minutes at lunch, fifteen minutes in the afternoon, etc. However, during this initial week, don't do the whole forty-five minutes first thing in the morning unless you have absolutely no other writing time. Why? Because this is a week to learn about how you work creatively. Perhaps the morning is when your hand moves the most freely across the page (or the computer keyboard). But you might surprise yourself if you sit down at the end of the day when you're tired. You might find that writing energizes you, that things happened during the day you want to get down on paper, that being a little worn out actually helps you be less inhibited creatively. *Where* a poet writes can also be important. Perhaps the café you pop into at lunch has the perfect blend of noise and solitude, allowing you to be bold on the page and to work undisturbed. Maybe the bus ride in the morning or the quiet of your house after ten at night inspires you in a particular and surprising way. You won't find out unless you give yourself the opportunity to be a writer in different settings at different times.

Of course, how one works is always idiosyncratic. You may know right away, without a doubt, that you must always write at a certain time in a certain place, the coffee at your side, the window open just so, in order to be able to access your imagination. But life doesn't always accommodate our creative routines, so if you find your schedule is thrown off, use the disruption as an opportunity to explore the way time and place impact the words you write, the images that come to you, the themes that bubble up on the page.

Finally, the beauty of committing to forty-five minutes of writing a day is that it defeats the notion that you don't have time to write. I promise you that no matter how busy you are, the pursuit of a creative goal is within your grasp. You may have to do some extraordinary juggling with your schedule. You may have to give something up. You may have to make a demand on the people in your life for help with child care, or for some peace and quiet. But if you want to write, you can.

I have nothing to write about, we poets often complain. Or we find we return to the same material again and again without really breaking through to something new, risky, and surprising. This week, break new ground by free-writing (just letting the words come in fragments, lines of prose, or possible lines of poetry without trying to make them coalesce into an integral whole) about what matters to you, what sticks in your mind as the day runs its course, what piques your curiosity, what makes you uncomfortable. Write about what you saw, what you tasted, a conversation you overheard, a feeling of dread that came over you, a face on a subway that inspired lust or sadness, a memory that popped up apropos of nothing.

As you write, try to make your details as particular as you can, but don't worry about writing a poem or even using proper syntax. If a poem happens, great, but the object this week is to wake yourself up to the way you experience the world. You, with your particular history, your foibles, your dreams, your loves, your hates. You, and the route you travel throughout the day, the sounds you hear, the food you taste or long for, the sensory physical details of your daily life that stick in your mind. Perhaps on Monday morning it will be the red wig the woman wore on the subway that inspires you; and Monday evening, the feeling you had, hand poised over the answering machine, before you picked up a call. Maybe Tuesday you'll write about the ticket stub you just found from a movie you went to with an old lover; and later in the day, the sound of the swing set when you took the kids to the park.

If, after the first day, you find that nothing stuck with you, that there was no urgency or energy to your experience (even the experience of memory and fantasy), ask yourself why not. <u>You must care about the life you lead and the world you live in.</u> Writing comes out of your passions. If you don't bring passion to your poetry, your reader won't care about what you have to say. Sometimes what we need in order to wake up to ourselves is just practice. Here are seven suggestions to get you going this week. Some are writing tips, some are living tips to help you connect with your creativity.

1. Read a newspaper and free-write about something you find there.

2. Write a letter to an old lover. (Don't send it.)

3. Do a physical activity you've never tried before.

4. Say no to plans with someone who bores the heck out of you.

5. Read one of your favorite poems aloud five times, choose one phrase from it, and use it as a springboard for free-writing.

6. Look at family photographs. Imagine the photo that was never taken. What might it have revealed? Write about it.

7. Use persona as a writing tool. Choose either a stranger you saw during the course of the day or someone you know well. Make up (or remember) a childhood event in that person's life. Imagine how he would remember it or tell it. Write it down.

Walt Whitman is a great poet to read as you begin your daily writing for much of his poetry began as daily jottings in his notebook. There he recorded some of what he saw and heard and felt throughout his day, as well as what he imagined and what he wanted his poetry to become. In his actual poems you can find passages that are unchanged from a notebook entry. You can also see how much he worked and reworked other initial scribblings into poetry. Read this excerpt from the 1882 version of "Song of Myself," a book-length poem that he never stopped revising.

8

The little one sleeps in its cradle,
I lift the gauze and look a long time, and silently brush away flies with my
    hand.

The youngster and the red-faced girl turn aside up the bushy hill,
I peeringly view them from the top.

The suicide sprawls on the bloody floor of the bedroom,
I witness the corpse with its dabbled hair, I note where the pistol has fallen.

The blab of the pave, tires of carts, sluff of boot-soles, talk of the prom-
    enaders,
The heavy omnibus, the driver with his interrogating thumb, the clank of
    the shod horses on the granite floor,
The snow-sleighs, clinking, shout jokes, pelts of snow-balls,
The hurrahs for popular favorites, the fury of rous'd mobs,
The flap of the curtain'd litter, a sick man inside borne to the hospital,
The meeting of enemies, the sudden oath, the blows and fall,
The excited crowd, the policeman with his star quickly working his passage
    to the center of the crowd,
The impassive stones that receive and return so many echoes,
What groans of over-fed or half-starv'd who fall sunstruck or in fits,
What exclamations of women taken suddenly who hurry home and give
    birth to babes,
What living and buried speech is always vibrating here

There is a lot here for the student writer to learn from, but for now, notice specifically the list quality of the passage. It creates the illusion of the poet wandering through the world and simply listing, without forethought, what he encountered along the way. "Parallel structure" is the term given to the repetition of syntax Whitman uses. Use it yourself as one more option for your own free-writing. Finish the following sentences.

I saw
I heard
I carried
I followed

The slap of the door
The call of the child
The steps in the hall
The crowd on the corner
I witness
I stop by
I touch

Now go back and look, as we might do with Whitman's passage, at the juxtapositions you've created. Perhaps they begin to resonate as a poem-in-the-making. Maybe certain sounds start to repeat themselves in an interesting way. Maybe a theme or themes pop up unexpectedly as might be the case in this brief example.

The crowd on the corner parts for the blind man.
I witness the shuffle in his steps and turn away.
I stop by the roses in buckets on the corner.
I touch a gift I haven't given yet.

Go back and look at Whitman again. He is a poet of wonderful sounds; blab, sluff, clank, clinking. He also stands a bit aside from the world he depicts. Where do you want to stand in your poem? What does the world of your poem sound like, smell like, taste like? Maybe "shuffle" is too general a term in line two above. Maybe the blind man has a loose sole on his right shoe and it slaps the pavement each time he lifts his foot up. Maybe the roses in the bucket are wet from a storm, their scent a bit muted, their buds still closed tight. And the last line, "a gift I haven't given yet." Maybe the real story here is a gift that has not been received. I haven't given it, because I haven't gotten it. This may seem like a digression, a kind of poetic rambling, but playing around with image and line—adding, exploring, shifting—is what writing a poem is about.

WEEKLY READING

Is there a poet—one of the greats—you've always felt too intimidated to read? Emily Dickinson, maybe? Shakespeare, perhaps? Wallace Stevens? Li Po? Pablo Neruda? Make a list of challenging poets you've been too scared or lazy or distracted to read, choose one, and begin to investigate his work. Get a collection of his work out of the library or at a bookstore. (Relatively speaking, poetry is a bargain, and sometimes buying the book can be a great incentive to really dive in.) Begin with a single poem by your poet of choice, and after you have read the poem at least five times (preferably aloud), spend a good half-hour writing about the poem in your writing journal. If you must, you can break up the half-hour into ten-minute increments throughout the week, returning to the poem, rereading it at different times. Do this every week for the next four weeks, choosing a different poem by the same poet each week.

To be a serious poet, you have to be an active reader of poetry. You have to challenge yourself. Read what you love and who you love, but read also, as you would in an MFA program, writers who you might not initially be drawn to or "get." These poets have something to teach you. When you write about a poem in your notebook, say anything about it and everything. *I don't like this because ... What does he mean here?* Look at the rhythm of the poem. The structure. The line length. Take as much of it as you can into your heart.

Then, become a poetry detective. Read about the poet. (Do an online search about him.) Look up words you don't understand. Stay with this poet for the next four weeks, reading one of his poems each week, doing your detective work, and writing in your journal. If you absolutely hate the writer you start with, you may make a different choice next week, but don't give up too easily. If you only read poets who are "easy" for you, you may get in the habit of turning away from mystery, depth, deep feeling, complication, and conflict because they require you give too much of yourself—too much time, too much courage.

Just as you can share the eight weeks of writing in this chapter with other aspiring poets, you can also start a mini reading group. Read poems with a poet friend. Talk about them. Read aloud, loudly aloud. Puzzle over the poems, critique them, feel your way through your own response to them. What pulls you into the poem, what keeps you locked out?

Week Two: Writing Poems

By now, you've filled up several (perhaps many) pages in your writer's notebook. You've begun reading like a writer, like a student of writing, which you are and will always be as long as you write. Maybe the work of the past week has made you conscious of a few changes you need to make in your life so that you can better nurture yourself as a writer. Maybe you've begun to see ways you've been holding yourself back. Remember, commitment is the best antidote to fear. Commit to another week of hard work and delight in language. Make yourself accountable. Tell a fellow poet (or friend or spouse or partner or counselor or teacher) that you've decided to embark on an eight-week independent study. Tell her you want to check in weekly with her just to say you got the job done. If you procrastinate, ask yourself why.

DAILY WRITING

Again, write at least forty-five minutes each day. This week, it's best (though not mandatory) to work in one sitting each day in order to give yourself the benefit of extended focus. Your goal for the week will be to generate a poem from some phrase, image, or experience you recorded the week before. Begin by reading your free-writing from last week. Maybe you already have the bones of a poem there. Maybe you have a word or a phrase that you can feel contains energy, deserves further exploration. Maybe you wrote something last week that you now see was self-deceptive. Tell the truth in a poem. Each successive day this week, expand on the poem you began on day one.

If you get stuck, start again with another phrase, image, or memory you recorded the week before. Are you prolific? Do you find that you can whip off a poem a day, maybe two? There's nothing wrong with that, but this week, slow down. Stick with one poem for the whole week (or for most of the week). Add to it, take away from it. Replace a general phrase or detail with a more specific image. Note where the subject starts to feel daunting, scary. Go to that place and write. Continue even when you think the poem is done.

This is not a beginner's how-to-write primer (though a beginning poet could learn a great deal from this chapter). The assumption here is that you've read poetry and tried your hand at writing it, and now want to learn to stretch yourself as a writer, to write the best poems you can and develop strategies for growing artistically. When thinking about how a great poem comes into being, it helps to look at a great poem. Here are the first eleven lines of "After Apple-Picking" by Robert Frost:

My long two-pointed ladder's sticking through a tree
Toward heaven still,
And there's a barrel that I didn't fill
Beside it, and there may be two or three
Apples I didn't pick upon some bough.
But I am done with apple-picking now.
Essence of winter sleep is on the night,
The scent of apples: I am drowsing off.
I cannot rub the strangeness from my sight
I got from looking through a pane of glass

The movement of this poem is both inward and outward. Frost is writing about (and out of) subjective feeling states both physical and otherwise (drowsy, strangeness) and also about an external activity (apple-picking). In a way, all of poetry is built on associative detail. Each word generates the next. Maybe you begin your poem with apple-picking, or riding the bus, or a memory of your father smoking his pipe. Let your focus drift between both the concrete experience or person or detail to the stranger, more daring, and perhaps more resonant language of your inner life. How does one do this? One great way is to imagine, with each line you write, someone beside you, asking you to *say more*. When we look at these opening lines of Robert Frost's poem, can't we say that his willingness to say more, to keep opening up that initial impulse/image, is what allows the poem to come into being, allows it to move beyond the concrete to something with more depth and mystery? A ladder, a barrel yet to be filled, two or three apples that didn't get picked, winter, sleep, night—suddenly a world is created, the world of the poem.

As you say more, don't worry too much about the shape of your poem. That's for next week. But do push yourself to exhaust the impulse that begins the poem. Say more.

Was your first week of free-writing a bust? Have you hunted through those pages for the kernel of a poem, finding that nothing jumps out at you? Try this: Write, as Frost did in his poem about apple-picking, about something left undone. It could be something concrete, or it could be more elusive: an apology you didn't make, a good-bye you didn't get to say. Write every day about this, push your poem until the end of the week. Write past the feeling that you've said it all. Write through the self-criticism that what you're writing is stupid, weird, or boring. As you write, don't be afraid to veer off the subject, as Frost does (from ladder to strangeness in his sight).

WEEKLY READING

Remember to pick your second poem from the work of your poet of choice and read it, reread it, feel your way through it, puzzle over it. If the poem you've chosen has you stumped, take a leap in your journal and write down your wildest guess about the meaning of the poem. Because you're trying to take leaps in your own writing, see if the poem veers off a predictable course. Does it surprise you anywhere?

The beauty of staying with one poet over time is that you can get a greater feel for her use of language and the obsessions and themes that poet returns to. Emily Dickinson is often noted for her concern with death and defiance. Elizabeth Barrett Browning's love for Robert Browning enters into much of her work.

Are you frustrated by how daunting your poet is? Try this: Copy two lines of this week's poem and carry them with you everywhere for two days. Take them out during lunch, on the subway, while you're waiting for the dentist, and read the lines over and over. Read them until they are as familiar as an old shirt. Read them until you think you can't bear to look at them one more time. Then, when the two days are up, go back and read the entire poem again. You may be surprised at what you've begun to understand.

Week Three: The Devil in the Details

Why do poems move us? Not because the writer is explaining something to us, but because the writer is creating for us, showing us a part of his world. Sensory detail, images that capture and evoke your experience, are the primary tools you have to convey to the reader the feel of your life as a physical, feeling, thinking, dreaming being. Closely observed and felt detail has another benefit for the poet. Often the search for the right details allows the poet to stumble into the true heart of the poem. Searching for the right detail also tells you a lot about what you consider to be beautiful, poem-worthy, important. Some of the most fruitful work you can do as a poet is to challenge your assumptions of what is poetic.

DAILY WRITING

Below are seven prompts or springboards for your writing this week. (Yes, you should still be writing forty-five minutes a day, at least.) Use the prompts to start off your free-writing, and then move into poem-making if you can. Your emphasis here is on exploring and expanding your use of detail.

1. Describe a place you've never considered including in a poem.

2. Write out of a sound from childhood: your father's footsteps on the stairs, the slap of the screen door when your sister ran out to play, the shrillness in your mother's voice when she was angry.

3. Write about an article of clothing: the feel, smell, color of it.

4. Write about hunger.

5. Choose one object nearby and describe it as completely as you can.

6. Write about your hands reaching for something, touching someone or something or about cold hands in winter or how small your hands were when you were a child.

7. Close your eyes and think of color. Use the first color that comes to you as the starting point for your writing.

WEEKLY READING

This week, focus on the details your poet of choice uses in a particular poem. What feelings do the details call up inside you? Why do you think the poet chose one sensory detail over another? Write about this in your notebook. For instance, if I chose the following D.H. Lawrence poem to work with, I might begin by copying the poem into my journal.

PIANO

Softly, in the dusk, a woman is singing to me;
Taking me back down the vista of years, till I see
A child sitting under the piano, in the boom of the tingling strings
And pressing the small, poised feet of a mother who smiles as she sings.

In spite of myself, the insidious mastery of song
Betrays me back, till the heart of me weeps to belong
To the old Sunday evenings at home, with winter outside
And hymns in the cosy parlour, the tinkling piano our guide.

> So now it is vain for the singer to burst into clamour
> With the great black piano appassionato. The glamour
> Of childish days is upon me, my manhood is cast
> Down in the flood of remembrance, I weep like a child for the past.

Then I might make notes about each stanza; the *aabb* rhyme scheme for example, which makes sound echo through the lines the way memory does through the human heart. In the first line, the repetition of *s* in *softly, dusk* and *singing*, quiets me down, evokes the singing of the woman, the mother. Suddenly, I feel longing.

Moving to the second stanza, I notice the word *insidious*. I might actually look it up in my dictionary. I puzzle over its place in the poem. It makes the memory recounted in the first stanza seem somehow threatening, as if longing is a feeling that creeps up on one and must be guarded against. (What feelings do I try and keep at bay?)

For the last stanza, I might make a list of some of the words found there:

burst

clamour

great

black

appassionato

cast

flood

Looking at them plucked from the stanza, I see and feel more clearly how the poet evokes loss of control. The past is greater, in the moment of the poem, than he is, than his desire to distance himself from it. It clamours for recognition. Is it the singer who is vain in the poem, or the adult who believes his adult concerns can drown out early, primary feelings of love and loss?

I might then play around with the order of lines in the poem. What if "I weep like a child for the past" came earlier in the poem? It would cheat me, as a reader, of a feeling of recognition, of having traveled through memory to a destination that is rich and satisfying. Where in my own poems have I hurried to make a declaration and in the hurrying, cheated the poem and my reader out of a fuller experience?

Finally, I might set the poem aside for five or ten minutes and then, without rereading it, write a few notes in my journal about the details that stayed with me. Which images do I remember? Which details call up other details in my own mind? How is the language the poet uses triggering my own creative urge to make associations, leaps? I might find that I keep returning to the word "boom" and even though Lawrence uses it differently in the poem, it might remind me of how fast childhood ends—boom, it's done. Maybe the "small, poised feet of a mother" (and why "a" mother, instead of "my" mother?) make me cringe a little. Perhaps my own mother was not so delicate and my memory of her less tender. Have I written about it? Do I want to write about it?

When you read poems, ask yourself what the event of the poem is. Then ask again and again. Sometimes poems infer, correctly or incorrectly, an event in their title; Frost's "Death of A Hired Man" for example, or his "Stopping by Woods on a Snowy Evening." Yet, as you read the poem, think about it, write about it. You may find that the true psychic or internal event of the poem has little or nothing to do with the title or the overt story of the poem. This can be useful in your own writing. Look, for example, at the following list of events:

>   birth of a son or daughter
>
>   death of a grandparent or parent
>
>   first snow (of the year, or in your memory)
>
>   a betrayal
>
>   fight with a sibling
>
>   receiving a gift
>
>   a failure
>
>   learning as a child to ride a bike, skate, tell the truth, lie

Choose one and, in your notebook, try writing not the story of the event but the details of it. First snowfall: cold, changed world, dark, soundless. (I'm stopping here, but you, in your notebook, can continue.) Something else is stirring in these details, something about the way the snowfall is witnessed, experienced, not the story of it, the fact of it alone. Sometimes we approach poems with the idea that if we have a great subject or event to write about, the details of the poem will flow easily onto the page. Often though, it's the details themselves that tell the truer story if we let them.

Don't be daunted by reading this attentively. It doesn't take any more time than reading more casually, perhaps more superficially. The payoff is great. What you notice about the way other poets use language becomes part of your own tool kit for making poems. If you don't read like a poet, you end up with fewer choices and fewer creative breakthroughs.

Week Four: Shape

How you shape your poems—the length of your lines, the rhyme schemes you employ consciously or intuitively, the way you break a poem into stanzas (or keep it whole), the punctuation you use (or lack of it), your choice of end-stopped lines or enjambment—all create a poem that looks a particular way on the page, that has a particular set of sounds and a unique tempo. The more you know about how the poets who came before you shaped their poems, the more innovative you can be with our own poems. In addition, by studying formal poetry, you give yourself the option of working with a traditional form yourself; a sonnet, say, or a sestina.

All poetry was traditionally oral, meant to be spoken or sung, sometimes accompanied by music. And today that tradition continues. Performance poetry, poetry slams, and rap entertain, delight, educate, and inspire many of us. As a poet, there are many ways to train yourself to be alive to form. One way is to get to know formal verse from the inside out. Reading a sonnet by Shakespeare is one thing; writing your own sonnet is another experience entirely. Struggling to find words that will match a particular rhyme and metrical arrangement allows you to live in poetic history, to feel the tension and frustration and perhaps joy and discovery of imagination constrained (or liberated) by form. Looking for a particular rhyming word may force you to make a choice you might not have made. Using a particular meter—iambic pentameter for instance—you may notice the rhythm of language in a completely new way. If you're one of many aspiring poets who haven't yet really looked at meter (from the Greek "to measure"), *The Teachers & Writers Handbook of Poetic Forms* and *A Poetry Handbook* by Mary Oliver are great places to begin.

DAILY WRITING

By now you've probably guessed that the focus for this week is writing poems in traditional forms. This week, using your *Handbook of Poetic Forms* (or a similar text) you will write a sonnet, a sestina, a pantoum, and lyrics for a rap song. (Rap contains great examples of rhyme and parallel structure. If you haven't listened to any, now is your chance. You might also want to look at poet June Jordan's work to see how deftly she uses rap to give structure to some of her best poems.) You may choose to revise a poem you've already been working on into one of these forms, or you may start each from scratch. Four poems, four forms of poetry. Don't cheat! Even if you find, halfway through the sestina, that you're struggling and that the poem is bordering on ridiculous, keep going. What you will learn by this is akin to what you would learn by looking at the engine of a car with the hood open instead of shut. You'll get your hands dirty. You'll see what drives the shape of formal poetry, and you'll become more aware of the way form is a part of contemporary culture.

WEEKLY READING

This week you have two reading tasks. The first is to take a last look (for now) at the work of the poet you've been investigating for the last month. Look at one of her poems from the vantage point of form. Copy the poem into your notebook. Write down everything you notice about its form (or the lack of it). How does the poet use rhyme in the poem? If your poet is a formalist, track how closely she is able to follow the form. Where does the poem deviate, even slightly, from the chosen form? This is important because all poetry is ultimately a combination of repetition and variation.

As you get to know formal verse from the inside out, you'll begin to see, hear, and feel more readily how even free-verse poets bring formal elements into their work. Form is part of every poem. By studying it and writing about it, you will bring more richness to your own work. In addition, you'll continue to expand your capacity to read like a poet: with joy, but also with intention.

Your second reading task is simply the reading you'll have to do to get this week's writing done. If you're not used to working in form, you may have to use another poet's efforts as a kind of cheat sheet. If the first form you choose is a sonnet, for example, you might use a Shakespeare sonnet as your model. Or, you might seek out an anthology of formal poems by contemporary poets and pluck a sonnet from that. The *Handbook of Poetic Forms* mentioned earlier provides an example of each form it lists. Read those or other examples, and write. Listen to rap and read liner notes, and write. Four poems, four forms.

Here is a sonnet by Wilfred Owen that might give you some ideas:

1914

> War broke: and now the Winter of the world
> With perishing great darkness closes in.
> The foul tornado, centred at Berlin,
> Is over all the width of Europe whirled,
> Rending the sails of progress. Rent or furled
> Are all the Art's ensigns. Verse wails. Now begin
> Famines of thought and feeling. Love's wine's thin.
> The grain of human Autumn rots, down-hurled.
>
> For after Spring had bloomed In early Greece,
> And Summer blazed her glory out with Rome,
> An Autumn softly fell, a harvest home,
> A slow grand age, and rich with all increase.
> But now, for us, wild Winter, and the need
> Of sowings for new Spring, and blood for seed.

The rhyme scheme of this poem is *abbaabba cddcee*. If you like, use this rhyme scheme as your own cheat sheet to start writing a sonnet.

Owen is writing about war—World War I, in particular. When you're trying your hand at formal poetry for the first time, it can be easier to focus mainly on getting the rhyme scheme and line length correct than to worry about subject. If you need a subject for your sonnet, think of a current event that you care deeply about. Scan the newspaper; perhaps use a headline as the first line of your sonnet. Don't worry too much if what you write doesn't make perfect sense. Explore the form. Play. You'll be surprised by the word choices that occur to you because you are forced to make a certain rhyme happen. Keep your efforts in your journal.

Week Five: What's Free About Free Verse?

This week your writing and your reading concern free verse, line length, and risk. You'll see how, in free verse, using one type of line may open up more possibility for you than another. You'll begin to understand, if you don't already, that you can be intuitive and innovative in the way you work with the lines of verse your poem contains, but you cannot be arbitrary or your poem won't coalesce, won't become dimensional—won't, in short, become poetry. Why? Well, the proof is in the pudding, so to speak. Look at a free verse poem you love, a poem you wish you yourself had written. How do the lines work? How do they begin? How and where do they stop? Notice what sits on the end of each line. For instance, here is the first stanza of "The River Merchant's Wife: A Letter," adapted by Ezra Pound from the Chinese of Li Po.

> While my hair was still cut straight across my forehead
> I played about the front gate, pulling flowers.
> You came by on bamboo stilts, playing horse;
> You walked about my seat, playing with blue plums.
> And we went on living in the village of Chokan:
> Two small people, without dislike or suspicion.

Here, perched on the end of each line, are *forehead, flowers, horse, plums, Chokan,* and *suspicion.* Whether you are aware of it or not, what hangs out on the end of the line catches your eye and your heart. Pound's lines end with images that create a picture; a person (*forehead*), a season of blossoming and instinct (*flowers, horse, plums*), a place (*Chokan*), a foreshadowing (*suspicion*). These images are nuances of meaning that gather force as the poem continues. You've heard poems characterized as narrative poems (poems that tell a story) and lyric poems (poems that are more condensed, perhaps fragmentary, less literal minded). However, all poems tell some kind of story, though not always a story with characters or a plot. A poem might be the story of a moment of consciousness, a discovery your heart made. The way your lines of verse are arranged on the page makes your story—the tension of it, the drama and mystery of it—more or less knowable to the reader.

DAILY WRITING

All wonderful poems are, on some level, a mystery, so you can't dissect exactly the impact a particular line break has, but you can begin to notice that there is an impact, that where a line is broken creates part of the beauty and magic of the poem. Of course, it's just not how a line breaks, it's how it begins, how long it is, how short. So, going back to the beloved free-verse poem you've chosen this week, rewrite that poem twice. Each time, make different choices in terms of line length and line breaks than the poet did, and study the results you get; feel your way through them. I might, for instance, use a stepladder line with Pound's poem.

> While my hair
> > Was still cut straight
> > > Across my forehead

Or an alternating long and then short line.

> While my hair was still cut straight across my forehead I played about
> > the front gate,
> pulling flowers.
> You came by on bamboo stilts, playing horse; you walked about my seat,
> > playing with
> blue plums.

You can see not only that the last image on each of the lines has changed, but that the shape of the poem has changed as well. The world of the poem is different in each version, even though the words are the same. When I use a stepladder line, I almost hear the three lines as a march. They seem very methodical and matter-of-fact. When I alternate the long and short lines, the poem picks up speed. The story seems hurried and blurred to me. I'm not sure what (if any) feeling the details give me. In retrospect, I can see that Pound's choices about line, though they might have been made quickly and intuitively, work for the good of the poem and for the details the poem contains.

Spend time on your rewrites of the free-verse poem you choose to work with. You may want to use your computer for this (rather than your notebook) so you can move lines around on the page easily. Experiment. Play. Read your efforts aloud. Go back to the original poem. Perhaps you'll discover that you disagree with a choice about line breaks that your poet made. Perhaps you'll be inspired to incorporate a choice he made into a poem of your own.

Every choice you make about the length of a line is risky because it forecloses another possibility. If you are always making the same choice—always, for instance, using short lines—it's safe to assume that you might also be making certain repetitive choices about image and subject as well. Change the line length; change the possibility of the poem.

Sound too simple? Think of examples of this from your life. Most of us are creatures of routine and habit. Is there a certain restaurant you go to every Friday because you love the Friday apple pie? And does that routine anchor you, round out your week and create anticipation by Wednesday for a specific pleasure that will be pretty much the same as it was the week before and the week before? (You can see where this is heading.) What if, one Friday, *you* made the pie, or went to a different restaurant and had cake? Where else in your life has repetition of the familiar created predictability? *But I like predictability*, you might be saying. *I like writing poems a certain way. I like using only short lines or long lines. I like eating only apple pie.* Ask yourself why. The anxiety created, the uncertainty you might feel changing the shape of your poem, can be very fruitful (no pun intended).

Your second writing assignment this week is to play with the lines of one of the pieces of writing you did in week three. In your first version, you might have a mix of long and short lines, some enjambed and some end stopped. Enjambment, if you don't know or have forgotten, is when one line spills into the next.

> While my hair was still cut straight across my forehead
> I played about the front gate, pulling flowers.

End-stopped lines are complete at the end of the line; they don't continue on to the next. Punctuation often appears at the end of an end-stopped line.

> Two small people, without dislike or suspicion.

Read aloud as you try different line breaks, listening to the way your poem changes. After you have written and read this first revised version of your poem, write two more. In the second try, make all your lines short, enjamb as many of them as you can, and remove punctuation. In the third version, let the lines flow long, keeping the punctuation of your original version. Has the energy of the poem changed? Do you see it differently, feel it differently? Often poets resist focusing on line breaks because they feel they somehow won't get it right. Let yourself have some fun with it. Becoming adept at line breaks is a lot like developing any kind of talent or skill; it takes practice, practice, practice!

WEEKLY READING

Even though you'll be challenged over the next four weeks with various other reading assignments, you should continue to read one of the greats for another month. You may stay with the poet you chose in the first week, or pick a new one for four weeks. Read one poem a week by your poet and write about it in your notebook. Continue your detective work on your poet, old or new. If you chose a relatively recent poet, perhaps you can listen to a recording of a reading she gave. Maybe a poem that stumped you in week one is starting to resonate for you. Keep reading, writing, growing.

Week Six: More About Risk

The great thing about being in an MFA poetry workshop is that you get a pretty immediate reaction to new work. If the reaction is positive, it makes you feel you're on the right track. If it's negative, you might feel misunderstood or you might have fresh insight into your new poem and see that you haven't gone far enough or taken enough risks. You not only have your fellow students as readers, but you have your creative writing instructor, whose work you might love and want to emulate. Even if you don't want to write poems like your instructor's, you might want to know some of what she knows, and you might be excited at the prospect of working closely with her and listening to her talk about the writing process and your poem in particular.

The truth is that a writing workshop, both inside and outside an MFA program, can offer the aspiring poet a great deal. Working in solitude with no feedback at all can be crippling for a poet, but working in a group also has its drawbacks. The time frame of a workshop itself, regardless of the personalities and proclivities of the instructor and students, can be inhibiting because, simply put, most of us like people to like our poems. In a semester of a creative writing workshop, you have an opportunity to share your work with others six or seven or eight times, perhaps. You want to hit a home run each time. Therefore, without even being aware of it, you may very well try and write less ambitiously, more cautiously, so you don't end up just bringing a mess into class. It's hard to get that home-run type of praise for a piece of work that is wild and mysterious and unformed and that remains so week after week. It makes you feel better to bring in a poem that has a beginning, middle, and end. And in fact, it might make your fellow students feel better or more inclined to praise you, because they can understand the poem readily; it's satisfying. (A bit like that apple pie on Friday.)

Of course, you can be your own inhibitor. What is writer's block but fear? Fear of failing. Fear of committing to a deep and perhaps private desire. Maybe you've never admitted to anyone just how much writing means to you. Maybe you've never admitted it to yourself. When you really care about something, the stakes are high.

This week, you will read your own work. Go back and read your writer's notebook, all of it. Pay particular attention to the poems and free-writing that you've done, but read your commentary on the other poems you've read as well. Read aloud, read silently. Read in several sittings or in one great gulp. Then reflect for a few moments on your life as you live it. What preoccupies you, obsesses you, haunts you? What, out of all the things that people have said to you, stays in your heart and mind? What have you forgotten that you wish you remembered in greater detail? Take a brief inventory of the essential themes of your life. When you are done, ask yourself what, out of that inventory, you have completely left out of your writing to date.

Too often, taking risks as a writer is interpreted as writing about a particular subject—sex for instance, naming parts of the body. Sometimes a poet feels she has taken great risk when she has loosened the floodgates of feeling onto the page: great rage, great desire, great grief, great joy. But what if for you the flood of emotion on the page is what comes easiest? Maybe for you the risk is in omitting the obvious statement of emotion (as in *I want him* or *she hurt me*) from the poem and instead quieting the poem down, sitting with the impulse of the poem and working with it in a new way. Here's another quote from Ezra Pound, from the third stanza of "The River Merchant's Wife."

> At fifteen I stopped scowling,
> I desired my dust to be mingled with yours
> Forever and forever, and forever.

There is great feeling in this passage, but there is also something else: the dust of life, one might call it; a sense of time that is evoked, not explained.

(*Forever and forever, and forever.*) The feeling comes across through detail and sound rather than through explanation or statement of feeling. Perhaps all the great feeling you want to illuminate the page with is really a cover-up for emotion that is less understandable. The certainty of powerful emotion can sometimes shut a poem down. The poem may rage or lust or mourn, but it may ask no questions, demand nothing from the writer and offer little to the reader. If you let *I want him* become *Why him?* or *Who am I with him?* or *Who am I without him?* you may create a new trajectory for your poem.

In a way, you can celebrate anything that motivates you to write poetry. But if you are one of those writers who feels certain, each time you write, that you know the subject of your poem and all the feelings you have about it, force yourself to shift your focus to what is unknowable, elusive, perhaps almost unnamable. Here are seven prompts you can use each day this week to help steer you toward greater depth in your poetry:

1. *The last lie I told ...*
2. *I was mistaken ...*
3. *Whatever it was, I've forgotten ...*
4. *I said it, but I didn't believe it ...*
5. *In the dream I was ...*
6. *No, what I really meant ...*
7. *When you weren't listening ...*

Week Seven: Time and Space

Your writing last week should have generated quite a bit of material, some of it coalescing into early drafts of poems, some of it still in a free-writing stage. This week, choose two pieces of that writing and experiment with the use of the stanza. A stanza (which means "room" in Italian) is a unit, a tool, a way of evoking time in a poem. How does a stanza do this? The brief pause between stanzas of a poem slows the reader down ever so slightly. It introduces, if only for a second or two, silence amid the words of the poem. That resting place becomes as much of the music of the poem as the words are. If you're writing formal verse, in which the stanza requirements are

predetermined, you don't have to consider as deeply that aspect of shaping
your poems. However, if you're writing free verse, you do.

Here is "The River Merchant's Wife," by Ezra Pound, in its entirety.

> While my hair was still cut straight across my forehead
> I played about the front gate, pulling flowers.
> You came by on bamboo stilts, playing horse;
> You walked about my seat, playing with blue plums.
> And we went on living in the village of Chokan:
> Two small people, without dislike or suspicion.
>
> At fourteen I married My Lord you.
> I never laughed, being bashful.
> Lowering my head, I looked at the wall.
> Called to, a thousand times, I never looked back.
>
> At fifteen I stopped scowling,
> I desired my dust to be mingled with yours
> Forever and forever, and forever.
> Why should I climb the look-out?
>
> At sixteen you departed,
> You went into far Ku-to-Yen, by the river of swirling eddies,
> And you have been gone five months.
> The monkeys make sorrowful noise overhead.
> You dragged your feet when you went out.
> By the gate now, the moss is grown, the different mosses,
> Too deep to clear them away!
>
> The leaves fall early this autumn, in wind.
> The paired butterflies are already yellow with August
> Over the grass in the west garden—
> They hurt me. I grow older.
> If you are coming down through the
> narrows of the river Kiang,
> Please let me know beforehand,
> And I will come out to meet you
> As far as Cho-Fu-sa.

Each stanza of the poem concerns a unit of time, but the space between stanzas also lets the story of the poem sink in. It gives the sense not only of demarcated time (*at fourteen, at fifteen*, etc.) but of time passing. This week, look back at some of the free-verse poems by other writers you've read not just in the last seven weeks, but also over the past several years. Read five or six aloud to yourself, noticing what the poet is doing with stanzas. Is he using some couplets mixed with three-line stanzas? Are there no stanza breaks in the poem? How does that affect you as a reader? Borrow, in part, if you don't have your own inspiration regarding stanzas, a shape one of those poets is using and try it out in two pieces of writing you want to work with. (Again, using a computer for this can be helpful.)

Finally, one more word about "The River Merchant's Wife," along with two more writing assignments to round out your week of reading and writing. I mentioned earlier that Pound adapted his poem from an original by the Chinese poet Li Po. (Actually, Pound adapted or translated his version of the poem from a translation of Li Po's poem by the scholar Ernest Fenollosa.) In addition to being an adaptation, "The River Merchant's Wife" is a persona poem. Pound writes out of the persona of the river merchant's wife. Persona and point of view can be great tools for opening up your poems.

This week, write a poem in someone else's voice. (The contemporary poet Ai uses persona to great effect in much of her work.) That someone else can be a character you make up, someone you see on the street, or someone you know intimately. If you need a way into your persona poem, begin with *I remember*. (Obviously the *I* is the persona of the poem, not you.)

Your last writing assignment this week concerns point of view. Rewrite two times a first-person poem you began over the last six weeks, changing the *I* first to *you*, then to *he* or *she*. What happens to the poem when you shift point of view? How does the story of the poem change? Does the feeling, the tension, the conflict seem to drain out of the poem? Or is some new energy injected into the poem by taking the *I* away? Make a mental note (or an actual note in your writer's notebook) to use a shift in point of view the next time you get really stuck in a bogged-down poem that you know has potential. In the end, you may not stay with the new point of view, but fooling around with it might very well crack the poem open.

Week Eight: Endings and Beginnings

You've now spent almost two months challenging yourself as a poet: growing, falling back, moving forward, questioning your commitment to creative work, and discovering that commitment in a new way. If you've skipped sections of this chapter, don't beat yourself up, but do go back to those sections. If you've avoided what seems too difficult (or not as pleasurable as writing your own stuff in your own way), go back and cover the ground you missed. You'll never regret it.

Own what you accomplished and what you put aside for later. Consider, as well, what parts of your life really contribute to your ability to live your dream as a poet and what parts of your life get in the way. Some things are beyond your control. You have to work. You may have kids. You have complicated relationships with other people. You have responsibilities in your community. But ask yourself the following question and write your answer(s) in your notebook: Are you still afraid to really give yourself the chance to write? Are you still afraid of failing, and because of that, are you finding reasons not to try too hard? If the answer is yes, consider what would help you to move beyond that fear. One option would be to start this chapter over. Right away. Don't look at the end of this section as an ending, but rather as a beginning.

In a way, that viewpoint is also useful when you work with the end of a poem. *How do I know when my poem is really done?* students often wonder. Many times, the best question to ask yourself about your poem after you've been working on it for a while is *Have I really started my poem?* Whether it's because of pressure to succeed in a workshop setting or simply because of a need to feel validated by having a finished product for all your creative efforts, you may find yourself much too eager to get the poem done, to wrap it up. You may ask *Is it done?* before you ask *What do I have here? What route have I not taken yet?* You may ask *Is it good?* before you ask *Is it authentic?* (Not authentic in the sense of literal, perhaps biographical truth, but true to the essence of who you are, of how you live in the world, of the secrets your heart keeps, of the lies you tell, the dreams you have forgotten, the miles you've traveled.)

The best method for getting to the end of your poem is simply to keep revising it until you have worn out the impulse (at least for now) to work on it. This week, you'll work toward wearing yourself out with a favorite poem you've written. In your notebook, write about your own poem: what you like in it, what you love about it. Write about what you remember in terms of the process of writing the poem. Did it come all in a flash? Did it germinate slowly? Did a specific memory or incident prompt it?

Next, rewrite the poem—saving your current version, of course. In your first rewrite, take out of the poem what you love the most, and then keep writing the poem. Yes, take out what seems to you to be the heart of the poem, the most important thing, and continue. In your second rewrite, go to the place in the poem where another subject or theme started to bubble up and you quickly brought the poem back to center. Go back into the poem there and follow the detour, see where it leads. Finally, for the third and last rewrite, begin writing from the last line of your poem. That's right. Forget everything that came before the last line. Make your end your beginning, and see what happens.

Print out all these versions and read them aloud. Put them away for several weeks and then read them again with a fresh eye. You may find that the version of the poem you like best is the one you used as a template for these revisions. But you may also find that a poem you thought was done had the potential to be much more, and that your work on it gave you an opportunity to push it further, to make it truer, more beautiful.

In poetry, as in life, endings are slippery—sometimes hard to define, sometimes unexpected, and sometimes so real and pronounced that you know, without any doubt, there is nothing more to say; the poem is whole. Read the work of poets you love and the poets you are coming to love with an eye toward the endings of their poems. One useful (if somewhat superficial) way to think about endings in poetry is to ask yourself, after reading a poem, if the poem left you with questions or if it seemed to sum everything up. Sit with the end of a poem and try to identify the different feelings the end leaves you with. Is it enough? Are you, as a reader, satisfied? Or is it like a conversation with a friend that ended too early? Are you hungry for more of the poem? Do you feel, intuitively, that the poet whose poem you are reading somehow didn't quite jump off the diving board?

There is no formula for ending a poem. If any instructor in a creative writing class ever tries to give you one, look at her with disdain. Through careful reading of other poets—all sorts of poets—and by revising and rereading your own work, you'll begin to get a feel for endings. You'll have a sense of when you've held back, when you've said enough.

Finally, because a poet's work is never really done, here are some questions to consider in your notebook before you begin this chapter again.

CREATIVE CHECKLIST

- What is the strangest thing you've written during these last eight weeks?
- What is the least finished?
- Have you looked at the beginning, middle, and end of your lines in your poems?
- Have you faithfully done your outside reading?
- Go back and read the first poem you tackled by that intimidating writer. Is the poem more resonant for you?
- What have you written that truly surprised you?
- According to your own eye and ear, how has your writing changed over the last eight weeks? Is it messier? Deeper? Worse? Better?
- And finally, how has your sense of yourself as a poet changed?

Publishing Your Poetry

Publication, for a writer, is both a validation of your efforts and also part of the creative process itself. A poem lives not only in the mind of the writer, but also in the mind of the reader. It is the writer's gift to the stranger, who will open the magazine or chapbook or anthology and stumble upon the words he connects to, identifies with, or finds beautiful, strange, musical, harsh, or revealing. Publication gives the reader the chance to make the kind of discovery that you've made reading poetry, that *Gosh, I always felt that way, but never quite knew how to say it* moment, or that *I never noticed that about the world before, but now I'll never forget it* moment, or that *Someone else has been through this—this love, this loss, this doubt, this rite of passage—and I am not alone* moment.

Perhaps you've hardly thought about publishing. Or maybe it's all you think about. There are pitfalls to both stances. If you recognize a bit of yourself in one of the following characterizations, use that recognition as an opportunity to enlarge and adapt your perspective on publication.

THE BASHFUL POET

I could never show anyone my poems. I write for myself only. Rejection would kill me. I write only for my circle of friends and family.

First, there is nothing wrong with writing solely for your own pleasure and having no interest in becoming more professionally invested in your pastime. However, sometimes a fragile ego and/or a need to minimize one's gifts (perhaps from a fear of letting your voice be heard, or from a fear that you've written something a family member or friend might take issue with) can inhibit you from putting your good work into the world. No one should tell you what to do with your poems, but if your mantra is *I'll never try to publish my poems*, ask yourself *Why not?* Make a list of everything you're afraid of about trying to get published. Imagine, for a moment, what it would feel like to see your work in print in a literary magazine you like.

Why shouldn't your voice be heard? Why shouldn't you be proud of your work and want to show it off? Why shouldn't you be strong enough to weather the rejections that will certainly come, and to persist until your work is accepted? Talented poets who resist publication sometimes say *Well, that's the messy world of poetry commerce.* I say jump in. Get your hands dirty. Send the work out. (I'll discuss how a bit later.)

If you're afraid that you've written something too personal, change a name in the poem. If you're scared that someone close to you will be offended by what you wrote, check out your intention in the writing of the poem. As long as you wrote the poem without the intention to do harm, most likely, no harm will be done. The writers who pen a vindictive diatribe against someone they know are never the ones who question what would happen if their poems got published. So, if you're asking, chances are no one is going to take offense at what you've written.

THE OVERZEALOUS POET

Everything I write is fabulous. I don't have time to read anybody else's work, even the work in the literary magazines I'm sending my poems to. My work is so good, I don't even bother to revise before I send it out. All my poems are in the mail, all the time.

There is nothing wrong with a healthy appreciation for one's own creative efforts, but publishing your poems ultimately depends on the quality of the work you submit. Focus on the craft of writing. Revise. Read widely. If you do this, eventually, as you send poems into the world, they will get published.

Check your motives. Is your primary goal to write the best poem you can? Or are you so keen on getting your work in print that the actual crafting of your poems seems like a secondary endeavor? Remember, you want the poems you do publish to reflect your best effort at the moment of publication and suggest your potential as a writer down the road. If you get a thoughtful comment from a poetry editor when a rejection comes in, consider it carefully. Not every comment an editor makes is useful, but those who take the time to say something about your poems usually have something of value to impart and believe that your work shows promise.

PUBLISHING BASICS

There are three main venues for publishing poetry:

- Publishing individual poems in literary magazines in print or on the Internet in the form of e-zines
- Publishing a chapbook (a gathering of your work that is considerably shorter than a full-length collection of poems)
- Publishing a full-length collection of your poems

Most poets begin their publishing efforts by submitting poems to literary magazines. The best way to choose where to submit your poems is by reading literary magazines and choosing the ones that contain poems you like. If a magazine contains poems you like, the poetry editor may have a sensibility—an ear for poetry—that is similar to yours.

Never pay someone to publish your poems, and try not to fall into the trap of sending work out blindly, anywhere, just to see it in print. Every literary magazine lists, either in print or on its Web site, guidelines for submission: the number of poems the editors like to consider, the reading period for poetry, and the policy on simultaneous submissions (sending the same poems out to different magazines during the same time frame). Follow the guidelines. Keep your cover letter brief. Never begin with *I've never published a poem before.* Keep a record of where you send your work, what you send, and how long it takes you to get a response. If you get a rejection, consider yourself a real writer. Rejection stories are famous among writers. Now you have your own. Eventually, if you keep at it, the acceptance will come.

Look in the most recent edition of *Poet's Market* for a comprehensive listing of potential publication venues for your poems. You might want to begin your publishing journey by choosing ten literary journals from *Poet's Market* that seem interesting. Now do your homework. Go to a bookstore or library that stocks literary quarterlies and journals, and seek out the publications you've selected. If you don't see them on the shelf, *Poet's Market* will tell you how to order a sample copy of each journal.

Beyond choosing publishing venues that contain poems you like, educate yourself about the relative competition you face when you submit to a certain magazine or journal. *The American Poetry Review*, for instance, receives many more submissions than a local college's literary quarterly. A national publication like *Poetry* magazine will be harder to get published in than a quarterly published by your local arts organization. You might want to consider starting locally, then slowly, as you accumulate some publication credits, begin sending your work to the many fine quarterlies that operate from different colleges and universities around the country. If you can't be bothered to read a copy of the quarterly or magazine you're submitting your work to, then don't send it there. Reading before submission is not only a courtesy to the editors who work hard to showcase writers they believe in, it also protects you from getting revved up about an acceptance only to find that the publication that took your work is only a stack of copied pages stapled together.

Always keep in mind, though, that there is a certain wheel-of-fortune aspect to publication. A poem you consider your best might get rejected out of hand everywhere you send it. Conversely, a poem you don't feel as strongly about might fall into the hands of an editor who loves it. So, acceptance or rejection, keep your solid work circulating. You never know when a poem will find a home in print.

Poets & Writers magazine and *Poet's Market* are the best resources for chapbook and manuscript contest listings, all of which have specific guidelines for submission. Most of the contests also have entry fees. The fees serve as prize money for the lucky winner or may cover some or all of the cost of publishing the winning chapbook or manuscript. How do you know if you're ready to enter a chapbook or manuscript competition? Well, if you've been sending poems you consider to be your best out to individual literary journals you love and have yet to get an acceptance, chances are you need to grow more as a writer before you're ready to invest in entry fees.

There are many more opportunities for publishing work as a chapbook than there are for publishing a full-length collection. One simple reason for this is that, typically, major publishing houses have a small poetry list—meaning they publish a limited number of poetry books each year. Smaller publishers often rely on state and federal grants to get their books off the press and out the door, and so also publish relatively few titles each year.

Chapbooks, on the other hand, are less expensive to produce, and can be a stunning showcase for your work. Every year brings a diverse array of chapbook competitions. The guidelines for each of these are often quite different, so study your entry information carefully. And, just as you do for individual publications, send away for sample chapbooks published by the publisher or organization you're submitting to. Chapbooks can vary widely in length. Some contain as few as eight poems, some as many as twenty-five. Sometimes poets create thematic chapbooks; the poems explore a single central theme—parenthood perhaps, or the death of a parent. Important here is to remember that each poem should illuminate the theme further, rather than just repeat it.

Often, chapbooks are a kind of mini-sampling of what the poet's larger collection would look like. The poems in this kind of chapbook can vary in length and theme. However, any gathering of your poems, large or small, should not be arranged randomly or with a simple abstract notion of which poem should come first, second, third, etc. You could arrange your poems chronologically—in the order, say, that you wrote them, or in order by theme (poems about childhood first, then poems about adolescence, then adulthood). Try to think outside the box when it comes to structuring a chapbook or a larger manuscript. What images recur in your poems? What sounds? In the best possible arrangement of poems, each poem calls to the other, enhances the one that follows it and the one that came before. It won't matter to your reader that you wrote one poem last year and another two years before that. What will matter to your reader is the emotional resonance of the poems read singly, and then as a group. Think of the emotional journey the poems together make. A mature love poem might start out a collection that ends with a poem about a childhood betrayal.

A typical full-length manuscript of poems contains an average of sixty-four pages of poetry. Before you consider submitting an entire book for publication, ask yourself if you are truly satisfied with the work you've gathered together.

Scrutinize it. Read it aloud. Share it with poet friends, fellow writers. It's not unusual for poets to realize, once they've looked carefully at their book-in-the-making, that a good third of it is mediocre. Don't be afraid to put work aside for the new poems that will make your manuscript a standout and really represent the breadth of your talent.

Finally, consider the fact that creating a book of poetry, as opposed to just writing individual poems, is a whole art in and of itself. A commitment to reading like a poet (as illustrated throughout this chapter) will help you tremendously when you're ready to start putting a book together. You'll find that you have the reading muscle to look at the way whole books of poetry by the writers you love are put together. Just as you did with individual poems, make notes in your journal about the themes a particular book considers, the way the structure of the book impacts you as a reader, the poems you feel the writer might have left out, or the poems that seem to be the central poems of the manuscript. Go to poetry readings whenever you can. Be bold and ask the featured poet after the reading how his first book came to be. You might be surprised by how willing the poet is to share his story with you.

Aspire! Expect greatness from yourself. Do the work, of course. But dream big, always. Imagine your book in the hands of a reader. Eventually, it will be there.

RECOMMENDED READING

Ferguson, Margaret, Mary Jo Salter, Jon Stallworthy, eds. *The Norton Anthology of Poetry*. 5th ed. New York: W.W. Norton, 2005.

Hass, Robert. *Twentieth-Century Pleasures: Prose on Poetry*. New York: Ecco Press, 1984.

McClatchy, J.D., ed. *The Vintage Book of Contemporary World Poetry*. New York: Vintage Books, 1996.

Oliver, Mary. *A Poetry Handbook*. San Diego: Harcourt Brace & Co., 1994.

Padgett, Ron, ed. *The Teachers & Writers Handbook of Poetic Forms*. 2nd ed. New York: Teachers & Writers Collaborative, 2000.

The University of Michigan Press publishes a series called Poets on Poetry. Books in this series are invaluable reading for the aspiring poet.

234

Playwriting

by CHARLIE SCHULMAN

CHARLIE SCHULMAN received an MFA in playwriting and screenwriting from the Dramatic Writing Program at the Tisch School of the Arts, New York University. His off-Broadway productions include "Angel of Death," "The Ground Zero Club," and "The Birthday Present." His plays are published by the Dramatists Play Service and in several anthologies. He has completed a new musical, "The Fartiste," based on his original screenplay. He is co-founder and artistic director of the Drama Center, a theater company in New York City dedicated to new plays. He has taught at New York University, Spalding University, and the Writer's Voice at the West Side YMCA. He is a founding member of the New York Writers Workshop.

Introduction: A Good Play and a Good Class

I like plays that get to the point. They may luxuriate in language and poetry, dwell on nuanced aspects of characte, or revel in moments of intense beauty, pain, desire, or other aspects of the human condition, but they should not bore or be self-indulgent (perhaps the worst crimes a dramatist can commit against her audience). A play should also provoke, compel, and inspire. If it is unable to do any of those things, the playwright has failed. A play is not a history or an ethics lesson. If audiences wanted that, they would stay home and watch the History Channel or, God forbid, read a book.

All of this is easy to say. The real goal is to find a way to put these concepts together in an organic and fully realized way. This chapter is an attempt to engage, compel, and inspire you, the aspiring dramatist, to write an intelligent, entertaining play.

I have participated as a student in numerous playwriting and screenwriting workshops over a twelve-year period spanning high school, college, graduate school, and beyond. I probably learned something worthwhile from every one of those classroom experiences, but only two or three instructors have had any real and lasting impact on my own writing. These instructors instilled in me the value of craft and structure. Under their tutelage I learned how to develop a solid premise and to dramatize conflict. They helped me to consider different choices and to create compelling characters with a clear dramatic action. In short, they showed me how to tell a story that feels like it needs to be told.

Most importantly, however, their courses taught me to appreciate how difficult it is to write a good play—and the discipline that it takes to do it. Great plays don't appear out of thin air. Someone has to will them into existence. Over time, I have learned the purpose of revision and editing—and I have come to terms with the amount of work required to create numerous drafts. Writing a good play requires a relentless drive toward greater and greater clarity. You must sort the productive from the nonconstructive to make the play as fully realized on paper as it is in your mind's eye.

One of the many reasons to pursue an MFA in playwriting is that a graduate program can be a good place to learn the tools of the trade. There are many playwrights working in the theater who learned their craft the old-fashioned way: They read plays and saw plays, wrote their own, and found ways to get them produced without the aid of a graduate school education. However, a quick look at the top playwrights working in the United States over the past several years reveals that an increasing number attended MFA programs. What these playwrights have in common is a close association with a theater company, producing organization, or influential person who helped to bring their works to the public eye. An MFA program puts you directly and instantaneously in the midst of a community of peers and mentors all working toward the same goal as you are. A good program will also expose you to a variety of writing styles, methods, and approaches to mastering the craft of playwriting. Some instructors may be more experimental or language-based, others will have a more traditional take on story, character, and structure.

Making contacts and developing professional relationships are the best reasons for going to graduate school for your MFA. Connections help you to get your foot in the door, and then to stay in the room once you've managed to get in. But all the connections in the world won't help you in the long run if you aren't able to deliver the proverbial goods. Conversely, all the talent in the world won't take you anywhere without the necessary contacts. Some people have the ability to make connections anywhere they go. Other people can be at the right place at the right time and still come away empty-handed. The important thing is to realize that it is very difficult to accomplish your goals all alone. If you want to be a playwright, it helps to live somewhere with a lively local theater scene and to immerse yourself in that scene any way you can. The goal is to meet talented people with whom you want to work and who want to work with you.

Unfortunately, there are many MFA programs that do not foster such a collegial atmosphere: Political infighting between faculty members can often trickle down to the students. Also, there are some universities (I won't name names) in which MFA students in acting, directing, design, and playwriting have little or no interaction with each other. It seems against reason for these departments to be so balkanized as to deprive their students of the opportunity to form valuable artistic collaborations, but it happens far too often.

Whether you attend an MFA program, form your own theater company, or find a sugar daddy to produce your plays, openness to collaboration and input from others can help make your work better. Participating in some form of a playwriting workshop can help you to realize the play you've struggled with unsuccessfully on your own. Some playwrights thrive in the classroom because they feel creatively stimulated by feedback, appreciate having deadlines, and find themselves motivated by exposure to the work of their peers. The best programs provide a collegial and supportive environment in which the intelligent insight of others emboldens you to take chances and to grow as a writer.

Despite what I gained from all of the classes and workshops I've attended, I have always learned the most in the theater—from actors, directors, designers, producers, and other playwrights. Plays are not academic exercises: They are meant to be performed. In my experience, playwrights discover more about their work when a play is read out loud or performed in front of an audience for the first time than from any classroom experience or reader's comments. The audience is either rapt with attention or not. The jokes are funny or not. The drama is crackling with tension or not. The action moves the story along, or it doesn't. The characters are specific and believable, or they're not. Once you know these things about your play, you can begin the process of revision and focus more clearly on your objectives.

In the years that I've been writing plays and teaching playwriting workshops, I have also read numerous books on the playwright's craft. Almost all of these instruction manuals are helpful in one way or another. Many of them also tend to be wordy, repetitive, theoretical, dry, and just plain unengaging—ironically, not all that different from many bad plays.

In this chapter, I have tried to buck this trend by creating a simple, informative guide to writing plays. I have found that whether I'm teaching junior high school students or a graduate-level seminar, the same basic elements of drama apply. A good instructor—and a good playwriting guide—helps the playwright to identify her subject matter and guides her through the process that takes her from an undeveloped idea to a fully realized play. I've dedicated the following pages to providing the reader with just such assistance. After some general remarks about content and process, you'll find a step-by-step explanation of the different components that make up a good play, along with writing exercises and samples from students I've worked with over the years. I hope that you find them to be fun, engaging, and helpful.

Why Write a Play?

Before you write a word, it's important for you to consider why you would like to become a playwright. One reason to write a play is to change the world. Another reason is to make a million dollars. Probably the best reason is that you have a burning desire that absolutely no one can talk you out of to write a work for the theater. Sure, I would like to change the world and make a million dollars, but those are not the primary goals that inspire me. My goal when I sit down to write a play is to create a world with consistent rules of its own. This world must be inhabited by compelling characters and tell a good story that expresses my thoughts, feelings, insights, and opinions in a coherent and complete way. I want to create a provocative, entertaining, informative work of art that makes the audience laugh, cry, and contemplate the meaning of their own existence—no small task. While this journey can at times be thrilling, it is often frustrating and difficult. Having said all that, it's best not to think too much about it. Just roll up your sleeves and write.

For me, the theater at its best remains our most supreme art form and our greatest interactive medium. Precisely because it is flesh and blood, it lives and breathes. It gives us a sense that life begins and ends—that we are living it now, not alone, but in a world shared with others. Theater incorporates all the arts—poetry, dance, music, and design—and it has become the only place where texts can be presented to a live audience without electronic media or corporate sponsorship (though this is becoming rarer and rarer).

Some of the best plays I have witnessed or heard about were not performed in professional theaters. Instead, they took place in inner-city public school classrooms and community centers. Sometimes you can have a theatrical experience just walking down the street. One playwright I know taught a workshop to a group of disinterested prison inmates who leapt into action when he spontaneously suggested that they improvise breaking into a car. Once he had hit upon a subject that these students knew about and had a passion for, the experience immediately became collaborative, thrilling, and dangerous—like all good theater.

I have also discovered that plays are often well received when audiences have intimate knowledge of the subject at hand. This is why skits performed on the last night of summer camp almost always go over tremendously well, no matter how weak the material. The performers and the viewers relate to the shared frame of reference. Conventional plays should aspire to replicate this experience in the theater. The playwright must be able to relate not only to her characters, but also to the audience that watches the dramatic action unfold. Try to keep this in mind as you come up with a concept for your play.

The Subject

Unfortunately, it is impossible to teach content. The instructor can only make suggestions to help students make stock characters more dimensional, identify predictable setups, invent ways to reverse expectations, and avoid tired clichés. A play can be about anything, even a peanut butter sandwich, as long as that sandwich is highly personalized, imbued with a sense of urgency, and made more relevant than any other peanut butter sandwich previously known to man. So how does the aspiring playwright do all of that?

First of all, it's not really a play about a peanut butter sandwich—or about jelly, or about any other subject you write about, whether familiar or arcane. The sandwich play, like all plays, has to be about people—people whose struggles we can all relate to. Perhaps your characters haven't eaten in weeks, or are profoundly moved by the sensation of eating well. What would happen if you limited the availability of peanut butter? Perhaps there is only one sandwich, and everybody wants it. You might imagine multiple, competing interests creating obstacles to the attainment of this sandwich.

This is obviously a silly example, but it helps to illustrate how to set up an objective and an obstacle, thereby creating dramatic conflict—the primary ingredient of any good play. Now you can heighten this conflict by raising the stakes, pushing the conflict to its furthest believable extreme. You can also sustain tension and increase the stakes by making your characters' hopes and fears manifest in every scene. In the case of the sandwich, as obtaining it becomes more urgent, the consequences of losing it turn increasingly dire—thus making the stakes more and more personal. If the characters cannot attain this urgently pursued objective, their failure should have resounding psychic and emotional implications and, by extension, universal ramifications. Along the way there must be a few reversals and revelations. Someone has a deadly food allergy; someone else doesn't want the sandwich after all because she really wanted something else; a third person wants to use it to kill the person with the food allergy. Through these plot twists, the dramatic tension builds until you get to the unpredictable, climactic ending that, in hindsight, was inevitable from the start. Voilà! You have a recipe for a play about a peanut butter sandwich—or anything else for that matter.

The Premise

Once you've determined what your subject will be, ask yourself a series of questions to help develop this idea into a viable premise. What do your characters want? What are the obstacles preventing them from getting it? What are they willing to do to get it? When you think about your premise, you also need to consider why you are showing us these particular characters on this particular day. Why can't your play start a day earlier or a day later? The play should start on the day that something extraordinary or unusual happens in the lives of your characters.

Something compelling has to occur at the beginning of your play—something that activates your characters and sets up the ensuing actions and conflicts. This inciting event actively propels your protagonists toward what they urgently want or need. You must make sure that this objective (this urgent need or desire) is tangible, obtainable, and grounded in some reality. It must also be an objective fraught with obstacles that your characters confront and, possibly, overcome. Once you have set up this clear and simple premise, you have the basis of your play.

Topical subject matter often does not translate well into theatrical situations (with some notable exceptions, such as Tony Kushner's *Angels in America*). So-called issue plays tend to feel removed and didactic—or to have a superficial, generic, TV-movie quality about them—and are quickly dated. It's always preferable to write about personal stories that may have larger, more universal reverberations.

This is not to say that plays cannot be political: Some of the best political plays deal with intensely personal relationships that are microcosms or metaphors for larger social concerns. The plays of South African playwright Athol Fugard, for example, deal with race, culture, and politics while functioning on a very simple level that can be boiled down to familiar interpersonal dynamics—thus allowing audiences in New York, London, or anywhere else to understand what it was like to live under apartheid.

Theatricality

What makes a play theatrical and specific to the stage? Unlike film and television, which tend to be literal, theater remains a genre in which the well-placed suggestion has the potential to fuel the imagination. In the theater, change and transformation can occur right before our eyes without any tricks or pyrotechnics. How can you use theater's limits—the fact that everything happens live, within the "four walls" of the stage—as an advantage?

I first experienced the kind of theatricality specific to live performance at the off-Broadway premiere of Bernard Pomerance's *The Elephant Man*, which went on to become a huge Broadway hit, as well as a movie starring John Hurt. In an early scene of the play, Dr. Frederick Treves lectures to an audience of physicians about John Merrick, a man with severe deformities, while Merrick stands beside him, on display. The actor playing Merrick was not deformed at all, but was instead quite handsome. Treves speaks in detail about Merrick's "enormous head," "the huge bony mass like a loaf" projecting from his brow, which "rendered the face utterly incapable of the expression of any emotion whatsoever." As he did so, the actor playing Merrick slowly twists and contorts his body until he begins to take on the characteristics of this unspeakably grotesque and pitiful character. By the end of the monologue, the perfectly healthy, handsome actor transforms himself into the Elephant Man before our eyes—a brilliant device that made this monologue profoundly theatrical. This process influences our sympathy and identification with Merrick. It takes the authority away from Treves's seemingly factual description of him and forces the viewer to take the hideous Elephant Man's humanity into account. Later in the play, even when the Elephant Man appears repulsive, the memory of this opening transformation continues to remind us of his fragile humanity (as well as our own).

In one such scene, Mrs. Kendal, who has been brought in to help educate Merrick, reveals her nude body to him. As in Treve's monologue, this scene is particularly theatrical because the audience fully accepts the premise that Merrick is physically repulsive—despite the actor playing Merrick not being visibly deformed in any way. This adds to the dramatic and sexual tension in the scene: It allows the audience to more clearly experience both Mrs. Kendal's repulsion and attraction to Merrick.

This complex dynamic was entirely absent from the less successful, film version of *The Elephant Man*. In the movie, Merrick is made up with an absurd-looking, misshapen pumpkin head. In providing this visual reality, the film diminished the viewer's ability to sympathize and imaginatively project himself into Merrick's predicament.

When you are contemplating the writing of a new play, it is imperative to consider what makes it theatrical and specific to the theater. Why must your idea be a play rather than a movie or a television show?

The Process

Assume that a play will require several drafts before you're done with it (and it's done with you). Some people like to just start writing and see what happens next—allowing the play to emerge as it is written. There's nothing wrong with doing that, as long as you are willing at some point to take corrective measures. In all probability, some (even most) of your preconceived notions about the play will change while you are writing it. Sometimes you will go down the wrong path. There's nothing wrong with allowing new ideas to take you in new directions. It is important to write with a sense of urgency, but it is equally important to take the time to let your ideas develop and evolve.

An aspiring playwright once asked George S. Kaufman if he had any advice to improve his play. Without looking at the script, Kaufman replied, "Make it shorter." Like Kaufman, you need to be artistically ruthless. At any point you may be forced to make choices and sacrifices. When you make a choice that doesn't work, you can't be afraid to go back and get it right. It doesn't matter how long it took you to write a specific scene or section of your play, or how much you love a particular monologue or exchange of dialogue. Everything you write should be up for grabs, with nothing being untouchable. As the old adage about playwriting puts it, you have to be willing to kill your babies—willing to make the necessary cuts.

Some plays are easier to write than others. When you are very clear on the story and the characters, a play can take on a life and momentum of its own. Every writer lives for the play, story, or novel that feels like it wrote itself. However, most writers—even the most successful ones—have productive and unproductive writing days. It's also important to remember that everyone is different. Clifford Odets wrote *Waiting For Lefty* in one weekend. Henrik Ibsen would often think about a play for a full year before writing the first words. John Osborne once claimed that he only wrote seven days a year. Whether it takes you two days or ten years to finish the play you want to write, the ultimate goal is to make it the absolute best it can be.

Even for writers whose motto dictates that it should come fast and easy or not at all, it doesn't always work that way. But it's equally true that if you take too long, you can lose your initial impulse and get bogged down in an over-thought quagmire. Sometimes a play-in-progress takes on the weight of too many other peoples' ideas, or gets workshopped to death. Eventually you become aware of diminishing returns on your efforts.

Finishing is one of the most difficult moments facing a playwright. I once asked the playwright Lanford Wilson about this problem when he visited a class I was taking at New York University. At the time, I had stopped writing a play that I had been working on for a while. I was stuck—the play wasn't going anywhere, and I had begun to lose my enthusiasm for it. I asked Wilson if he ever tossed aside plays that he had been working on for a while. He sighed and answered, "Eventually I abandon them all." Sometimes playwrights have the opposite problem: For example, Maria Irene Fornes has been known to revise her plays all the way up until their final performance, and Jean Genet revised *The Balcony* well after it had been produced and published internationally. Usually a play is finished when the playwright tears herself away and moves on.

Keep It Simple, Stupid

Ever since a professor of mine once offered me these four words of wisdom, I've passed them on to my own students. This has occasionally ended up in some mishaps—as when a student in my class told me that he had taken my suggestion and "kept it stupid." *Keep it simple* doesn't mean to keep it simplistic or dumb it down, but to keep the premise urgent, present, and always clear. A good story is easy to tell in a few sentences. A bad story goes on and on, and we quickly lose interest. Complexity emerges out of simplicity and not out of a morass of complications. That is to say, the multilayered nuances of human relationships can be best fleshed out if a clear and simple premise is established. Romeo and Juliet are in love, but their families oppose the union because of a long-standing feud. Nothing could be clearer or more elemental. Emulate Shakespeare: Be smart enough to keep it simple.

Some playwrights say that they can't start writing a play until they know what happens in the end. That way, the entire nature of the exercise becomes something like a road trip. You have to get from here to there, and the important question becomes what route you are going to take and why. Even if you get lost along the way, if you know what the end is going to be, you can keep reorienting yourself and get back on the right track. And just because you know the end before you start, it doesn't mean you can't change your final destination while you're en route.

A playwright does not have to reinvent the wheel with every new play. My favorite example of this occurred when I used to teach an advanced playwriting workshop for a select group of New York City public high school students as part of a program offered by Young Playwrights Inc. As part of the class, I would wrangle free tickets to take the students to see plays, and I would often ask the playwrights to come to our class afterward and speak about playwriting. In one of these sessions, with the playwright David Henry Hwang, one of the students asked the question that everyone wants to know: "How do you know how all the scenes will fit together so that it all works out in the end?" Hwang unexpectedly responded that he finds another play that has a structure that would work well for his subject. For example, when writing his Tony Award–winning play *M. Butterfly*, he adapted the structure of Peter Shaffer's play *Amadeus*. The students' mouths dropped open at this stunning revelation. Clearly Hwang is an original and immensely talented writer. There is nothing hackneyed or shopworn about the plays that he writes. But even a great talent like his doesn't start from scratch—we all use basic concepts of dramatic structure to help us construct a play that works.

Once you have a good idea of your characters and a compelling idea for a play, you should do your best to write a first draft as quickly as possible. A lot of people can't write the first draft because they feel like it's not going to be good enough: The characters might sound alike; the story might run out of gas. The point is to push on through to the end and get a first draft down on paper. Writing a play, like most worthwhile endeavors, is a big leap of faith. Know that your first draft is probably going to have some weak spots. Don't let that stop you. You can always fix it later.

The Setting

The set of a stage play should be described in concise detail that best conveys the definitive production that exists in the playwright's mind's eye. Remember that theater is a collaborative art form and the description of the set is the playwright's contribution to what will ultimately reflect the director's and production team's concept for the production. My advice is to keep your description of the setting clear and simple so as not to leave it too open for interpretation.

The choice of a play's setting(s) is an important and often overlooked dramatic decision. Think of choosing the setting as an opportunity to help yourself out by selecting an environment that will introduce conflict and drive the dramatic action. Tennessee Williams's play *The Glass Menagerie* is about memory—so the walls of the family home materialize and disappear in a way that allows the protagonist, Tom, to step in and out of the action. When he is in the house, it is cramped and claustrophobic. The fire escape and the lights of New Orleans in the distance suggest a waiting and alluring world outside. The photograph of the father, watching over the household, activates the play's drama and infuses it with conflict. While the father, who abandoned the family years before the play starts, never appears in person, the photograph provides Tom and the audience with a constant reminder of Tom's desire to emulate his father and flee the unhappy family. The hovering presence of the absent father thus makes visible the shame and guilt Tom feels when he considers his responsibility and obligation to stay and help his mother and sister. Eventually, the father's picture also provides him with the motivation he needs to leave the family and lead his own life.

Craft and Structure

Instructors can't teach content—or talent for that matter—but they can help you to gain a basic understanding of dramatic craft. Like any other skill (say, algebra or crocheting), there are a lot of fundamental rules and concepts that you must extrapolate from and apply to your own work. Every play attempts to put these concepts together in an organic, invisible, and fully realized way, and some turn out better than others. The ultimate goal is to absorb and implement dramatic structure in such a way that it does not feel artificially imposed upon the play you are writing. There are exceptions to every rule, but only after you fully understand dramatic structure can you legitimately transcend or reject it.

There are reasonable arguments against traditional dramatic structure. At its worst, it can seem formulaic and predictable. Sometimes you can almost hear the wheels turning as the structural mechanics creak and sputter. But at its best, dramatic structure is a skeleton upon which to hang the flesh of the playwright's unique thoughts, feelings, ideas, and insights.

The notion of dramatic structure has a long history: It was first set down by Aristotle in his fourth-century B.C. text *Poetics*. Written more than a century after the great Greek playwrights Aeschylus, Sophocles, and Euripides died, Aristotle's *Poetics* set out the philosopher's observations on the elements that make a great tragedy in their works. For Aristotle, the most important component of a play was its plot, which he believed had to progress in a linear fashion in order to function successfully. Plays must, he believed, be whole and unified; they must be universal and comprehensible to all viewers; and they must recognizably imitate life. In order to fulfill these goals, the play must be structured as an evolution, with a clearly identifiable beginning, middle, and end. While Aristotle was not known to have ever written a play, these ideas about dramatic structure set the standard for traditional theatrical form for several centuries.

However, a number of influential twentieth-century dramatists rejected the continuing utility of Aristotelian dramatic structure. Many of these artists challenged traditional concepts of linear narrative with compelling, thought-provoking forms of theater. But traditional Aristotelian ideas remain useful for playwrights—even those who are interested in nonlinear theatrical forms. The success of plays and movies that break all the classic rules of dramatic craft depends upon the writer's knowledge of the rules that are being broken.

Elements of a playwright's craft—dramatic structure, character development, objectives and stake, etc.—are really just mechanisms for making sure that the audience follows the onstage action. Some playwrights today seem to feel that this craft is not worth learning. They view the idea of telling a story as hackneyed—they believe that all stories have been told before, or that character development and dramatic conflict are old hat. They may be right, but far from being innovative or iconoclastic, many of these playwrights simply fail in their task to compel, entertain, and provoke. Even a bad doctor had to go to medical school; anyone can be a bad playwright.

The exercises I provide have proven to be a useful tool to help students begin the play that they want to write and to clarify their plays-in-progress. Some of these exercises (the ones that may be difficult to understand) include sample responses, written by my students, followed by a brief analysis.

The Basic Elements of Dramatic Writing: Objective, Obstacle, Conflict, and Action

The playwright's primary job is to dramatize conflict, so the first step toward writing a play is developing a grasp of the basic elements of drama. Conflict stems from a character's desire to act on an urgent want, need, or desire, which is commonly referred to as the character's objective. This objective may be connected to a larger emotional or abstract idea—a desire for love or a sense of well being, a search for enlightenment. However, in order to clearly define the character's pursuit of his objective, that objective must be made specific and concrete. Once you have established an objective, conflict can emerge when obstacles are placed in your character's way. To put it mathematically, objective + obstacle = conflict. This formula is very simple in theory and can also be simple in practice—provided that you convey the objective with clarity and urgency. Unfolding events compel your characters to actively seek their objective in a journey known as their dramatic action.

Here are some familiar examples of objectives and their corresponding dramtic actions: Hamlet's objective is to avenge his father's death. His dramatic action is the pursuit of this objective by contriving to trick his uncle into revealing himself as the murderer. Romeo and Juliet's objective is to be together. Their dramatic action is the journey they must take in order to achieve this objective. Tom's objective in *The Glass Menagerie* is to find his sister Laura a gentleman caller. He hopes against hope that by achieving this objective he will finally be free of his mother's unreasonable expectations of him. Upon the realization that finding a suitor for Laura was truly impossible all along, Tom determines that the only way to be free of his family is to abandon them. His dramatic action is the journey he must take toward this realization.

Conflict is created by the interaction between a character's dramatic action and the obstacles to his objective. In real life, many of us are conflict averse, choosing to avoid direct confrontation. However, in the theater, playwrights who do not know how to embrace, build, and manipulate conflict—how to dramatize conflict—cannot succeed. The astute dramatist skillfully moves his characters toward a breaking point; and at that point, he reveals new information that makes further conflict unavoidable. This conflict builds to an inevitable final confrontation, which results in a moment of truth in which the character either attains or fails to attain his objectives, thus resulting in the creation of a new world order.

Dramatic action should not be confused with the physical activities onstage. A play can be chock full of compelling events or actions, but if it lacks dramatic action, eventually it will become stagnant and dull. Aristotle argued that the core of drama is the imitation of an action. He was referring not to a specific physical action, but rather to an internal, psychological need.

HOW NOT TO DRAMATIZE CONFLICT

Here are a few guidelines for what *not* to do when attempting to dramatize conflict. I have come across examples of each of these points in the work of beginning students, experienced playwrights, and even myself.

1. Do not write scenes, either long or short, in which characters convey exposition of past events without engaging an objective and obstacle in the present.

2. Omit scenes and characters that do not further the dramatic action of your play.

3. Stay away from scenes with characters who talk about offstage characters and events that do not relate to the scene currently taking place.

4. Avoid the trap of creating central characters who passively react to events rather than act upon the world around them. You do not want your main character to be a void at the center of your play—or to be surrounded by more interesting minor characters.

Character

How do you create characters that ring true? Often by creating characters who *are* true. Many of the best characters in modern drama are based on real people from the playwright's own life. Characters you know intimately are easiest to write about, for you know what they sound like and you know their behavior—even their irrational actions and speech seem believable and fully motivated. Sometimes it is easier to watch and listen than to invent or imagine. However, a character is rarely based on only one person. Many are composites of various people, or even combinations of real people, fictional characters, and the playwright herself. Most of the time, a piece of the playwright's psyche makes up some part of each character she creates.

If you want to create a fully dimensional character, it helps if you respect the character—even if this character is hateful. It is easy to dismiss a character you dislike and have already on some level dismissed. These characters tend to be one-dimensional and one-sided, whereas real people are complex and multifaceted. Our own characters are often paradoxical and hypocritical. You might like to think of yourself as good and virtuous, but do you always feel that way? Do you always behave that way? What happens under intense pressure and extenuating circumstances? For example, a man might be gentle and loving to his wife and children but act cruelly toward his enemies. Is this person good or bad? It is best not to stand in judgment of your characters. Instead, try to see them through your own eyes. How would you feel if you were in their situation?

As corny as it might sound, you have to love all of your characters—or at least try to put yourself in their shoes. I like to imagine that I am each character, and that someday I might find myself in a similar situation. Even if a character's feelings, thoughts, fears, and desires are completely abhorrent, the goal is to depict her as fully human. Otherwise, you are simply confirming preconceived notions. It is usually obvious when a playwright has an axe to grind or harbors a grudge against a character. Such one-sided representations are best suited for satire and propaganda, and flat characters are precisely what severely limits these genres. It's best to show a character in her full complexity and let audience members decide for themselves what to think.

Characters perform tasks and speak words to further the plot and to reveal their thoughts and feelings. If they do not serve these purposes, they should not exist in your play. Since drama boils life down to its absolute essence and pushes it to the furthest believable extreme, everything in a play should have a dramatic purpose. Nothing—not even characters—should be extraneous or arbitrary.

SENSE AND MEMORY

This exercise helps you to create believable, complex characters based on people you know by writing a scene that is inspired by an event in your life.

   I. Focus on an event in your life that had significant emotional impact on you.

2. Describe a single setting where this event took place in great detail, including everyone who was there at the time.

3. Jot down a few words to describe the feelings that thinking about this place evokes in you.

4. Put these feelings in the mouth of your character. Have your character start the scene with a line (or several lines) of dialogue explaining how she feels and why.

5. Have another character present disagree or contradict what your character has just said.

6. Continue writing the scene for twenty minutes. These characters are based on your memories of real people, but once they start speaking, they can say anything you want them to say. They are, in effect, becoming fictional characters rooted in people you know. Don't be afraid to allow the scene to go in any direction that it takes you. When you read the scene over, take note of which parts are "real" and which are "fictional." Can you easily tell the difference? Where did you feel the impulse to invent? What did that accomplish in the scene?

WRITE A MONOLOGUE

In a monologue, one character speaks for an extended time without being interrupted. The monologue may incorporate stage directions and the on-stage presence of another character who does not speak.

For the following exercise, create a character and a monologue for that character based on a photograph of a real person. You can use any photograph you like; I often use the provocative, haunting images of the photographer Diane Arbus. This exercise may not work if you use a photograph of a model, a famous person, or someone you know. The photograph is supposed to be a springboard to the imagination and should not be weighed down by facts that place limitations on creativity. However, this exercise also can be done without the use of a photograph at all.

I. Look at the photograph or imagine a character and answer the following questions. You can write down the answers or not. The important thing is that you know the answers and that you incorporate them in the body of the monologue. Your answers should be brief.

- Who is this person?
- Where is she right now?
- What is she doing there?
- How does your character feel about what she is doing there? Use one or two words to describe the feeling (e.g., *happy, sad, scared, angry, horny*).
- To whom is your character speaking? For the purpose of this exercise, make sure that she is speaking to another person. Do not have your character speak to herself, to an animal, to an inanimate object, to the audience, or to God.
- What does your character urgently want?
- What is keeping the character from getting what she wants?
- What is your character willing to do to get what she wants?

Take a minute to feel the feeling that you wrote down for your character. Give yourself fifteen minutes to write the monologue. Make it at least one page long. Don't censor yourself or cross anything out. Try to address all of the questions above.

After writing your monologue for fifteen minutes without stopping, incorporate the next instruction.

2. Have the character who is speaking reveal a secret that she has never told anyone else. The secret does not necessarily have to be earth shattering, but it must ring true. A secret often helps to make your character's objective more urgent and personal. Your character's dramatic action needs to intensify as she moves through the story. If the character's action becomes increasingly personal and meaningful, the dramatic stakes are raised.

Now that you have written your monologue, you have created a character with an urgent objective, a conflict, and a dramatic action. You are ready to dramatize this conflict. Take the next steps to imagine how this monologue, or parts of it, might fit into a longer play.

3. Turn the monologue into a dialogue. Add a person for your original character to speak to, and rewrite the monologue as a scene between two

people. Be willing to use some lines from the monologue in this scene, to throw away other lines, and to invent new ones as you see fit. The addition of the new person might take you in a new direction, but you will still have an objective, an obstacle, and a revelation. By the time you get to the end of this scene, you should resolve the conflict and introduce a new one.

4. Decide what would happen in the scene before the monologue. Who would be in it?

5. Decide what would happen in the scene after the monologue. Who would be in it?

6. Build a play from the scenes before the monologue and after the monologue. You may want to add new characters along the way. Make sure that each new scene has conflict, including an objective and an obstacle. Does each scene move the characters closer to achieving their objectives?

Constructing a Scene

As you learned in the last exercise, a scene is a segment of a play that dramatizes conflict and drives the action forward. Every scene has a core objective and obstacle. The friction created when these dramatic elements collide creates drama. When your character's quest for his objective is impeded by an obstacle that has been placed in his way, the conflict that results can be resolved in one of three ways: the objective is achieved, it is not achieved, or it is rendered irrelevant and superseded by a new objective. Whatever the resolution, it should spark a new dramatic question or objective for the next scene. The objective of each scene must be connected in some way to the overall dramatic action of the play and move that action forward.

The easiest way to think about scenes is to begin with the premise that every scene answers one dramatic question, then poses a new question that raises the stakes. The new dramatic question propels the action into the next scene, where it will be resolved one way or another and a new dramatic question will be introduced—and so on.

A scene also consists of numerous dramatic beats. These beats are not to be confused with a pause in the play's dialogue, which is also termed a beat. In this context, a beat is a small dramatic unit, several of which make up the scene. Actors often use beats to break down their character's overall objective in a scene into shorter, "actable" dramatic moments. These beats can consist of the various tactics used by a character in a scene to achieve the overall objective, and thus help to delineate the scene's shifts or moments. For example, if the objective of a scene is for one character to keep another character at a restaurant, the first beat might be ordering lots of food and wine; the second beat, seeking advice about a personal matter; the third beat, feigning illness. Each beat represents a different way of enacting the larger objective of the scene, allowing the actor to envision the scene as a series of mini objectives.

The playwright's approach to writing a scene can mimic an actor's, breaking a scene down into various beats. Often the dramatic beats in a scene come into existence naturally and instinctively, while the scene is being written, but it still can be helpful to be consciously aware of where beats exist. Doing so helps you to keep the overall objective of the scene in your sights and, later, to fine-tune a scene during the revision process.

Every scene must also contain dramatic tension—a condition that is created when a character confronts obstacles in pursuit of his overall objective. Smaller, individual objectives may be pursued in each scene, as long as they are connected to a larger, more important objective. In order to sustain this tension, the playwright finds ways of raising the stakes—that is, of making the character's achievement of the overall objective, and the consequences of not achieving that objective, increasingly more urgent.

One major way of magnifying the urgency of an objective is to make that objective more personal, specific, or necessary to the character's well-being. Establishing what is called a tension of opposites in a scene allows you to heighten the viewer's awareness of the character's reasons for achieving the objective (and the potential consequences of his failure to do so). This tension of opposites is the conflict between a character's hopes and fears, a conflict that should appear in every scene. Hope provides a tangible motivation that drives a character to pursue an objective. Fear is the palpable reminder of the outcome that would result from a failure to reach the objective. These two principles are always intertwined. As hope builds, fear increases—with the resulting conflict sustaining dramatic tension.

TWELVE LINES OF DIALOGUE

Write a short dialogue between two characters, following the instructions below.

1. Decide where the scene takes place.

2. Have each character speak six times.

3. Each line of dialogue must be four words or less.

4. By the end of the scene, the relationship between the two characters must be permanently changed.

The following sample, a student's response to this exercise, is a dialogue that takes place in a shoe store.

> **FEMALE CUSTOMER:** It doesn't fit.
> **SALESMAN:** What hurts?
> **FEMALE CUSTOMER:** The insole.
> **SALESMAN:** I fixed it.
> **FEMALE CUSTOMER:** No, you didn't.
> **SALESMAN:** Yes, I did.
> **FEMALE CUSTOMER:** I relied on you.
> **SALESMAN:** I tried to help.
> **FEMALE CUSTOMER:** Well, you didn't.
> **SALESMAN:** Let me try again.
> **FEMALE CUSTOMER:** I'm shopping somewhere else!
> **SALESMAN:** Good riddance.

This dialogue contains all of the basic elements of a scene. In it, you can identify an objective, an obstacle, a raising of dramatic tension, and, finally, a reversal. In this particular sample exercise, the author establishes a relationship between the two characters that shifts permanently at the end of the scene. This change results directly from a conflict that was created through the confrontation of an objective and an obstacle. In this case, the relationship of the customer and the salesman is established in the customer's pursuit of her objective. The customer wants her shoe to be fixed, and she has come to the person she expects will be able to fix it. The obstacle to the objective is that the shoe still hurts her foot after the salesman has worked on it. Tension is generated when the salesman insists that he fixed the shoe. The customer raises the stakes by making it personal: "I relied on you." The scene's dramatic tension reaches its highest point when the customer exclaims, "I'm shopping somewhere else!" With this line, the objective in the scene is resolved—through a failure to achieve that objective. The once harmonious and mutually beneficial relationship between the customer and salesman is forever changed because the shoe is not fixed. As a result, the customer's faith in the salesman is dashed: She initiates a reversal. A new world order emerges, and instead of getting her shoe fixed as she had expected, the customer is left with a broken shoe and no immediate recourse.

If this scene were part of a longer play, the playwright might have concerned herself with how the objective of the scene fits in with the protagonist's overall dramatic action. Perhaps the customer expects to attend an important event (a party, job interview, funeral) where she has to meet a specific person (a potential love interest, boss, relative) for a special reason or meaningful event (to have sex, get a job, meet her birth mother). She needs to get her shoe fixed before this can happen. It all would have worked out fine if only the salesman had been able to repair her shoe! Now she's running out of time. What will she do next? What led her to this point? The playwright has to decide how the scene's objective connects with a larger dramatic action. If the customer needs to fix her shoe so that she can continue to pursue her objective, then she has a dramatic action.

DRAFTING A SCENE YOU DON'T KNOW HOW TO WRITE

In this exercise, you will put an idea for a scene down on paper. The way to begin is to write it for only two characters. Once you have a grasp of your scene with two characters, you can add as many other characters as you wish.

1. Start the scene by having one character state specifically what he urgently wants—that is, explicitly define the objective. It might help if he wants something from the other character in the scene.

2. Have the second character disagree with or contradict the first character—that is, explicitly define the obstacle.

3. Continue writing the scene. Now that you have set up an objective that is being directly confronted by an obstacle, you have created conflict. How this objective will be resolved is the dramatic question of the scene.

4. Resolve the dramatic question by having the objective achieved, not achieved, or deemed irrelevant.

5. End this scene by posing a new dramatic question that will lead you into the next scene.

Inventing Dialogue

Some people have a natural facility for writing excellent dialogue. Their dialogue may be lyrical, witty, authentic, and crackle with wit, economy, energy, irony, or sexuality. Dialogue can do all of these things, but it must above all dramatize conflict.

In other words, writing a play requires more than having an ear for dialogue. A playwright must use dialogue to develop character, instigate conflict, convey dramatic action, provide exposition, and dramatize subtext. The trick is to be able to use your knowledge of craft to make all of these dramatic elements appear to be effortlessly working for you.

In real dialogue, people often use a kind of shorthand with each other and leave out exposition. When this type of shorthand is used in a play, the performed dialogue can be compelling simply because the audience is trying to understand what the relationship is between the characters and what they are talking about.

THE OVERHEARD CONVERSATION

For this exercise, you will eavesdrop on a conversation in which you are not a participant, one that is not intended for your ears. Do not use telephones, take notes, or record this conversation. I hereby absolve myself of any responsibility or liability if you do anything that is illegal or that will result in your getting punched in the nose.

1. Overhear a conversation.

2. After you have overheard the conversation, do your best to reconstruct the conversation word for word. It's okay to guess if you can't remember a word or two, but do not make up or embellish the conversation. The goal is to be as accurate as possible.

In the following sample from a student, the speakers are a young couple on the subway.

> **HER:** Baby, I just don't understand why it's such a big deal?
>
> **HIM:** It is a big deal, man. How you gonna act like you didn't see me there? I'm gonna keep talking to him, but that shit ain't right.
>
> **HER:** Look, all I know is that he doesn't like me. He doesn't like me, Joe. And I can't lose you.
>
> **JOE:** Shit, Nancy, but that's my boy.
>
> **NANCY:** And I'm your girl, okay? I'm your girl.
>
> [Joe moves his head in the other direction, upset, and says nothing to her. Nancy grabs his hand and kisses him on the neck.]
>
> **NANCY:** I need you, okay? I *need* you. I'm sorry. Look, I can't lose you; you're all I have. [She kisses him on the lips.]
>
> **JOE:** I don't want to lose you either, but look, that shit's fucked up.
>
> **NANCY:** I'm sorry, I'm sorry. I promise I'll try. Just as long as I'm with you.

This exercise is a listening exercise that, when executed properly (as in this example), reveals certain truths about the way people speak.

1. People speak with their own distinctive voice. They may use similar language or slang, but their individual personalities usually break through.

2. People interrupt each other and repeat themselves.

3. People don't always speak in complete sentences or use proper grammar.

4. People who know each other use a kind of shorthand when conversing. They don't reveal exposition. Often, this is precisely what makes a conversation compelling in a play, when the audience must try to make sense out of what is being said by listening and using deductive reasoning.

5. People don't always listen to each other. Conversations jump around. However, they also tend to maintain a coherent through-line.

THE SNIPPET SCENE

Write a scene that makes sense out of five random overheard snippets of dialogue.

1. Overhear five random lines of dialogue in five separate situations and write these lines down.

2. Write a scene that uses all five lines of dialogue. Like all scenes, it must include an object and an obstacle and end on a dramatic question. Make sure that the scene resolves its dramatic question and introduces another.

In the sample below from a student, the five overheard lines of dialogue were:

1. "Mommy's supposed to call me today but she didn't call me."

2. "I know, but what's it gonna take, like a year?"

3. "Check that sucka out! He looks like a terrorist!"

4. "My wife is home sick. And she better have dinner ready when I get home."

5. "That was a fun commute."

[An airport curb. A BROTHER (age fourteen) and a SISTER (age ten) stand there waiting.]

BROTHER: That was a fun commute. I can't believe the baby puked on me.

SISTER: Eew! ... You smell. Can we go now?

BROTHER: Mommy's supposed to pick us up any minute. We have to wait.

SISTER: I know, but what's it gonna take, like a year?

BROTHER: Stop your griping. It's not even that cold.

SISTER: Is too.

BROTHER: Is not!

SISTER: Anyway, where's Mommy? Did you even talk to her?

BROTHER: Ummm no. Mommy's supposed to call me today but she didn't call me.

SISTER: Well, what are we gonna do?

BROTHER: Let's see if one of the baggage handlers can help us.

SISTER: [Pulling him back] No! Check that sucka out! He looks like a terrorist!
BROTHER: Oh, would you relax. And watch your mouth. [To Baggage Handler] Sir, could you help us? Our mom is supposed to pick us up but she hasn't shown up yet and it's been over an hour and a half.
BAGGAGE HANDLER: Maybe she's home sick. My wife is home sick. And she better have dinner ready when I get home. Speaking of sick, you stink, kid.
BROTHER: Sir, we just need to get home. My sister is freezing.
BAGGAGE HANDLER: All right, kid, you're breakin' my heart. Here's a couple of dollars for a cab for you and your sister. Go home and get cleaned up.
BROTHER: Thank you so much!

In this sample exercise, the playwright effectively uses random snippets of dialogue to create an objective, an obstacle, and a resolution to the scene's conflict. The objective is introduced when Brother says "Mommy's supposed to pick us up any minute. We have to wait." Prior to this, the tension of waiting for Mommy has been set in motion by the fact that Brother has been puked on, and Sister can't stand the way he smells. The obstacle to the objective is that Mommy hasn't shown up yet, and the conflict reaches its highest point when Brother says "Mommy's supposed to call me today but she didn't call me." The tension is sustained when Brother turns to the Baggage Handler for help, and he resolves the conflict by giving the kids money for a cab. What remains is the dramatic question of what actually happened to Mommy. If this were a longer play, perhaps that would be addressed in the next scene.

Dramatizing Exposition and Creating Subtext

Exposition is like cholesterol within the body of a dramatic work in that there are both good and bad types. Good exposition provides the audience with vital information that contextualizes the character in her back story and activates the dramatic conflict occurring in the present. Good exposition elevates the urgency of a scene's dramatic conflict and interacts with the character's objective. Bad exposition, on the other hand, digresses from the immediate conflict and prevents the playwright from dramatizing effectively. It lends a scene no new exigency or increased understanding. Bad exposition drains tension from a scene by taking the characters and the viewer out of the present dramatic conflict.

In your play, a character might recount something that happened long ago, thus providing the audience with crucial information. This expository information must, however, relate back to the conflict taking place in the current scene. If the exposition you are imagining can fuel the dramatic conflict, move your story forward, raise the stakes, and increase the tension of opposites, then it can be a useful tool.

When it comes to writing exposition, the contemporary playwright has been dealt a difficult hand. Generally speaking, blatant use of exposition is often frowned upon—although there are exceptions to this rule. There is little patience for exposition in new plays—perhaps because of the fast pace of modern life (and film and television writing), or simply because there is a perception that it is boring and nonessential. However, it is important to recall that the plays of Shakespeare and Ibsen contain scenes composed almost wholly of exposition. In these scenes, the audience learns essential information and is exposed to personal histories without which the drama cannot begin to unfold. Where these writers took their time to orient the audience to the world of the play, contemporary playwrights tend to jump directly into the dramatic action. You should feel free to experiment with various ways of using exposition in your play.

When working exposition into your text, don't forget that important information should always be conveyed at least twice. If a fact, condition, or situation is absolutely necessary in order for the audience to follow the plot, you must guard against the possibility that some audience member will cough over the one line that reveals this information. It has even been suggested that viewers do not really pay attention to anything that happens in the first seven minutes of a play. While this may or may not be true, keep in mind the process of acclimation and settling down that audiences undergo at the beginning of a play. Most viewers come to the theater at the end of a long day; they may be tired, digesting a meal, or distracted by their lives. It is your job to provide a compelling alternative to all these reasons for them not to be fully present.

Dramatic subtext is the opposite of and complement to dramatic exposition. This term refers to the unspoken objective that lurks beneath the surface of an explicit or clearly stated objective: the deafening silence of what is not being said. Subtext is unconscious, instinctive, and subtle—it exists in our everyday lives and interactions—and it activates the drama by lending an emotional urgency to superficial and tangible circumstances or events.

THE NEUTRAL SURFACE SCENE

When writing dialogue, exploring the unsaid can be a very effective form of communication between characters. The following exercise gives you a simple recipe for experimenting with subtext by adding an unspoken objective to what is otherwise a clearly stated objective.

1. Begin with the following simple dialogue, or a similarly neutral exchange between two people.

    A: Hi.
    B: Hi.
    A: How are you?
    B: Not bad. And you?
    A: How is Bill doing?
    B: He's good.
    A: Tell him I say hello.
    B: I will.

2. Now provide a subtext by adding to each neutral line of dialogue the unspoken thoughts of the character as he is speaking, as in the sample from a student, below.

    A: Hi. [*Uh, oh. What should I say?*]
    B: Hi. [*Well, I guess this meeting was inevitable.*]
    A: How are you? [*Do you still hate me?*]
    B: Not bad. And you? [*You've got a lot of nerve.*]
    A: How is Bill? [*I know I haven't called for six months.*]
    B: He's good. [*Like you care.*]
    A: Tell him I say hello. [*I wish I had been nicer to Bill.*]
    B: I will. [*Wait till I tell Bill who I ran into today!*]

Here, subtext gives dimension and nuance to a conversation that was otherwise perfunctory and banal, helping to flesh out the relationship between these two people. In this scene, the objective, or central question, revolves around *How is Bill?* The subtext is that A feels guilty about past actions that involve Bill and affect the current interaction between the two characters on stage. If the neutral surface scene is like tofu, then subtext is the unseen ingredient that gives it flavor and spice (that is, conflict and greater significance). If you can make the unsaid clear enough, an actor should be able to convey the subtext of the scene to the audience. The neutral surface scene has no clues in the text to what the subtext might be. Sometimes double meanings to seemingly innocuous statements or questioning can give both actors and audiences clues to the subtext. Other times what has come before or after can give clues. Often, actors and directors imbue texts with subtext the playwright was either unaware of or did not intend.

Dramatic Reversals

Dramatic reversals exist in all media—not only in plays and films, but in fiction, poetry, and even nonfiction. In the theater, reversals increase the urgency of the dramatic action by turning it in a new direction. Major reversals often occur at the ends of acts or in the climactic scene near the end of a play, but reversals also crop up in individual scenes. Technically speaking, all reversals function the same way and work together in a play. However, they can have slightly different purposes. Reversals within individual scenes tend to reinforce the overall object of the act. Reversals that occur at the ends of acts or in climactic final scenes resolve objectives and propel the dramatic action in a new direction.

In Clint Eastwood's movie *Million Dollar Baby*, Eastwood's character is Frankie Dunn, an aging boxing trainer who runs his own gym. Hilary Swank plays Maggie Fitzgerald, the eager young woman who wants Frankie to train her to be a professional boxer. But Frankie doesn't train girls—not to mention that he still struggles with his estrangement from his own daughter. In one scene, Frankie sees Maggie using his personal speed bag for training purposes. He asks for it back and Maggie returns it, explaining that Morgan Freeman's character, "Scrap," lent it to her because she can't afford one of her own. Frankie gets the speed bag back from her, but then feels guilty and gives her back the speed bag on loan. Frankie's objective in this scene is to dissuade Maggie from training in his gym, but through this reversal he ends up encouraging her. This pivotal scene is the first chink in his armor: By the end of the act, Frankie has begun training Maggie. Dramatic reversals are extremely useful for propelling your story forward and demonstrating character development through dramatizing conflict.

A dramatic reversal occurs when a character attains an objective—only to recognize that the reality of the situation is completely the opposite of what she thought to be true. This change in perception propels the character to reverse her dramatic action. This phenomenon is commonly called recognition and reversal, stemming from terms in Aristotle's *Poetics* to describe, for example, Oedipus' realization that his actions to evade the fate that had been predicted for him were the very actions that caused him to fulfill it. In *Million Dollar Baby*, Frankie achieves his objective for the scene—he gets the speed bag from Maggie—but upon achieving his objective, he sees things more clearly, regrets his behavior, and recognizes that he wants to help Maggie after all.

SHIFTING GROUND

Write a scene that contains at least two dramatic reversals.

1. Write a scene where there is a power shift between two characters.

2. Once the power shift is clearly established, find a way to shift the power dynamic again.

Here's an example from a student.

> [Two men are sitting on a bus. MAN 1 is reading a magazine. MAN 2 surreptitiously looks over MAN 1's shoulder and reads along with him. MAN 1 makes a subtle annoyed gesture, and MAN 2 briefly looks away before gravitating back to reading over MAN 1's shoulder.]
>
> **MAN 1:** Do you mind?
> **MAN 2:** I don't if you don't.
> **MAN 1:** Well, I do. People should mind their own business. [He goes back to reading.]
> **MAN 2:** I'm sorry. I've forgotten my manners. It's just that I have a personal interest in that article you're reading. Would you mind if I take a look at it when you're done?
> **MAN 1:** Just take it. [He hands the magazine to MAN 2.]
> **MAN 2:** Really? Are you sure?
> **MAN 1:** Yes.
> **MAN 2:** Gee, thanks.

[MAN 2 opens the magazine and begins to read the article. MAN I rifles through his own briefcase in search of reading material. When he finally gives up, he fastens his briefcase and sighs. He looks around and notices MAN 2 reading the magazine.]

MAN I: Excuse me.
MAN 2: What?
MAN I: I've changed my mind. [He snatches the magazine out of MAN 2's hands and begins to read, then slides two seats away from MAN 2 and turns his body away.]

In this example, Man I's objective is to read undisturbed by Man 2. He abandons or fails to achieve this objective when he hands the magazine over to Man 2. This is the first reversal in the scene: With the immediate objective resolved, Man I's dramatic action is reversed. He had wanted to read undisturbed. Now he's willing to give up reading the article if it means that Man 2 will stop bothering him. However, when he finds his new status unacceptable, he reverses his dramatic action again and takes back the magazine.

Revision

The lessons up to this point were designed to help you write a first draft of your play—or at least the first a few scenes. Now you may face problems that all writers confront after they've gotten to the end of their first draft. You may like some of what you've done so far, but feel that overall the play doesn't hang together or build in dramatic tension. Perhaps the story peters out or drags in places. Maybe the stakes aren't high enough, or the premise is faulty to begin with. Your main characters may not be well defined, the conflict not clearly set up or not fully developed. Perhaps exposition needs to be eliminated or used more effectively, or subtext needs to be magnified. Your task now is to go through your play and edit ruthlessly, asking yourself questions based on the lessons of this chapter. Cut anything that doesn't fuel the dramatic conflict or move the story forward. Find a way to activate exposition and emphasize the underlying subtext. Does every scene have an objective and an obstacle? If not, why not?

A good idea for a play will always call you back. Sometimes, when you feel like you've hit a wall, you may need to put a play-in-progress on the back burner for a while. A good rule of thumb is to focus on whichever play you can work on most productively at the moment. After a while, you will have several plays in various stages of completion. However, everyone is different: Some people can only work on one project at a time, while others like to take time away from a play so that they can come back to it with a fresh, more objective eye.

Sometimes external events help you to revise. Once, during rehearsals for a public reading of a two-character play I had written, the actors were struggling with some of the lines, claiming that some of the speeches were long-winded or just difficult to say. I felt that they just didn't get it. Then one of the actors dropped out two days before the reading, and the remaining actor suggested that I play the opposite role myself. He believed that it would be a valuable learning experience for me, and he was right. Even I didn't want to say some of the lines that I had written for the character, and I was forced to rewrite about half of the dialogue. Now, whether I am working with actors or not, I use this test to help me revise my work.

It is in your best interest to find a teacher or a theater professional with significant dramaturgical skills to assist you in the all-important revision process before your play goes out into the world. Showing your work to an influential person who knows theater can be helpful, but what you need at this point is someone who can help you heighten conflict, edit exposition, set up and reverse expectations, and/or or create an unpredictable ending that was inevitable from the start. You may want to find a playwriting teacher by signing up for a writing class in an adult continuing education program or at your local community college.

As you proceed in your career as a playwright and find yourself in various professional situations, it will become easier to encounter such knowledgeable people. The goal is to develop your skills so that you can attract theater professionals (playwrights, agents, directors, actors, producers, and literary managers) who will serve as sounding boards for your work.

CLARIFY THE DRAMATIC ACTION

This exercise is a way to begin the revision process for plays-in-progress, but it also can help to clarify your ideas for a new play. Follow the steps below to write an outline of the basic structure of the play.

1. List all the characters.
2. State their objectives—what each character wants.

3. Outline their obstacles—what is keeping each character from getting what he wants.

4. Lay out the dramatic action—what each character is willing to do to get what he wants.

5. State what each character's secret or great realization is (if he has one) by the end of the play.

Item five is completely optional. Not every character has a secret, but it can sometimes be helpful to think about this possibility. A characters usually experiences some form of significant change by the end of the play, some sort of realization or a revelation of his true inner self. Here's an example of how I completed this exercise with one of my own plays-in-progress.

The Great Man

CHARACTERS: the Biographer, the Famous Author, the Author's Wife, the Author's Agent

The Biographer

OBJECTIVE: The Biographer wants to write a biography of a Famous Author he greatly admires.
OBSTACLES: the Famous Author's initial reluctance to consent to a biography; the Famous Author's spin on the events of his life; the Famous Author's use of influence to impede the Biographer's research.
DRAMATIC ACTION: The Biographer will do whatever it takes to complete the biography and become the definitive authority on the Famous Author.
SECRET OR REALIZATION: Once he really gets to know his hero personally, the Biographer feels betrayed and sets out to destroy the Author by writing. By the end of the play he realizes that he doesn't have what it takes to be a great man.

The Author

OBJECTIVE: The Author wants his version of his life to be told by the Biographer.
OBSTACLE: The Author's version of his life contradicts reality.
DRAMATIC ACTION: The Author is determined to have the Biographer's opus dismissed as irrelevant by the literary establishment.

SECRET OR REALIZATION: The Author is determined to leave his legacy to no one—not his wife, children, agent, or biographer. His legacy, the end product of his life's work, is the only thing that really matters to him.

The Author's Wife

OBJECTIVE: The Wife wants the biography to position her as the Author's one true love and as the sole heir to his legacy.

OBSTACLE: The Biographer, the Author, and the Agent all have agendas that compete with hers.

DRAMATIC ACTION: She will thwart her competition by any means necessary in order to end up as the sole heir to the Author's legacy.

SECRET OR REALIZATION: Contrary to her appearance of being a loving and devoted wife, she can't wait for the Author to die so that she can go off with her lover.

The Agent

OBJECTIVE: The Agent wants to sell books.

OBSTACLE: The Author is making the biography difficult for the Biographer to complete. The unexpected new novel from the Author further complicates matters.

DRAMATIC ACTION: To pit his clients against each other and go with whomever will help him further his own career.

SECRET OR REALIZATION: None. The Agent is what he always claimed to be from the start—a person whose agenda is to cultivate authors and sell books.

All the characters in this particular play-in-progress have an objective, obstacles, and a clear dramatic action. Nevertheless, the Biographer is the protagonist because his dramatic action is what drives the play. Everyone else's objective and dramatic action serves to either fuel the Biographer's story or put obstacles in his path.

Writer's Block, Procrastination and Getting Stuck

We all experience frustrating pauses in our writing process. However, there is a big difference between having a full-blown case of writer's block and just being stuck. Writer's block means that, for some reason, you are unable to access any of your ideas, or that you just don't have anything to write about. If you think you may be suffering from writer's block, you should pause until your writing calls you back. (However, if your problem is procrastination, then welcome to the club: All writers procrastinate. Sometimes procrastination is absolutely necessary, but sometimes it really is just a complete waste of time.)

There is often a point during the writing of a play, novel, short story, or work of nonfiction when the author feels stuck. Sometimes she simply cannot figure out what to write next. I offer five solutions to overcoming this problem:

1. **STRUGGLE THROUGH IT.** Being stuck is a rite of passage. It happens to everybody at some point. We all have good writing days and bad writing days. You can soldier on through the bad days in the belief that you are laying the groundwork for a good writing day in the not-too-distant future.

2. **PUT THE PROJECT ON THE BACK BURNER.** Sometimes you need to temporarily put aside what you are working on. A good idea eventually will call you back. Start something else or give yourself a few days off—it might give you the fresh perspective needed to start up again. Sometimes when I give up on a project, it frees up my imagination. I suddenly discover solutions that I couldn't come up with earlier. By giving it up, I am able to keep going.

3. **RETHINK WHAT HAS COME BEFORE.** Sometimes you get stuck because you've written yourself into a corner. Just because you are unsure about how to go forward doesn't mean that you are stuck with what you've written. Be willing to change or even eliminate pages and entire scenes. It's scary, but it can be a liberating experience. With one stroke you can break down walls that have stifled you and open up new possibilities.

4. **GET FEEDBACK.** It can be very helpful to get feedback from somebody who knows what she's talking about, although it may be difficult to find this person for any number of reasons.

> Even very intelligent and insightful people may not have what I like to call a dramaturgical IQ. Find a person who does and stick with her.
>
> 5. **ABANDON THE PROJECT.** Sometimes diminishing returns bring your writing to a grinding halt, or you completely lose interest in writing a particular play. Some relationships end because they should, and so do plays that were not meant to be. It's hard to make this executive decision—playwrights often stick with a play that isn't working simply because they don't want to waste all the time and effort that they've already spent on it. But sometimes you just have to cut your losses.

Getting Produced

All playwrights want their plays to be produced. Getting to see your work performed by talented actors onstage, with live people in the seats, is the ultimate reason to write a play. More than anything else involved in writing a play, the task of getting produced requires relentless determination and thick skin. If you meet these requirements, consult the most recent edition of the *Dramatists Sourcebook*, an excellent resource guide for playwrights who want to take a play to the next step. Contests and development workshops such as the National Playwrights Conference at the Eugene O'Neill Theater Center are also good opportunities for unknown playwrights to get their work out into the world.

You can do certain things to make the possibility of a production a reality. One thing to keep in mind is the size of your cast. Theaters and producers often look for small casts for economic reasons: Each additional salary makes a play harder to finance. A prolific and widely produced playwright once told me that the best way to get produced is to write a two-character play with one set. You can also solve this problem by writing several parts to be played by the same actor. Plays like Paula Vogel's *The Baltimore Waltz* and Terrence McNally's *A Perfect Ganesh* feature a new character in every scene. When these plays are produced, one actor often assumes all of these roles, and it's fun for the audience to see this actor change into different characters throughout the play. The same is true of Robert Schenkkan's *Kentucky Cycle* and Thornton Wilder's *The Long*

Christmas Dinner. In these multigenerational plays, characters die; the actors return later as their children, grandchildren, and great-grandchildren. The effect is very theatrical and helps make a play specific to the theater.

Conversely, university theater groups, community theaters, and some theaters with acting companies attached look for plays with a large number of roles, so that everyone in the company can have a part. Other theaters look for very specific themes to further their theater's mission—for example, plays about colonial America or plays that celebrate scientific innovation. The best rule of thumb is to write the play that you need to write. If it calls for a large cast, so be it. Any choice that you make can either make a production more difficult or make your play exactly what someone is looking for.

It is difficult to write a good play. A play can't be fixed in the editing room or improved by a terrific soundtrack. To write a good play, you must be willing to reveal a very human part of yourself. All great plays reveal an obvious truth—often one that turns out to have been evident from the start, even though the protagonist (and hopefully the audience) refuses to see it. It is this painfully honest portrayal of human behavior that makes a play universally valued and revered. All of this may come at some personal cost or sacrifice to you—symbolic or literal. Nevertheless, I encourage you to take this challenging, and ultimately rewarding, plunge.

RECOMMENDED READING

RESOURCES

Brecht, Bertolt. Translated by John Willett. *Brecht on Theatre.* New York: Hill and Wang, 1964.

Dramatists Sourcebook: Complete Opportunities for Playwrights, Translators, Composers, Lyricists and Librettists. New York: Theatre Communications Group, updated annually.

Egri, Lajos. *The Art of Dramatic Writing.* New York: Simon and Schuster, 1960.

Hatcher, Jeffrey. *The Art & Craft of Playwriting.* Cincinnati, Ohio: Story Press, 1996.

Spencer, Stuart. *The Playwright's Guidebook.* New York: Faber and Faber, Inc., 2002.

PLAYWRIGHTS AND PLAYS

Albee, Edward. *The Zoo Story.*

Beckett, Samuel. *Waiting For Godot.*

Brecht, Bertolt. *The Threepenny Opera.*

Churchill, Caryl. *Cloud 9.*

Fugard, Athol. *"Master Harold" ... and the Boys.*

Hwang, David Henry. *M. Butterfly.*

Ibsen, Henrik. *A Doll's House.*

Kushner, Tony. *Angels in America.*

Mamet, David. *Glengarry Glen Ross.*

Miller, Arthur. *All My Sons.*

O'Neill, Eugene. *Long Day's Journey Into Night.*

Pinter, Harold. *Betrayal.*

Strindberg, August. *The Dream Play.*

Wilde, Oscar. *The Importance Of Being Earnest.*

Wilder, Thornton. *Our Town.*

Appendix

by **TIM TOMLINSON**
& **CHARLIE SCHULMAN**

Ten MFA Dos and Don'ts

by **TIM TOMLINSON**

1. *Don't* expect to learn anything from your workshop instructors. *Do* educate yourself. The best way to educate yourself is to write, and the second best way is to read. Do a healthy mix of these two practices, and you can't help but improve. If you're lucky, you will wind up with a workshop instructor (perhaps even an entire program) that actually teaches something, but you can 'tcount on that.

2. *Don't* expect to "become" a writer through your work in the MFA program. *Do* enter as an already working writer, with the habits of

writing already established. Those habits are writing every day (or at least frequently), revising, and reading.

3. In workshops, *don't* be a critic. In other words, don't provide the academic history of a genre, its connection to other genres, its relation to political consciousness in Southeast Asia, etc. *Do* comment on manuscripts constructively and honestly, with an eye toward the craft, not the meaning.

   Some workshops devote a lot of time to the meaning of the story, and to the writer's intention. But what if the writer came up with a wonderful piece that she hadn't intended? The poet Elizabeth Bishop says that she frequently wound up publishing poems that meant the opposite of what she'd intended. Meaning, politics, philosophies—these can all be enormous censors of the imagination, and to an emerging writer, the burden of saying the right thing is too heavy to bear. Besides, what does a bird intend when it sings, and what is the meaning of a flower, and what is the politics of a dream?

   Instead, comment on the elements of the piece the writer *can* control: pace, contrast, exposition, clarity, motivation, verisimilitude. Help the writer master her craft; let the writer worry about her own political consciousness.

   When political consciousness is foregrounded in the workshop, the writing begins to reflect the "correct" politics, and potentially provocative work (think Céline's *Journey to the End of the Night*, or J.M. Coetzee's *Disgrace*) might never make it out of the classroom.

4. *Don't* listen to everyone. If you were a painter, you wouldn't listen to someone who said "I love your green painting, but can you make it blue?" Some workshop comments are just as (un)helpful. In his excellent book on story structure, *Narrative Design*, Madison Bell claims that 95 percent of what you hear in a workshop will be worthless. That's a rather high percentage; we like to think that that percentage is a bit lower in our own workshops. But the point is, you can't write by committee. Ultimately it comes down to you, and to your own aesthetic.

   Do learn to identify those voices in the workshop that do provide insight, and that do help you get through material, generate pages, and solve story problems.

5. *Don't* be afraid to make changes others suggest. *Do* keep your original manuscript intact. One of my students, T. Glen Coughlin, whose workshop material eventually became the novel *Steady Eddie*, used to go home after workshop meetings and enter every change the participants suggested. (This was an advanced workshop in which the participants generally offered useful, constructive critiques—more on that later.) He would then print out the changes and compare them with the original manuscript. As per Madison Bell, many of those pages wound up in the wastebasket. But more than he would have expected actually worked to the novel's advantage. The point: Editorial insight from outside readers can be a wonderful asset. Often other eyes can see what the writer's cannot because the writer is so immersed in the material and in the original expression. It is rare that I quote the late President Ronald Reagan, but in considering workshop suggestions, it is useful to trust, but verify.

6. *Don't* ignore others' tastes. *Do* identify what others admire, and what you admire. If you're working under the influence of William S. Burroughs or Terry Southern, you might not get the most sympathetic read from an admirer of A.S. Byatt or George Eliot. And vice versa. Establish who likes what and remember those likes when you listen to or read comments.

7. *Don't* feel as if you have to read *Finnegans Wake*, *The Man Without Qualities*, or *The Waves* before you can contribute to or have an opinion about literature. *Do* read, and read around the genres, regions, eras. Try to read the books that make you want to write, the ones that you have to put down in order to get something of your own down. Read the books that make you want to read more. Conversely, toss across the room anything that makes you dislike reading or that makes you want to retire your pen (or keyboard).

8. *Don't* give up because you get a rejection. *Do* send out. Get rejections, and get revenge: Publish. When you peruse the shelves of the bookstores and the pages of the literary magazines, you can reach the indisputable conclusion that there is no reason to suppose that editors and publishers are in possession of anything but questionable taste.

Therefore, when you're rejected by one of these philistines, think of it as an indication of the merits of your piece, rather than its flaws.

9. *Don't* worry. *Do* write. What if you set out to write *Doctor Zhivago* and you wind up with a manuscript that more closely resembles *Charlotte's Web*? So what? It is what it is. Your job as the writer is to get out of the way of the characters so that they can show us their own truth. If that truth is more clearly etched across a spiderweb than the frozen tundra, so be it. And remember, worry is interest paid in advance on a debt that may never come due.

10. *Don't* procrastinate. *Do* daydream. When it was siesta time, a Spanish poet used to hang a sign on his door that said "Do Not Disturb: Writer at Work."

Feedback

by CHARLIE SCHULMAN

Giving and receiving constructive feedback is an essential part of the revision process. Like with writing itself, there is a fair amount of trial and error involved, and your skill level will increase with (good) experience. The following guidelines will improve the quality of your experience in giving and receiving critique, once you've found your audience.

HOW TO RECEIVE FEEDBACK

Once you've finished a draft of your work, you will want to see what kind of response it gets from other people. You may be able to gauge from their response whether the work is compelling, funny, or sad. This kind of general response can be very helpful, but to get a more specific and nuanced take on your piece, you should show it to someone who knows what she's talking about. And, since a fair amount of personal opinion is involved, try to get a second or even third reader for your work as well. A writing group works well for this purpose: It allows you to receive a constructive critique. But if you live in an isolated area, you can look to online classes and instructors for hire.

I. **LISTEN, AND DON'T BE DEFENSIVE.** Part of the problem with feedback in general is that most writers really only want to hear that their hard labor has resulted in an unparalleled work of genius. It is often somewhat shocking when the response falls short of unanimous praise. Therefore, most writers are defensive, and rightfully so. You must stay true to your unique, singular vision, but try to be open-minded—if only because this might lead you to improve your work. Don't dismiss anything out of hand. In my experience, writers who defend their work during a feedback session are not making productive use of the critique experience. If those critiquing your work have read your work, then they have heard what you have to say. The only time you really need to speak is when requesting clarification, and even then you should be brief. Take everything in and sort it all out later. Taking notes can help you to do this and to maintain self-discipline while you're hearing feedback.

2. **LISTEN TO THE PROBLEM, EVEN IF IT'S PRESENTED WITH THE WRONG SOLUTION.** Sometimes respondents are way off base. But when they point out some aspect of your work that is unclear, illogical, confusing, repetitive, or lacking in some way, they are usually on target. This can be incredibly helpful if you have lost your objectivity and ability to see the obvious (in other words, if you're like most of us). However, while their identification of a problem may be correct, responders often shoot themselves in the foot by serving up a solution that in no way correlates with the writer's vision. When this happens—and in my experience it happens a lot—your immediate instinct may be to reject not only the off-putting solution, but also the initial critique. Avoid this pitfall—don't throw out the baby with the bathwater. Try to identify problems with your work and to separate these flaws from the suggestions that readers offer up as potential solutions.

3. **DON'T DISMISS ANYTHING OUT OF HAND.** A suggestion that seems to have a lot of merit at the moment it is given may seem much less appropriate when you're back at your desk. Conversely, a suggestion that seems to make no sense when offered may seem ingenious later. A suggestion might morph into a better idea or make sense in a different context. It's in your best interest to consider all suggestions as having some sort of potential.

4. **BUY INTO IT BEFORE YOU WRITE IT.** Sometimes you will receive suggestions that you truly believe are useful from the beginning. But unless you can make sense of the suggestion and know how to implement

it, moving forward will be a useless exercise. It is fine to experiment with new concepts and directions, but unless you are fully motivated and grasp what you want to do, the results will reflect your ambivalence.

5. **DON'T LISTEN TO TOO MANY VOICES.** Feedback is a balancing act. One of the dangers of getting feedback is that you start to hear a lot of voices in your head telling you what to do. Unfortunately, these voices have a tendency to drown out your voice—the voice that drove you to write in the first place. Sometimes you can lose touch with the impulse that motivated you. Counteract this influence by remaining true to yourself. In the end, you are the person who has to be satisfied with what you have written.

HOW TO GIVE FEEDBACK

Giving productive feedback can be as important as receiving it, because it helps to create an environment where everyone involved can do their best writing. Keep the following in mind:

1. **BE CRITICAL IN A POSITIVE AND CONSTRUCTIVE WAY.** It's easy to tear a piece of writing to shreds, but being critical in a positive, tactful, and constructive manner takes time and careful consideration. As a respondent, your job is to inspire the writer to improve. You cannot and should not treat any work in progress with contempt, no matter how offensive or poorly written it may be. It is crucial that you establish a safe place for the writer to express himself and take chances.

2. **VIEW EVERY WORK AS A WORK IN PROGRESS.** You can be critical and tough, but remember that when a work is in its incipient stages, it has to be nurtured into existence. A work in progress should not be evaluated as though it were a finished product. Balance support with challenging suggestions.

3. **TALK ABOUT WHAT WORKS.** More often than not, we overlook what might be working well and go directly to what isn't working. Writers need to know what they are doing right just as much as they need to know what they are doing wrong.

4. **DON'T REWRITE OTHER PEOPLES' WORKS.** Respondents often experience a strong impulse to impose their will on other peoples' work by offering suggestions that would make the work in question look

and sound like something *they* would write. Look at the piece from the inside, and help the writer create what he wants to write—don't impose your own style or sensibility.

5. **SEPARATE WHAT ISN'T WORKING FROM YOUR SUGGESTION TO IMPROVE IT.** When you're receiving feedback, you must separate the identification of a problem from any misguided suggestion for solving it. When you're giving feedback, identify the problem thoughtfully before offering up a solution to fix it. You don't want the writer to be so put off by the suggestion for improvement that he discards your brilliant criticism.

Index

Love the LORD
your God with all
your heart and
with all your soul
and with all your
strength.

—Deuteronomy 6:5

This doodle devotional
belongs to:

Delaney Bruns

Love is patient, love is kind.
It does not envy, it does not boast,
it is not proud.
It does not dishonor others, it is not
self-seeking, it is not easily angered, it
keeps no record of wrongs.
Love does not delight in evil but
rejoices with the truth.
It always protects, always trusts,
always hopes, always perseveres.
Love never fails.

—1 Corinthians 13:4-8

The love you share with God is the greatest love of all! Write down or illustrate the ways you strengthen your bond with God.

God shows kindness to everyone because He loves us all! Think about how you show kindness to the people you love as you doodle faces and outfits for the people shown here.

What is your favorite hymn or praise song?
Write your favorite lyric here and fill any
empty space with swirls, flowers and hearts!

But let all who take refuge in you be glad; let them ever sing for joy. Spread your protection over them, that those who love your name may rejoice in you.

—Psalm 5:11

Color in the hearts below and fill them with words that remind you of how much God loves you!

GOD IS
LOVE

CHOOSE
TO LOVE

LORD,
I love the house
where you live,
the place where
your glory dwells.

—Psalm 26:8

Decorate this church with
tons of bright colors and add
trees, flowers, birds and people
who are excited to love God!

Love must be sincere. Hate what is evil; cling to what is good. — Romans 12:9

Let love light the way! Brighten up this page by filling in this stained glass with different colors.

Make this the brightest, most colorful sun you can! Don't limit yourself to oranges, reds and yellows—make it a rainbow of sunrays!

Your love, LORD, reaches to the heavens, your faithfulness to the skies. —Psalm 36:5

God loves you for more
reasons than there are
stars in the sky!
Doodle in more stars
and use glitter for
some extra sparkle!

By day the LORD directs His love, at night His song is with me—a prayer to the God of my life. —Psalm 42:8

Think about the Lord's song in your life while you doodle around these musical notes and fill them with brilliant, happy colors!

PATIENT

FO

Love is lots of things!
Color in these words that
describe a loving person
and add some more
descriptions of your own!

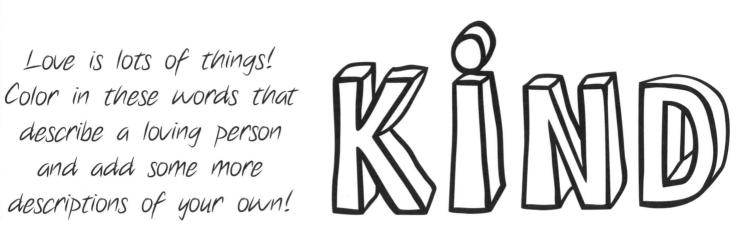

KIND

RGIVING

Give thanks
to the LORD,
for He is good;
His love endures
forever.
—Psalm 107:1

Reflect on his amazing love for you while you turn this infinity symbol into a dazzling piece of art!

God loves you for all of eternity!

God gave us rainbows because He loves us. As you fill this rainbow with bright, beautiful colors, think about all the other incredible gifts He has given us and doodle some of them around the rainbow!

Wear your love for God on your sleeve-or better yet, around your neck! Add more charms to this necklace that demonstrate your love for the Lord!

Let love and
faithfulness never
leave you; bind them
around your neck,
write them on the
tablet of your heart.
—Proverbs 3:3

Fill each letter with a different pattern using bright, bold colors!

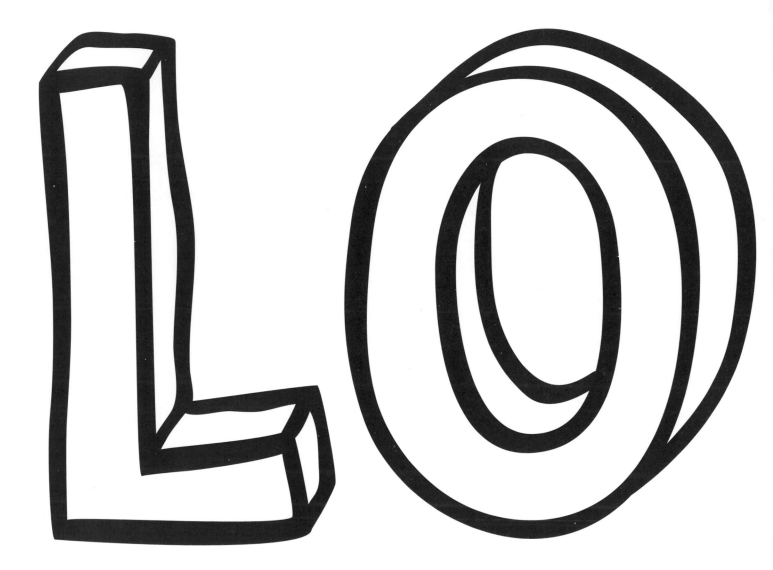

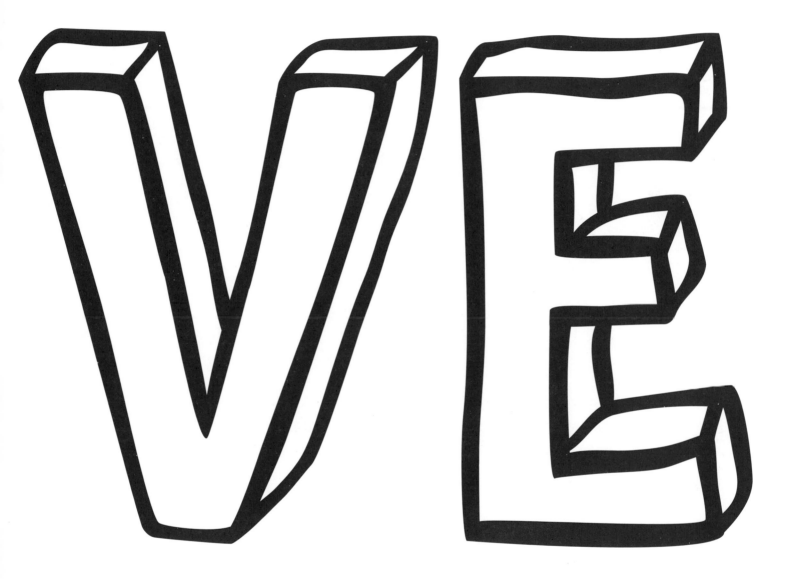

Fill each heart with stripes, polka dots or zig-zags in all different colors! Draw or paste in a picture of someone you love and doodle more hearts around it. Fill one heart with another heart, and fill that heart with another heart (and another and another) until your heart is bursting with love!

NEIGHBOR

—Mark 12:31

Think about your neighbors and all the ways you help each other as you doodle decorations for these houses! Add trees, windows, bright colors and even people to fill them.

Nobody loves you like your family!
Doodle in details (and more people and pets, too!)
to create a portrait of those you cherish the most.
If you like, cut out pictures of family members to
use instead and draw a fun setting. You can be at
the beach, your backyard or even on the moon!

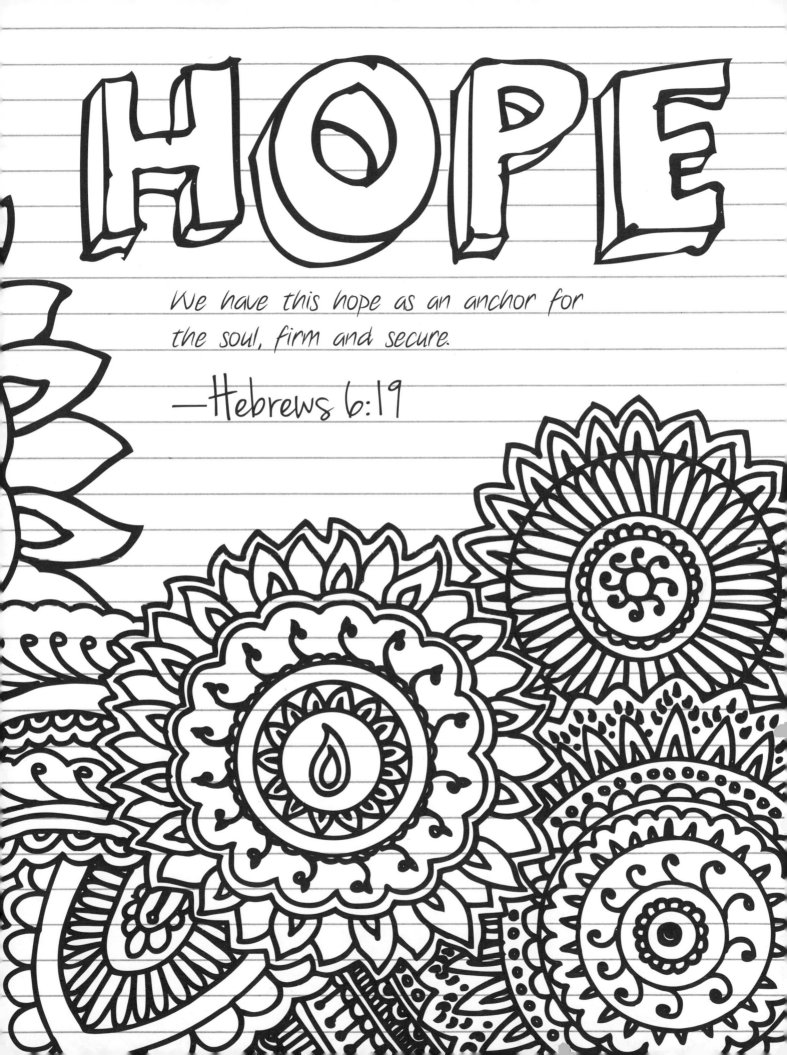

HOPE

We have this hope as an anchor for the soul, firm and secure.

—Hebrews 6:19

"For I know the plans I have for you," declares the LORD, "plans to prosper you and not to harm you, plans to give you hope and a future. —Jeremiah 29:11

God has big plans for you! What things do you hope to achieve with the help of the Lord?

1

2

3

4

5

Hope is an unshakeable confidence in God, regardless of your circumstances. Think about all the ways you can strengthen your confidence in the Lord while you doodle more swirls, flowers and designs to create a colorful collage.

From sunrise to sunset, have hope in the Lord!
Add a sun and all the brilliant colors of a sunset to this
picture and doodle in beachgoers to enjoy this daily gift.

Guide me in your truth and teach me, for you are God my Savior, and my hope is in you all day long. — Psalm 25:5

Hope in the Lord teaches us patience! This page will take a long time to carefully color, but the final product will be worth it.

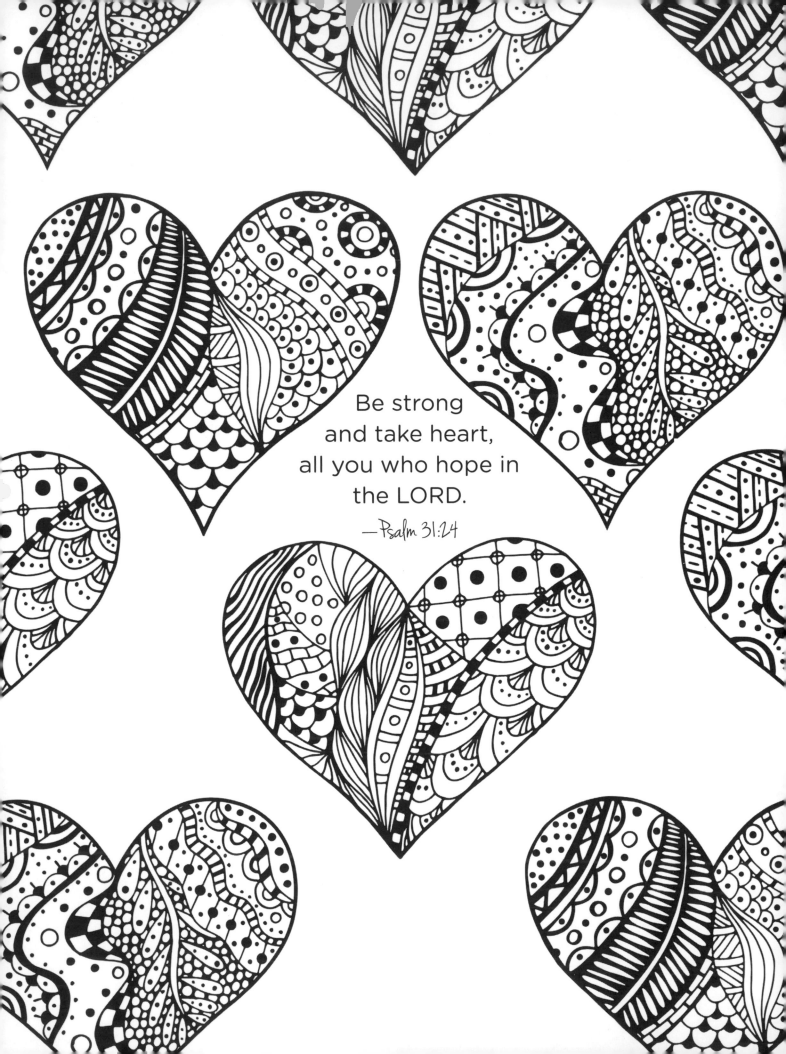

Be strong
and take heart,
all you who hope in
the LORD.

—Psalm 31:24

STR
ENG
TH!

Hope requires strength!

Doodle different patterns in every letter of this word.

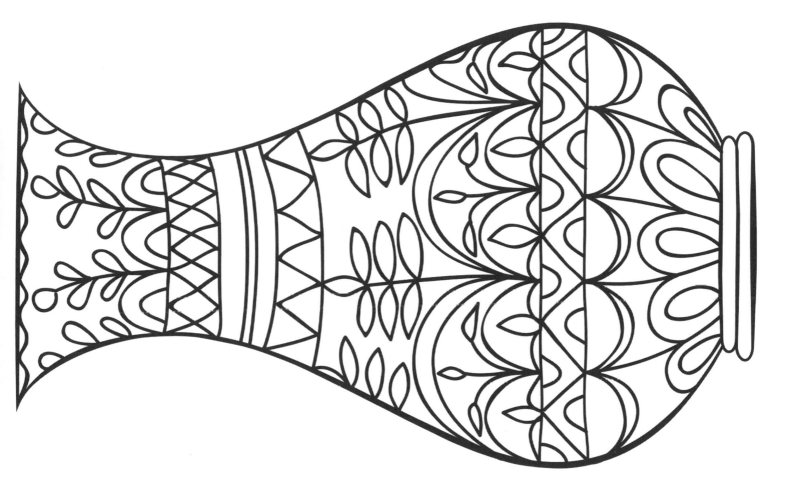

Having hope brings encouragement, just like a bouquet of flowers! Doodle in some flowers to fill the vase, and then decorate it as brightly as you can!

Create your own coat of arms!
Doodle in patterns, animals, your family—
whatever gives you strength!

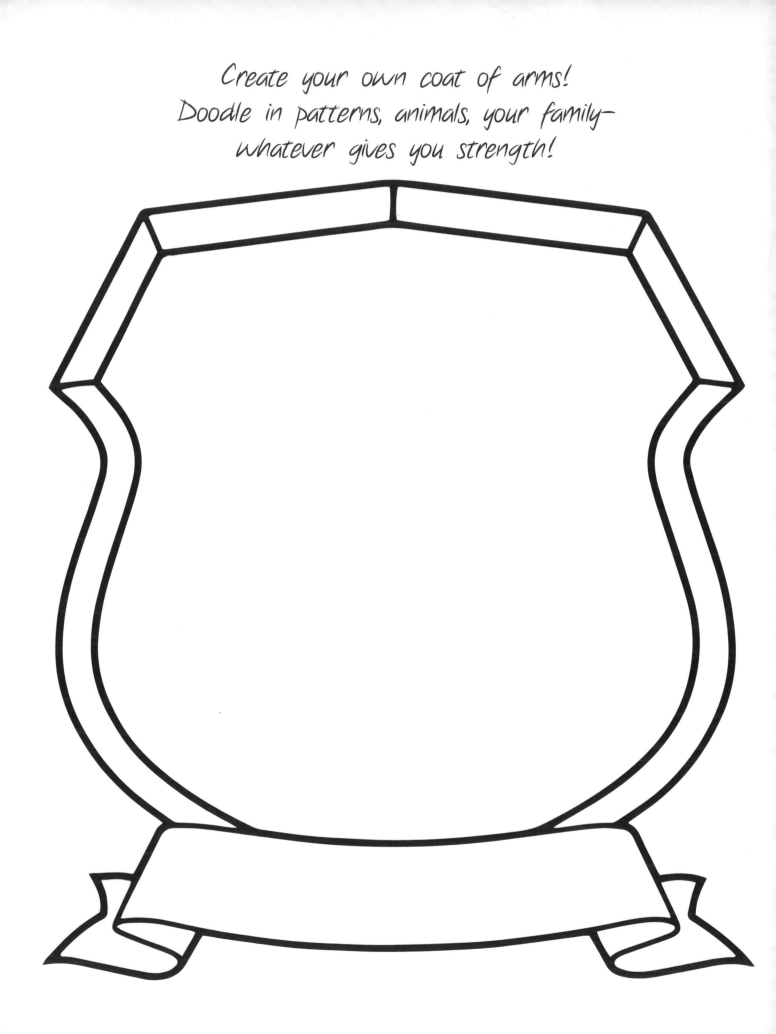

We wait in hope for the LORD;
He is our help and our shield.

—Psalm 33:20

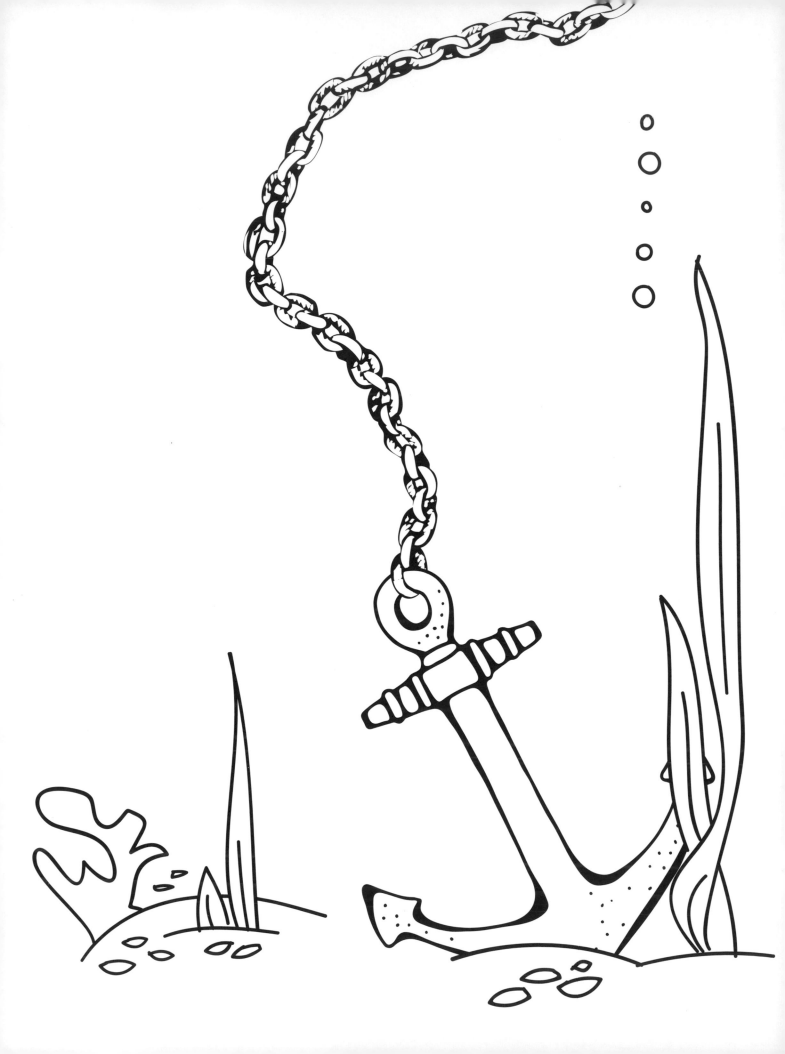

Hope is like an anchor keeping us safe in a storm!
Doodle more details into the picture below, like
fish, shells or even treasure!

Even youths grow tired and weary,
and young men stumble and fall;
but those who hope in the LORD
will renew their strength.
They will soar on wings like eagles;
they will run and not grow weary,
they will walk and not be faint.

—Isaiah 40:30-31

Having hope can help you soar! Color in this majestic eagle and doodle in clouds, mountaintops or whatever you dream up!

Hope helps us feel secure and protected, like having a guard dog with you at all times! Doodle in some more animals or other things that make you feel safe.

But as for me, I watch in hope for the LORD, I wait for God my Savior; my God will hear me.

—Micah 7:7

When you pray to God, what do you hope for? Doodle the way the world would look outside your window if God answered all your prayers!

The more you hope, the more your love for God blossoms! Doodle leaves, flowers and even birds and squirrels—or a pig if you want!—on the branches of this tree.

Most doves are white, but you can turn these doves any color you want! When you're done, doodle in a beautiful background.

Be joyful in hope, patient in affliction, faithful in prayer.

—Romans 12:12

There's nothing more illustrative of hope than a flower that's about to bloom! Doodle more and more flowers on this page until it's completely covered in bunches of blossoms!

Hope in the Lord is pure, like the clear waters of a mountain lake. Doodle in more of the Lord's natural gifts, like trees, fish and other animals!

All who have this hope in Him purify themselves, just as He is pure. —1 John 3:3

Hope means trusting God to guide you on your path!
Doodle flowers, trees and even family and friends
along your path to make it beautiful!

Hope is the light in the darkest of moments. Color this leaf with the brightest colors in your arsenal to show how hopeful you are! The colors don't need to match how leaves look in real life—be creative!

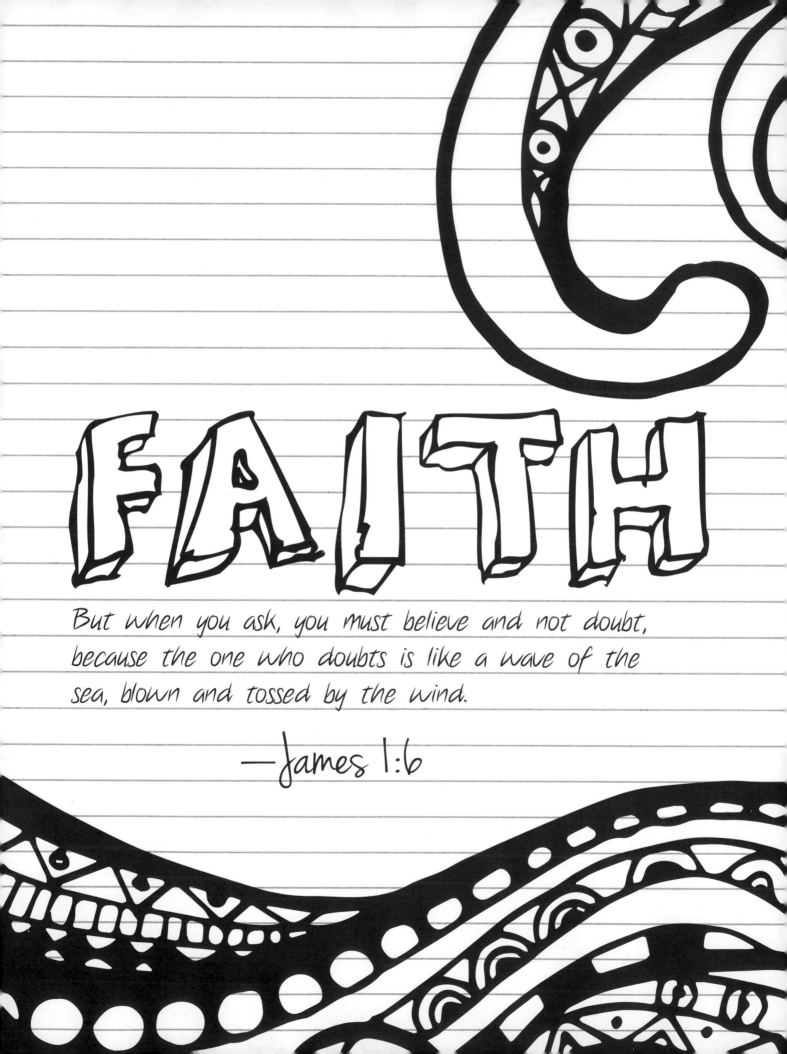

FAITH

But when you ask, you must believe and not doubt, because the one who doubts is like a wave of the sea, blown and tossed by the wind.

—James 1:6

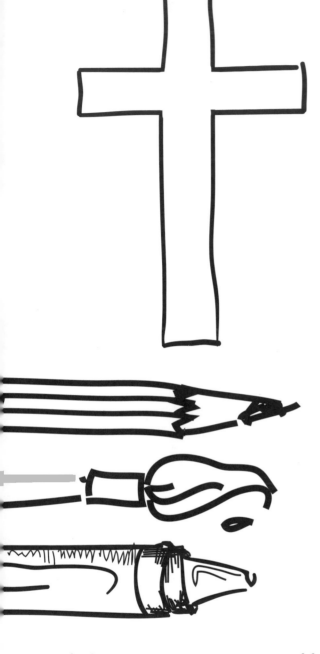

Make each cross a different color and play with using different coloring tools (like pens, markers or crayons), creating different patterns or even using found materials (cut up magazines, cloth or washi tape) to make each cross unique—just like your relationship with God!

Putting your faith in God is a little bit like learning to ride a bike: As soon as you stop thinking about falling, you won't fall. Have faith that God will keep you upright, and He will!

Draw yourself on this bike and then doodle around it to put yourself anywhere you imagine: in the mountains, on a boardwalk or even underwater or in space!

Trust in the LORD with all your heart
and lean not on your own understanding;
in all your ways submit to Him,
and He will make your paths straight.
—Proverbs 3:5-6

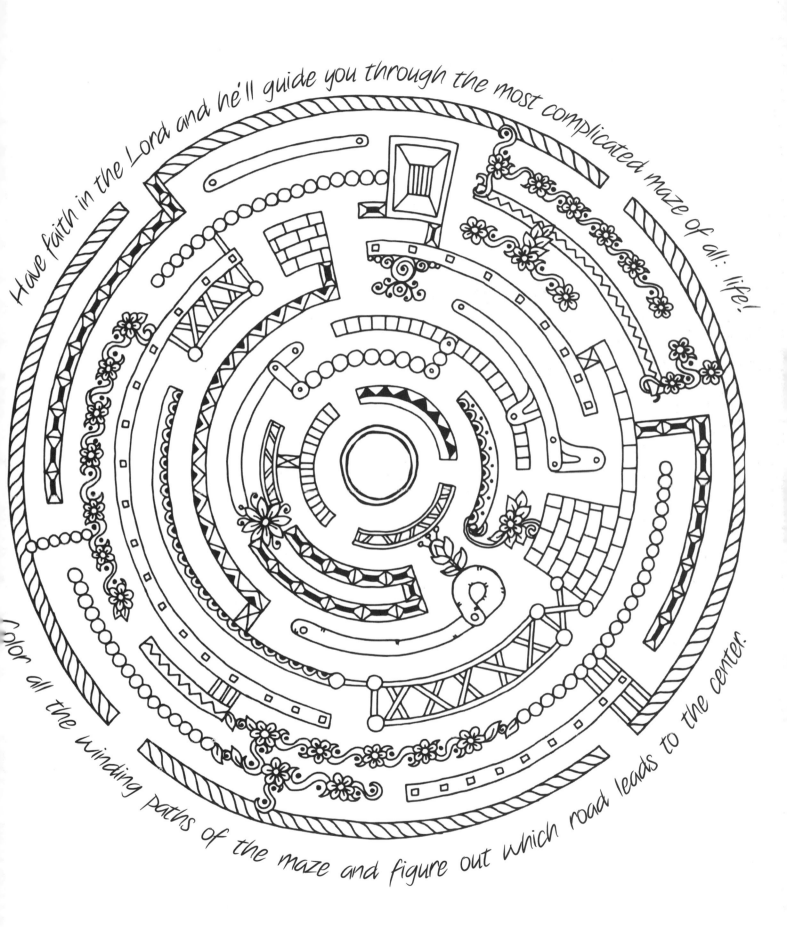

Have faith in the Lord and he'll guide you through the most complicated maze of all: life!

Color all the winding paths of the maze and figure out which road leads to the center.

Faith is great because it holds us together, just like stitches on a quilt! Color in the different designs on each patch to turn this quilt into a wonderful example of your faith in the Lord.

God sacrificed
His only son for
us, and all we can
do in return is
have faith! Color
in each pane of
stained glass with
a vibrant hue, and
think about the
incredible sacrifice
the Lord made
for us.

For it is by grace you have been saved, through faith—and this is not from yourselves, it is the gift of God—not by works, so that no one can boast.

—Ephesians 2:8-9

Your faith can move mountains!
Draw a big range behind these
hikers, then cover it with trees
or snow caps or flowers!

He replied,
"If you have faith as
small as a mustard
seed, you can say to
this mulberry tree,
'Be uprooted and
planted in the sea,'
and it will obey you."
—Luke 17:6

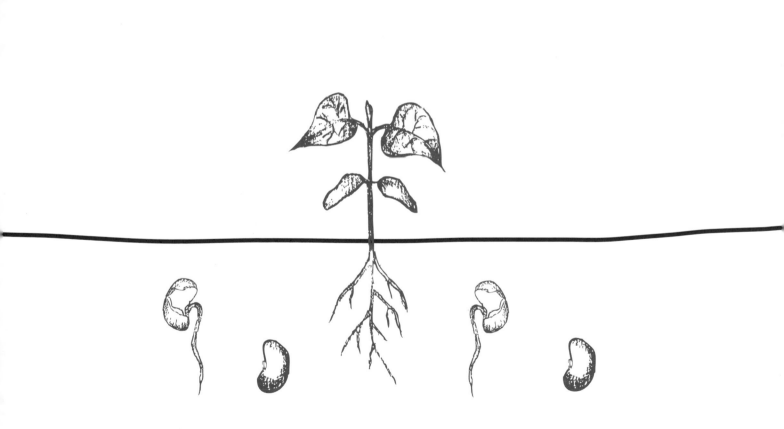

Seeds are tiny, but they can grow into something enormous! Doodle in more plants and bugs as you think about how far your faith can take you!

Ripples start small but become much larger! They just need somebody to start them.

Doodle in more and more ripples in bright, dazzling colors!

Rely on your faith and
it will grow as tall and
strong as a tree! Use
colored pencils, crayons or
watercolors to cover this
tree with vibrant hues.

Be on your guard; stand firm in the faith; be courageous; be strong.

—1 Corinthians 16:13

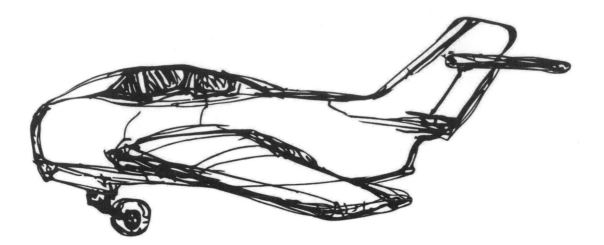

You need to have a lot of faith in your parachute to jump out of a plane! Doodle clouds to fill out this scene and fill them with swirls, patterns or whatever design you like.

For we live
by faith, not by
sight.
—2 Corinthians 5:7

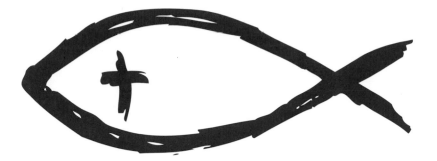

Having faith means knowing God is there even though you can't see Him! Fill this page with colorful fish symbols as a symbol of your own faith in the Lord!

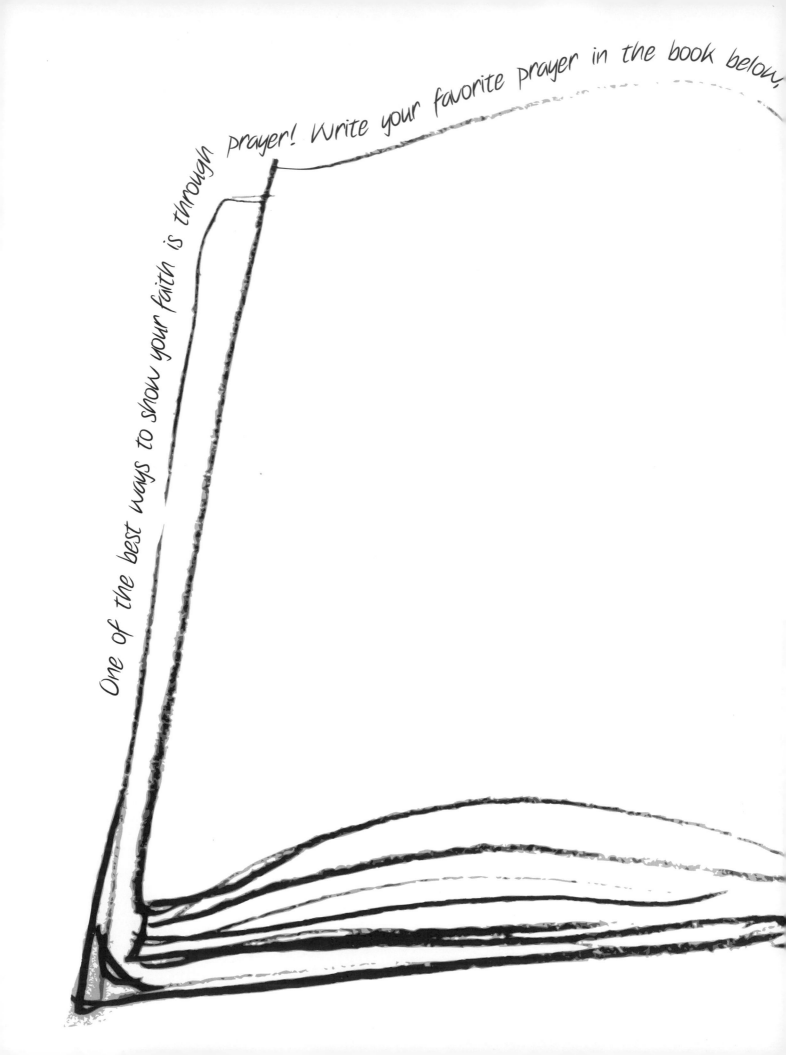

One of the best ways to show your faith is through prayer! Write your favorite prayer in the book below,

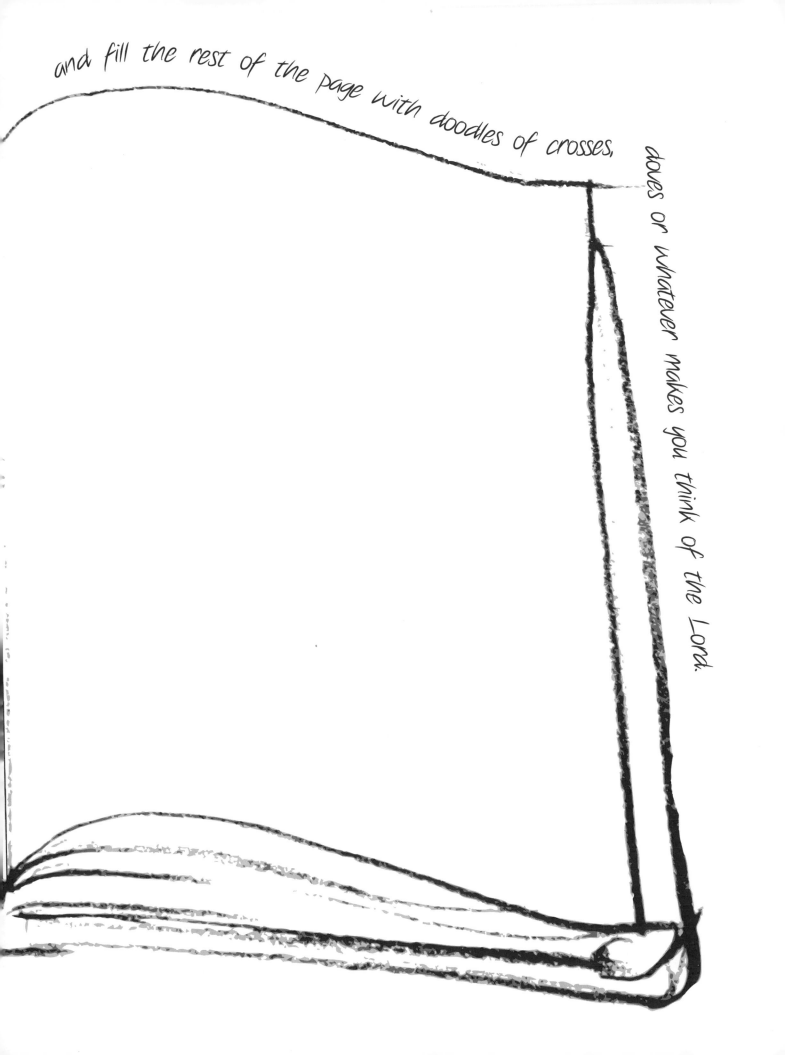

and fill the rest of the page with doodles of crosses,

doves or whatever makes you think of the Lord.

Think about ways you can strengthen your faith in the Lord while you fill each letter with different materials! Use washi tape, markers, colored pencils or even patterns cut out from magazines—get creative!

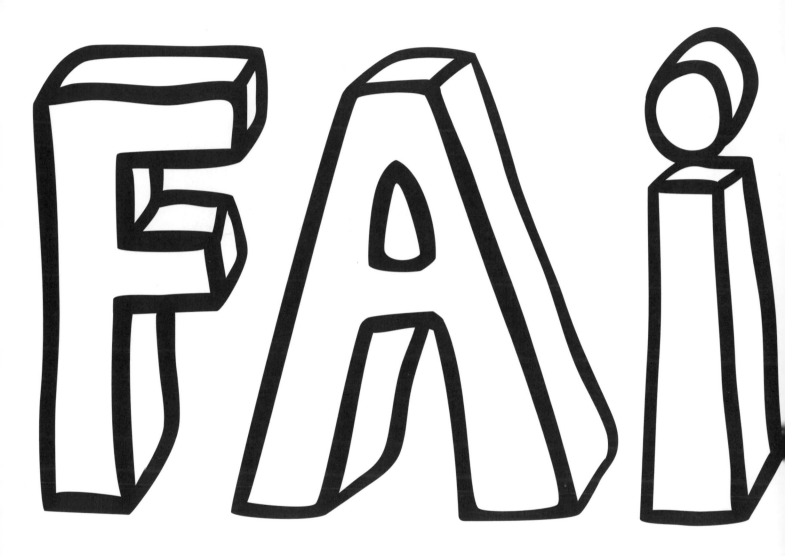

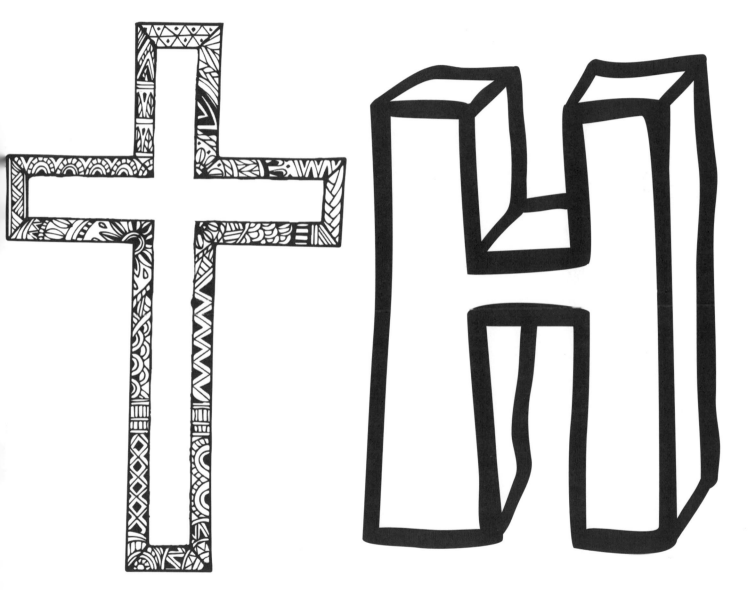

A caterpillar follows its instincts and forms a cocoon, and sure enough, it turns into a butterfly!

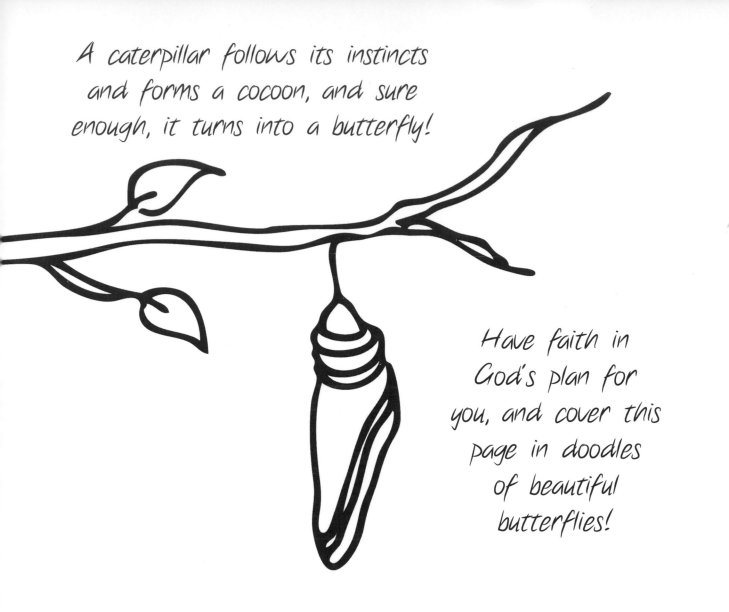

Have faith in God's plan for you, and cover this page in doodles of beautiful butterflies!

Use this page to brainstorm ways you can lead others by example and exude love, hope and faith to the people in your community.

Don't let anyone look down on you because you are young, but set an example for the believers in speech, in conduct, in love, in faith and in purity.

—1 Timothy 4:12

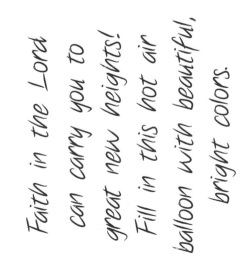

Faith in the Lord
can carry you to
great new heights!
Fill in this hot air
balloon with beautiful,
bright colors.

"But ask the animals, and they will teach you,
or the birds in the sky, and they will tell you;
or speak to the earth, and it will teach you,
or let the fish in the sea inform you.
Which of all these does not know
that the hand of the Lord has done this?"

—Job 12:7-9

Reflect on this quote
while you use colored
pencils, crayons or
even gel pens to
make the colors of
these birds soar!

As you color in these words, think
about all the ways love, hope and
faith work together to strengthen
your relationship with the Lord!

Media Lab Books
For inquiries, call 646-838-6637

Published by Topix Media Lab
14 Wall Street, Suite 4B
New York, NY 10005

Printed in Huizhou, China
March 2017
1

ISBN-10: 1-942556-60-8
ISBN-13: 978-1-942556-60-2

▲▼▲

CEO *Tony Romando*

Vice President of Brand Marketing *Joy Bomba*
Director of Finance *Vandana Patel*
Director of Sales and New Markets *Tom Mifsud*
Manufacturing Director *Nancy Puskuldjian*
Financial Analyst *Matthew Quinn*
Brand Marketing Assistant *Taylor Hamilton*

Editor-in-Chief *Jeff Ashworth*
Creative Director *Steven Charny*
Photo Director *Dave Weiss*
Managing Editor *Courtney Kerrigan*
Senior Editors *Tim Baker, James Ellis*

Content Editor *Kaytie Norman*
Content Designer *Michelle Lock*
Content Photo Editor *Catherine Armanasco*
Art Director *Susan Dazzo*
Assistant Managing Editor *Holland Baker*
Designer *Danielle Santucci*
Assistant Photo Editor *Jess Wendroff*
Assistant Editors *Trevor Courneen, Alicia Kort*
Editorial Assistant *Isabella Torchia*

Co-Founders *Bob Lee, Tony Romando*

Also by this publisher

Tree of Life: Art Therapy for Adults

Combine stress-relieving coloring with images and inspiration from the Bible. Follow selected scripture passages as they were written. This inspirational coloring book is meant to be uplifting with beautiful designs—perfect for color enthusiasts of all ages who want to create works of beauty and devotion. Perfect for Bible Study or as a personal devotional, each of these delightful designs is printed on its own page, so it's easy for you to remove and display individual images.
List ISBN: 9781942556558

Available wherever books are sold